The Origin of Subjectivity

The Origin of Subjectivity

AN ESSAY ON DESCARTES

BY HIRAM CATON

New Haven and London

Yale University Press

1973

Library of Congress catalog card number: 72–91291
International standard book number: 0–300–01569–0

Designed by Sally Sullivan
and set in Granjon type.
Printed in the United States of America by
The Colonial Press Inc., Clinton, Mass.

Published in Great Britain, Europe, and Africa by
Yale University Press, Ltd., London.
Distributed in Canada by McGill-Queen's University
Press, Montreal; in Latin America by Kaiman & Polon,
Inc., New York City; in Australasia and Southeast
Asia by John Wiley & Sons Australasia Pty. Ltd.,
Sydney; in India by UBS Publishers' Distributors Pvt.,
Ltd., Delhi; in Japan by John Weatherhill, Inc., Tokyo.

For Sophia and Stanley . . . each in different measure

Contents

Preface

Since the present study on occasion strays from the well-marked thoroughfares of interpretation, some anticipatory indications of what the reader might expect are in order.

The term "subjectivity" has been introduced to make good a deficiency of Descartes's nomenclature. Because his terms "mind" and "soul" are borrowed from the traditional philosophic vocabulary, they insinuate a continuity with traditional conceptions that bear the same names, whereas Cartesian mind is conceived as "I think," or consciousness. Yet consciousness is susceptible of many interpretations, of which Descartes's is only one. To emphasize that Cartesian mind is consciousness of a specific kind, I have supplied a term to characterize it uniquely.

With full knowledge of the cause, Descartes undertook to lay new foundations for philosophy, the exact understanding of which must be the final aim of all commentary. That the foundations can be understood only by following the "order of reasons" has been generally recognized since Gueroult's valuable study. It is argued here that the founding of philosophy is identical with the principle of order that governs the order of reasons, and that the ordering principle is the genesis of philosophy stated in the "history of his mind," the *Discourse on Method*. The origin of subjectivity is accordingly the parthenogenesis of dualism from those seeds of wisdom, mind and body.

There is broad agreement that interpretation should be based as far as possible upon Descartes's directives concerning the correct approach to his writings. That substantial hermeneutical disagreements remain despite this consensus indicates that the directives are not sufficiently clear or that they have not been adequately canvassed. I have taken pains to show that certain directives have been overlooked or ignored because, when accepted in good earnest, they prescribe an approach based upon criteria counter to those now in use and yield substantive results contradictory to prevailing opinion. This circumstance has obliged me to pay more than usual attention to hermeneutics.

The principle of order easily gives the impression that the foundation emerges as the peak of a genesis, whose antecedent steps, like the transition from youth to maturity, are not visible in the final stage. The conspicuous movement from method to metaphysics, whose interpretation is the watershed of all commentary, is usually said to be of that character; metaphysics is the foundation that the mature Descartes realized his method did not provide. I have attempted to show, however, that Cartesian philosophy has but one foundation, and that the movement from method to metaphysics is a discursive elaboration of the static coherence, under the dualist principle, of the parts of philosophy.

The reduction of the principles of philosophy to reason and extension requires the reduction of physics to mathematics. The theoretical kernel of Descartes's thought is the execution of this program and the response to the problems it engenders. The program, which is intended to explain how the real world of extension is accessible through experience or sensibility, is executed in two stages. The first is a mathematical explanation of vision and its generalization in a mechanistic physiology. The foundational function of these dualist physical theories is to confirm the methodological distinction between sensibility and extension not only by explaining the genesis of sensibility from extension, but by explaining it such that just how the mind has access to extension from sensibility becomes evident. Metaphysics recapitulates method after the fact of dualist physics with a view to consolidating the latent unity of objective physics and subjective thinking. The recapitulation establishes reason and extension as the irrevisable coordinate principles of philosophy by showing that the elements of the dyad reciprocally mediate one another. It therefore becomes clear that not merely is there a continuity between method, physics, and metaphysics, but that these parts of philosophy are inseparable. Admittedly it does disconnect the scholastic edifice of the *Meditations* from the core of Cartesian thought. The nonarbitrary removal of this mask is one of the consequences of attending to the neglected hermeneutical directives.

The present work owes a great debt to the secondary literature, especially to French scholars from Liard forward. I am also happy for the opportunity to acknowledge the writings of Richard Kennington and Gerhard Krüger, from which my studies took their initial orientation. Many improvements in the final draft were occasioned by the discerning comments of an anonymous reader for the Yale Press, and by the insistence of Jane Isay, of that establishment, upon clarity and conciseness. My colleague E. M. Curley graciously placed at my disposal the bibliography that appears here as an appendix. The large number of titles that have appeared in the decade since Sebba's *Bibliographia Cartesiana* was issued testifies to the current interest in Descartes and the need for a continuation of Sebba's labors.

I have also the History of Ideas Unit, of the Research School of the Social Sciences, Australian National University, to thank for the fine facilities and leisure it has afforded and continues to provide me.

My friend and former colleague at the Pennsylvania State University, Stanley Rosen, provided the counsel, encouragement, and philosophical direction without which my efforts would not have borne fruit. I am content if this study approximates his outstanding scholarship.

H.C.

Canberra, Australia
February 1, 1972

Note on Texts and Abbreviations

In order to cite a large number of works expeditiously, I use the following system of abbreviations. The Adam and Tannery edition of the *Oeuvres de Descartes* is cited as "AT." The Adam and Milhaud *Correspondance* is cited as "AM." The Haldane and Ross English translation is cited as "HR." To reduce as much as possible double citation of AT and HR, the *Principles of Philosophy* and the *Passions of the Soul* are cited by Descartes's paragraph numbers. Since the paragraphing of the HR translation of the *Meditations* corresponds to the AT Latin version, I have usually cited them by the Meditation number and paragraph, while abbreviating *Meditations* to "MM"; thus, the second paragraph of the First Meditation becomes "MM I, 2." The interpolation of F.V. into a quotation means that the words that follow are from the French translation. I have cited Gilson's edition of the *Discourse on Method,* which is abbreviated to "DM." Classical texts are cited according to the standard numbering systems; the Bibliography shows the translations that have been quoted. The secondary literature is identified by the name of the author, the date of publication, volume, and page number; for the interpretation of the name and date, see the Bibliography.

In quoting texts contained in HR, I have often retained the HR translations, which are reproduced with permission of the Cambridge University Press. Other translations are mine. I have David L. Anderson of the Pennsylvania State University to thank for assisting occasionally with translation difficulties.

Chronology of Descartes's Life

The following chronology is adapted from Sirven, 1928, and Alquié, 1950. The dating of events up to 1630 is frequently conjectural.

1596   Born March 31 at La Haye, Touraine, to a family of minor nobility.

1606   Enrollment at La Flèche, a prestigious Jesuit college whose curriculum was based on Aristotle and St. Thomas.

1614   Graduation from La Flèche.

1616   Bachelor's degree from the University of Poitiers, with license in civil and canon law; first meeting with Mersenne.

1617   Service with Prince Maurice of Nassau, in Bréda, Holland; first meeting with Beeckman.

1619   Journey to Denmark, Poland, and Hungary; attendance at the coronation of the Emperor in Frankfurt.

        10 November, probably in Ulm: The day in the *poêle* and the dream of a "marvellous science," recorded in the *Olympica* and *Discourse on Method*.

        Writings: *Compendium musicae, Olympica, Opuscula,* mathematical sketches.

1621–22 Return to La Haye.

1623–24 Journey to Italy; pilgrimage to Loretto and visit to Rome. There is no record of the persons Descartes met on this journey.

1625–28 Paris years; association with Cardinal Bérulle, founder of the Oratory.

1629   Move to Amsterdam. Excepting two visits to France, Descartes remained in Holland until 1649.

        Writings: *Regulae ad directionem ingenii, Studium bonae mentis.*

1633   Completion of *Le monde, ou Traité de la lumière* and *Traité de l'homme;* suppressed owing to the condemnation of Galileo.

1636   Correspondence begun with Constantine Huygens.

1637   Publication of *Discours de la méthode,* together with *Dioptrique, Météores,* and *Géométrié,* at Leyden.

1641   Publication of *Meditationes de prima philosophia,* at Paris.

1642   Condemnation of Descartes's philosophy by the Magistrates of Utrecht; Jesuit opposition intensified.

1644   Publication of *Renati Des-Cartes Principia philosophiae,* at Amsterdam. Publication of the Latin translation of the *Discourse* and Essays.

1645–47 Continued opposition to Cartesianism in Holland. Descartes addressed defenses to the Curators of the University of Leyden, and to the Magistrates of Utrecht and Groningen.

1647   Publication of the French translation of the *Meditations* and the *Principles of Philosophy.*

1649   Publication of the *Passions de l'âme,* at Paris; journey to Sweden to tutor Queen Christine.

1650   Death by pneumonia on February 11.

1667   Descartes's remains removed to Paris from Stockholm.

1 The Order and Intention of Descartes's Philosophy

The Order of Philosophy

Descartes's emphasis on the importance of correct order for understanding his thought has sufficed to render it one of the recognized principles of interpretation. From time to time disagreements about the character of the order have been significant for interpretive disputations. But with the publication of Alquié's *La découverte métaphysique de l'homme chez Descartes* (1950) and Gueroult's *Descartes selon l'ordre des raisons* (1953), the problem of order emerged as perhaps the key to all other interpretive disagreements. Alquié adopted the chronological order which arranges the texts according to their date of composition, and which imposes the obligation "never to explain a text by a text chronologically posterior, and to endeavour to read each work of Descartes as if one did not know those that follow." [1] This method was designed to recover the coherence of Descartes's thought by showing that a development from a physical interest to a metaphysical interest accounted for the inconsistencies upon which the interpretations of Liard, Gilson, and others had seized. [2] It was also intended to reveal that Descartes had no "system," and that attempts to interpret his philosophy systematically were bound to produce an artificial one-sidedness.

Gueroult's Descartes, on the other hand, is an uncompromisingly systematic thinker. There are many texts in which Descartes emphasizes the significance of the order and connection of his thinking, not only in metaphysics, but in physics as well. It is characteristic of him to say that all his natural philosophy is false if one or another of his assumptions is false. [3] Thus it seems that Descartes thinks of himself as a systematic thinker. Yet the unsystematic or inconsistent nature of the texts obtruded upon Gueroult and compelled him to adopt a principle of organization to adjudicate the inconsistencies. His principle is that the *Meditations* present the authoritative statement of Cartesian philosophy; it is a privileged text that "may not be weakened, still less contradicted," by any other text. [4]

By this he means that it is always possible to find a reason for preferring the reading of the *Meditations* to passages in other writings that might contradict them.

One of the premises of this dispute is that the task of the interpreter is to expound Descartes as he "understood himself."[5] So long as the interpreter is a commentator rather than a critic, this premise naturally guides his study, for it merely directs that he discover what Descartes meant. But necessary as this premise is, it can be maintained with complete fidelity only on the condition that one suspend his critical faculties, or become deliberately unintelligent. The office of commentator cannot be separated from the office of judge and critic. To understand requires drawing conclusions about what the author intended to say but did not quite say, or about what he said but obscured by other inconsistent statements—not to mention the possibility that the author did not wholly understand himself or his subject. The commentator therefore has no alternative but to interpret the texts, and hence to change them. His notion of fidelity is not that of the printer, but of the student who will take great pains to secure the coherence and integrity of his master's thought, although his apprenticeship must never be slavish. The necessity for departures from the texts is easy to illustrate with respect to the hermeneutical principles adopted by Alquié and Gueroult. Alquié cites no text to support his chronological procedure, and he admits that Descartes tends to project back to an earlier date later thoughts.[6] There is no text that endorses the privileged status that Gueroult attributes to the *Meditations*; like Alquié, he arrives at this position by way of argument. This circumstance does not mean that either or both interpretive principles are erroneous, but only that the arguments that support them must be examined.*

The present interpretation amends the letter no less than others, but it does so only by invoking an argument, based on the letter, that the emendation corresponds to the spirit or intention. This commentary is therefore an interpretation, if you will, a "one-sided" view of Descartes; the apology is, as always, that the view taken is correct. The claim to truth is, however, a qualified one. The condition for believing in the possibility of a single true interpretation is that Descartes's philosophy is itself in all respects true and determinate. Yet Descartes's philosophy is incomplete and harbors certain unresolved problems.

---

* Alquié's extensive use of the correspondence to interpret the published writings takes no cognizance of Descartes's remark that his letters are usually written "with too little care to merit being seen by others than those to whom they are addressed" (AT I, 178). His first chapter, which discusses themes drawn explicitly from the *Discourse,* appears to offend at once against the chronological principle. For a critique of Gueroult's hermeneutics, see Alquié, 1956, 403–18. For Gueroult's restatement of his hermeneutics, see Gueroult, 1962, 172–84.

Owing to these gaps and hesitations, there may be a variety of interpretations with equally well-documented claims to have identified the gaps and classified the hesitations. But no interpretation can cover all the ground and reconcile all the contradictions—or at least none has until now. A true or, better, a sound interpretation is one that carries the uncompletable interpretive work a significant distance while obeying the discipline of the texts.

THE ORDER OF STUDY AND ITS INTENTION

Neither Alquié nor Gueroult bases his interpretive principle of order upon explicit textual sanction. Yet there are two texts—the Preface to the *Principles of Philosophy* and the more elaborate *Discourse on Method*—that present outlines and a synopsis of Cartesian philosophy as a whole. By establishing the rule of order from them and by examining the Preface here and the *Discourse* in the next chapter, we shall attempt to show that the order that emerges generates our principal interpretive thesis that self-consciousness is the fundamental and unifying motif of Cartesian philosophy.

Descartes prepared the Preface for the French translation of the Latin original. This bibliographical datum is of some consequence. To write in Latin is to address the learned, who are the heirs and guardians of the philosophical tradition, especially the tradition of Aristotle. The division of the *Principia* into brief paragraphs was a deliberate imitation of the accepted style of scholastic instruction, for Descartes hoped that it might be adopted in the schools.[7] To write in French, however, is to address the man or woman of "good sense," the *honnête homme,* who has not received the scholastic instruction. Addressing this audience, Descartes expresses embarrassment that his readers might mistake his philosophy for one of the scholastic kind, so he seizes the occasion to explain how it differs from the received Aristotelianism. He cheerfully anticipates that the French version of the *Principles* will be "better understood" than the Latin, for "those who have learned least about all that has hitherto been called philosophy, are most capable of apprehending the truth."[8] The Preface is therefore written expressly for the authentic recipients of Cartesian philosophy, who may or may not know Latin.

The perspective of the Preface is a moment of rest that looks backward at the successful completion of a great labor, and forward to future labors of a different kind. The peak upon which he stands to take in the grandeur of this prospect is the goal of philosophy, wisdom. He begins with a mixture of conventional definitions of wisdom as "perfect knowledge of all things that man can know, both for the conduct of life and for the conservation of his health and the invention of all the arts; and that in order that this [perfect] knowledge should serve these ends, it is necessary that it should be derived from first causes." [9] The statement is Aristotelian in its retention of the ideal of knowledge of all things through principles; the stress on the utility of theoretical knowledge echoes many strands of the philosophical tradition, although Descartes fails to mention what the useful was traditionally thought to be useful for, namely, happiness. A decidedly untraditional, but not unprecedented, note is sounded by the connection of theoretical knowledge with the "invention of arts." Traditionally, the utility of theory was the light it gave the *ars vitae* and knowledge of the good, which was conceived to be a disposition of the soul that was attained by contemplation or theory. Health and the arts, on the other hand, were "external goods" to be enjoyed by anyone, regardless of the condition of his soul. The coupling of theory with the arts links Descartes with what might be called the "Archimedean tradition," which was revived by Descartes's contemporaries Galileo and Bacon, and especially the latter in his formulation of knowledge for power. The Preface only alludes to this aspect of wisdom. Here the Preface echoes the proclamation of the *Discourse* of a "practical philosophy," whose work is the "mastery and possession of nature," thanks to the fusion of the arts and sciences through a mathematically based mechanistic physics.

Looking back at the history of philosophy, Descartes observes that all philosophers strove to discover the "first causes and true principles" of things. Until his own time, however, that effort has been in vain, for only Descartes has at last succeeded in this momentous endeavor. The part of philosophy, or wisdom, which discovers first principles and causes is metaphysics. Descartes generously praises this knowledge as good for its own sake: "And this sovereign good, considered by natural reason without the light of faith, is none other than the knowledge of truth through its first causes, i.e., the wisdom whose study is [the task of] philosophy." [10] However, as he proceeds to explain the connection between first principles and knowledge of all the particular things in the world, he gradually shifts to a view of wisdom as consisting of "degrees," which entails a corresponding shift in his initial statement of metaphysical knowledge as the sovereign good.

Metaphysics provides the principles of physics, whose fruits, as the celebrated tree of knowledge metaphor has it, are medicine, mechanics, and morals. Since the tree is desirable for its fruits rather than for the roots (metaphysics) or trunk (physics), so now in a revised statement on the worth of metaphysics, it is considered only as instrumental for attaining the "highest point of wisdom in which the sovereign good of the life of man consists," which is described in two, not obviously consistent, ways. According to one account, the sovereign good is the "highest and most perfect moral science, which presupposing a complete knowledge of the other sciences, is the last degree of wisdom." [11] This formulation suggests that philosophy terminates in a traditional relation between theory and morals, perhaps along Stoic lines. The second statement, however, leaves the matter vague: "The last and principal fruit of these Principles is that by cultivating them we may discover many truths which I have not expounded, and thus, passing little by little from one to the other, acquire in time a perfect knowledge of philosophy and attain the highest degree of wisdom." [12]

The ambiguity about the terminus of Cartesian wisdom is caused by the progress of wisdom in slow degrees; i.e., by the progressive character of his physics upon which the "fruits" depend. In the course of discussing writings already published, Descartes mentions that he needs only to "treat exactly of medicine, morals, and mechanics" in order to "give mankind a body of philosophy which is complete." [13] But in the final paragraph of the Preface, the possibility of presenting a complete body of wisdom is ruled out. Because of the multitude and expense of the experiments that are required for the successful completion of physics, he declares that "many centuries" will pass before this design is brought to perfection; accordingly, he closes by commending his project to posterity.[14]

A cluster of difficulties is introduced by the ambiguity of the completion of wisdom, the principal of which seems to threaten the coherence of the claim: if the "last degree" of wisdom lies somewhere in the indefinite future, what is the present degree of wisdom that is able to certify the contingent future as wise? What is the character of wisdom that it *can* be augmented by degrees? In what way does moral science depend upon physics? And what is the present status of moral science, given that physics is incomplete?

These problems arise in the context of Descartes's treatment of the "whole body of philosophy" according to the order of its subject matter. Let us return to his statements on order in the hope that more exact scrutiny might bring to light some further indications of their meaning.

Hamelin examined this text and concluded that the "logical order of knowledge is . . . the chronological order of their generation in [Descartes's thought]; he affirms that it begins by establishing metaphysics, to pass subsequently to physics." [15] By subject, that order is, he thinks, metaphysics, physics, and mechanics, medicine, and morals, as the tree of knowledge metaphor has it.

Hamelin's reading of the text is of interest because it is quite common and yet mistaken.* There are two statements of order, not one, and neither statement conforms strictly to the tree of knowledge metaphor. Finally, the order in question is neither chronological nor logical, but the order of study and the order of publication.

The first statement on order begins with the remark that "in order to make very clear the end I had in view in publishing, I would like to explain here what seems to me to be the order which should be followed in self-instruction." [16] It is: First, get yourself some morals if you have none. Secondly, study logic— not school logic, but "the logic that teaches us how best to direct our reason in order to discover those truths of which we are ignorant." Then one is prepared for "true philosophy," which is metaphysics, followed by physics, finally terminating in medicine, mechanics, and morals. Morals do not constitute a part of philosophy in this scheme; so we are left with logic, metaphysics, etc. Logic, however, is merely an alternative name for method in Descartes's usage, so that the order is method, metaphysics, etc. The distinction between logic or method and "true philosophy" evidently reproduces the traditional concept of logic as propaedeutic, as distinguished from a positive ("true") science.

The second statement of order begins in a similar vein: he wishes to explain the end he had in view (utility) by publishing. This order consists of an enumeration of his published writings up to that time, listed in order of publication. The *Discourse* is said to summarize "the principal rules of logic and an imperfect system of morals." Thus, the *Discourse* corresponds to the first two items of the first enumeration of order. The *Dioptric, Meteors,* and *Geometry* are then cited as examples of the utility and progress of knowledge, and as touchstones that show the difference between true knowledge and scholastic learning. Next come the *Meditations* with this remark: "foreseeing the difficulty which would be felt by many in understanding the foundations of metaphysics, I undertook to explain the principal points in a book of Meditations." [17] This discrepancy of order—metaphysics prior to physics in the first enumeration, posterior to it in the second—is magnified many times in other writings and will be one of the fundamental facts upon which our interpretation turns. Finally come the *Principles,* which repeat metaphysics, and proceed from its principles to physics, but terminate short of the "moral science." Of this order—the order of publication— Descartes says: "By this means I believe myself to have commenced to expound the whole of philosophy in its order without having omitted anything which

* Hamelin notes that his reading of the passage is the traditional one, whose authority had been challenged by Liard's claim that physics is prior to metaphysics.

ought to precede the last of which I have written." [18] Lest there be any doubt about the deliberateness of this plan, he adds that he has published each work as he judges the minds of his readers to have been sufficiently prepared by that which preceded it. A comparison between these two orders reveals that the order of study is identical with the order of publication (excepting the discrepancy noted above). This indicates that the chronological order is of consequence only insofar as it is absorbed into the order of publication. As for the logical order, the "order of reasons," it is absorbed into the order of study.

There are several immediate and important consequences of the identification of the order of publication with the order of study. It shows that the "order of reasons" begins in the *Discourse* rather than the *Meditations,* and that we should not proceed to the latter without having understood the "reasons" of the *Dioptric, Meteors,* and *Geometry.* It has never been observed, I believe, that this unorthodox sequence is the recommended approach to the *Meditations,* yet it has a direct bearing on the discrepancy noted above about whether physics is prior or posterior to metaphysics.

The second consequence of Descartes's rule of order is that it identifies the writings he published as the core texts. The posthumous writings and correspondence must be appraised by using the core as the criterion. It would be a legitimate use of that core if we judge from it that the posthumous *Regulae* is indispensable for understanding the method. It may be further inferred from Descartes's statement on order that no text of the core is accorded a hermeneutically privileged position as containing the principal statement of his thought; in particular, the status of the *Meditations* within the core must be established by examination of those works in the proper sequence, which we shall do in the next chapter. Finally, the statement on order signifies that the essential coherence of Descartes's thought is bound up with its literary form—it is to specific books, rather than to topics, that we must first address our attention. It confirms Gueroult's view that a principle of order establishes the coherence of Cartesian philosophy, even if it is not the order that Gueroult had in mind.*

The first member of the series according to the rule of order is the *Discourse.* With the publication of this work, Descartes became the first philosopher to publish the history of his own philosophy, which is itself part of that philosophy, and which, contrary to the rules of sound historiography, was composed and published prior to the publication of the other writings, but in retrospect to their

---

* Despite his stress upon the order of reasons, Gueroult seems to have paid no attention to the problems these texts pose to his "valorization" of the *Meditations.* He also seems to be unaware of the denigrations of metaphysics that occur in the *Discourse.*

completion. This unusual perspective rules out any ascription of a sense of development to Descartes's conscious thought, since no later text retracts this claim to completion, although it does not exclude a genetic analysis of his thought either; for the *Discourse* is a history of the genesis of Cartesian philosophy. The sequence of the genesis also produces an order of philosophy, which we shall later show duplicates the order of publication, and provides the material for resolving the discrepancy about the order of physics and metaphysics.

It is natural to expect that such a history would provide a synopsis of the whole and, in the best case, an authoritative guide. Descartes seems to have had this purpose in mind, for he wrote in the *Discourse,* "[to those who] desire to follow a course similar to my own, it is not necessary that I should say any more than what I have already said in this Discourse." [19] It appears, then, that the Preface and *Discourse* are the writings from which the order and objective of Descartes's philosophy, as he understood it, must be determined.

Let us return now to the Preface to deal with the problem of the termination of philosophy. The only systematic work published after the *Principles* is *The Passions of the Soul.* There is reason to believe that this writing, which expounds *générosité* as "one of the principal parts of wisdom," presents as much of the perfect moral science as the nature of progressive Cartesian wisdom enables him to command. To establish this important contention, it is necessary to pay regard to literary detail. The *Principles* parade grandly through the whole of philosophy. Beginning with metaphysics, they pass on to consideration of the general principles and characteristics of the material world, then treat the visible cosmos, and finally descend to earth. But it is incomplete, as is noted both in the Preface and in the body of the work. It requires two additional parts, one on plants and animals, and one on man. A complete body of philosophy would thus terminate in a discourse on man based on principles "derived from first causes," and would in this way, presumably, exhibit the nature of the relation between physics and morals. Despite the restriction of the subject, the *Passions* answer this requirement. Part I is entitled "Of the Passions in General, and Incidentally of the Whole Nature of Man"; and in a prefatory letter Descartes remarks that he speaks of the passions "not as a rhetorician, nor as a moralist, but as a physicist." [20] In order to bring out the significance of the claim to speak of the "whole nature of man" as a physicist, we must revert to the *Discourse.* In the summary of metaphysics, Descartes announces himself to be exclusively a "thinking thing." The summary of physics follows the plan of the *Principles,* except that in the *Discourse* man is included in the physical schema. Of this inclusion

Descartes writes, "It is necessary that [the soul] should be joined and united most closely to the body in order to have sensations and appetites similar to our own, and thus to form a true man." [21] It would seem that, despite the metaphysical claim, the true man—one whose soul is united with body—would come to light only in a treatise on "sensations and appetites," i.e., passions. This inference is confirmed in another way by a comparison of the *Principles* and the *Passions.* In the midst of his discussion of the laws of motion, Descartes notes that he does not at that place consider whether the soul is able to impart movement to the body, and hence does not bind his principles to accounting for such effects.[22] Directly in the *Passions,* however, he asserts that "It is an error to believe that the soul supplies the movement and heat of the body." [23] This assertion is at once the necessary condition for Descartes's treating the passions "as a physicist" and the principle by means of which he exhibits the dependency of "wisdom," or perfect moral science, upon physics. The *Passions,* therefore, are the fourth and last member of a series that constitute a "complete body of philosophy."

The concept of wisdom that terminates in a moral doctrine is altogether traditional. But the notion of wisdom that reaches into the future for completion by generations to come is new and Baconian, and only the *Discourse* explains its meaning. This state of affairs, which would be strange in the absence of an authoritative guide to Descartes's thought, is fitting in light of Descartes's own directives, and follows from the character of the *Discourse.* It is fitting because, of all Descartes's writings, only the *Discourse* and Preface are written explicitly from the point of view of the whole of philosophy, and of these, the *Discourse* is by far more comprehensive. Only the latter announces the "mastery and possession of nature" as the highest, or at least ultimate, task of philosophy, and only from that work can we gather what that task implies for the attainment of wisdom.

In summary, it can be said that the problem of locating the correct orientation for the study of Descartes is solved in principle by the order stated in the Preface and elaborated in the *Discourse.* These sources provide the essential guide to the texts. The principle of order is the path of the acquisition of wisdom, although that path is traceable only by following it through a series of books. The literary dimension of the path cannot be replaced or set aside by what we might take to be the *ordo essendi;* the literary order establishes the interpreter's *ordo cognoscendi,* which is the only reliable way to the ordo essendi.

Descartes's Veracity

A FURTHER PROBLEM OF INTENTION

There is a second problem for interpretation of Descartes to which the rule of order is perhaps ultimately the key, but which nonetheless demands separate consideration. It is the presumption that Descartes misrepresented his actual views. There are two versions of the nature of the misrepresentation. According to that advanced by Balz, Beck, Röd, and Heidegger, the "exigencies of exposition" forced Descartes to distort his teaching by expounding his untraditional thought in traditional concepts.[24] Heidegger summarizes this conception when he observes that Descartes's "repeated efforts to make the novelty of the foundations of metaphysics understandable to his contemporaries forced [him] to speak on the level of tradition, and thus to explicate his position extrinsically, i.e., inappropriately."[25] Precisely what is new and essential is misrepresented. All the above-mentioned authors agree that the central conception of mind as *res cogitans* is distorted by the exposition of it as a substance.[26]

The other view, toward which the first tends, is that Descartes's misrepresentations are deliberate. This view lives a somewhat fugitive existence in Cartesian scholarship. It has been advanced by such respectable scholars and thinkers as Charles Adam and Leibniz, and nearly all of the most notable recent commentators have felt obliged to challenge it. But with the exception of Maxime Leroy, no one has attempted a systematic interpretation that shows the scope and character of the alleged dissimulation. Instead, there are scattered remarks, all the more provocative for their brevity. Such oracular utterances would deserve scant attention but for the fact that they are so energetically opposed. The reason for the opposition is not far to seek: if the oracles speak truly, we are confronted with a grave obstacle to Descartes's thought. The threat of dissimulation is especially menacing to an interpretation devoted to Cartesian self-consciousness. It is advisable, therefore, to bring the problem out of the shadows.

As mentioned, the only sustained argument for the dissimulation thesis is Leroy's *Descartes, le philosophe au masque*. This work failed to convince partly because of the weak argument that links the publicly visible Descartes with what Leroy detects behind the mask (a skeptical, agnostic, "Faustian" man); and it failed because Leroy was unable to show how his dissimulation thesis could provide a criterion for a nonarbitrary interpretation of Descartes as ironist. For these reasons an examination of Leroy's argument would be unprofitable.

It is better to sample the oracular utterances that drift through Cartesian literature. The selection has been chosen for the diversity of the philosophical and religious persuasions of their authors, as well as for the temporal distribution of the views from Descartes's day to the present.

After corresponding with Descartes about the beast-machine question, Henry More concluded that he was an "abundantly cunning and abstruse genius" who by "counterfeit and prestigious subtlety" insinuated that mind as an incorporeal substance is a "useless figment and chimera." [27] La Mettrie concurs in this judgment; the "real distinction" between mind and body is but a "ruse" which deceives "only the theologians." [28] Fathers Gassendi and Daniel found Descartes's portrayal of the spirituality of the soul so exaggerated as to be a fitting subject for satire. Leibniz, Locke, and d'Holbach doubted the sincerity of the proofs of the existence of God. In his Cartesian *Système de la nature,* d'Holbach declared: "Thus one is right to accuse Descartes of atheism, seeing that he very energetically destroyed the weak proofs of the existence of God that he gave." [29] In the midst of the reception of Descartes's philosophy, Leibniz protested that "when I hear these praises [of Descartes's metaphysics], I am astonished that the world is so easily deceived by those who but adroitly play with words while corrupting their sense . . . even as Descartes has abused these great words, the existence of God and the immortality of the soul." [30] The coeditor of the *Oeuvres,* Charles Adam, wrote in his biography of Descartes: "His protestations of respect for the religion of his country, sincere as they are, should not impose upon us"; and his metaphysics is a "flag to cover the goods," namely, his physics. [31] There are times when Gilson almost agrees with this view. Addressing the problem of dissimulation, Maritain dismisses as a "rather crude hypothesis" the contention that Descartes was insincere, but believes nevertheless that he "took wise precautions in the face of the excessive prejudice of the crowd and of the official savants" by developing a "strategy" of rhetoric for the presentation of his philosophy. [32] In different ways, Laberthonnière, Krüger, and Jaspers suspect Descartes's piety. Krüger sees in the self-assertion of the *Cogito* a defiance which marks the "beginning of the revolt against Christianity which we call the Enlightenment." [33] Heidegger's interpretation of Descartes is in full accord with Krüger's insight. One of the pillars of the Enlightenment, d'Alembert, anticipates Krüger, calling Descartes "one of the chiefs of the conspirators who had the courage to raise the banner against an arbitrary and despotic power, and who, in preparing a brilliant revolution, laid the foundations of a government more just and happier than any ever seen established." [34]

These statements and their implications are considerably at odds with the prevailing approach to Descartes.[35] They imply that in reality Descartes adhered exclusively to the first rule of the method—to give credence only to reason— and therefore rejected the claims of religion and also that he rejected Aristotle and everything in the tradition upon which a rational theology might be developed, replacing traditional theologico-metaphysical principles by mathematical principles as the foundations of the sciences. His moral philosophy is nonreligious in principle and perhaps deliberately hostile to religion. The virtues are nothing but passions, which are generated by entirely mechanical causes. He anticipates a new life for mankind made possible through the conquest of nature by a technological physics. These views Descartes more or less openly states, but then obscures by contradictory statements. He feigns submission to the Church and pretends to possess a metaphysics which upholds the existence of God and the immortality of the soul. This pretense is made necessary by his understandable desire to avoid persecution for heterodox opinions. But it is also dictated by a long-range strategy to replace Aristotle, and the ways of thought of antiquity generally, with his own teaching in the philosophical culture of Europe. The success of this extraordinarily ambitious scheme depended upon a pedagogy which muted the extent of his rupture with the past even as it emphasized novelty.

As is indicated by the periods of the sources quoted above, there is nothing particularly new about this interpretation; in fact it seems to have been the dominant view among the *philosophes*. In its main lines, the almost uniform opposition to it in the impressive Descartes scholarship that has grown up over the past fifty years or so is not new either. It claims, as a host of Cartesians have always claimed, that Descartes's method and physics are compatible with and require his metaphysics as well as religion.* And the importance of the problem is acknowledged: Gouhier urged, "The total interpretation of Cartesianism is at stake." † It is advisable, then, to consider what can be said for and against a hermeneutics of dissimulation.

BENE VIXIT, BENE QUI LATUIT

For the most part, criticism of Descartes as an ironist has not addressed the problem in a general way. Usually the argument centers upon particular cases, with the critic attempting to show that alleged instances of dissimulation can

---

* Bouillier's *Histoire* records the innumerable attacks and defenses of Cartesianism in its early years. See also Monchamp, 1886, and Bohatec, 1912.

† Gouhier, 1924, 11. Boyce Gibson wrote that the "question of dissimulation is more important than it seems at first sight, for it is impossible to understand or evaluate the system of Descartes unless we realize what he was trying to do" (Gibson, 1932, 50). Also Laporte, 1945, 299.

be satisfactorily explained in other ways. Fortunately, however, some scholars, chiefly Laporte, have made general observations that are useful to consider.

Laporte questions the possibility of a coherent hermeneutics of dissimulation by propounding a version of the Epimenides paradox as its logical implication. If one assumes that an author dissembles, all that he says is suspect. Yet in order to distinguish between an author's true opinions and what he affirms but does not believe, it is necessary to know that at least one assertion is reliable. Since, on the assumption of dissimulation, all are dubious, the assumption "is not only gratuitous, it is incoherent." [36]

Laporte's argument is an unanswerable objection to a hermeneutic that begins with a universal doubt. But is this Cartesian premise, with its implication of a deceiving demon, really necessary? One might compare the detection of dissimulation to the detection of a criminal. When the crime is manifest, the detective does not suspect everyone indiscriminately; he must establish suspects by evidence that creates a presumption of guilt; his investigation incorporates the legal principle of presumption of innocence. What is true in law has its parallel in the assumption that guides all reading and listening. Analogously, we assume that a person means what he says until and unless there is reason to believe otherwise. An acceptable hermeneutics of dissimulation would perforce begin with the commonsensical assumption that the author under investigation means just what he says. It must begin, in other words, with the simple trust that a would-be dissembling author necessarily assumes in his readers, for that trust is the basis upon which the author induces his readers to believe anything whatsoever. But knowledge that men sometimes lie is also commonsensical. Everyone who is not stupid distinguishes between trustworthy and untrustworthy men, as well as between irony, exaggerations for rhetorical effect, and literal statements. Might not a hermeneutics of dissimulation come into being merely as a systematic extension of the insight and prudence that commonly govern the evaluation of opinion? But the interpreter is distinctly more limited in his methods than the detective, for he must both establish the crime and convict the suspect from his own mouth. This condition can be met only if the author desired to reveal his opinions as well as to conceal them; it implies an author who "speaks from both sides of the mouth" or who "writes between the lines." Ex hypothesi, then, the interpreter has the advantage over the detective that his suspect cooperates in his own capture.*

---

* Leo Strauss has expounded the method of esotericism that seems to have been once in common use by philosophers and other writers. I am much indebted to his works, particularly to *Persecution and the Art of Writing*.

Since all interpretation must begin with simple trust, a hermeneutics of dissimulation can legitimately be based on the author's own words when they intimate or say explicitly that he does not always mean what he says, or that he does not say all that he believes. In addition, if he discusses the advantages or necessity of disguise in terms which make it clear that the necessity applies to his own situation, then the words provide the habeas corpus of a hermeneutics of dissimulation. Such remarks are frequent in Descartes's writings, not merely in letters and other more or less private documents, but in published writings intended for the eyes of all and, indeed, are the source of his reputation as an ironist. For example, in the *Discourse,* Descartes summarizes a physical treatise (*The World*) that, he says, "certain considerations prevented me from publishing." The consideration was the "disapproval" of a physical theory by "certain persons, to whose opinions I defer." [37] Although these persons are not further identified, nor the Copernican theory mentioned, no one doubts that the allusion is to Galileo's recantation. The question is, what is the cause of this deference? Is it an intellectual scruple about the truth of the theory, as Laporte maintains? Or is it prudential regard for his reputation and welfare? He goes on to write in this passage that the "authority" of these persons "has no less weight with my actions than my own reason has over my thoughts." But writing, or the public expression of one's views is, according to an immediately subsequent statement, an action, for he says that the rule which governs his writing is his desire "not to give expression to what could be disadvantageous to anyone." [38] "Anyone," however, includes himself. Considering the passage as a whole, then, Descartes suggests that the authority of the clergy, as manifest in the case of Galileo, caused him to refrain from publicly espousing a "certain physical theory," although he reserves judgment as to its truth to himself. This interpretation seems to be confirmed when, a little further on, he as it were reminds the reader of the import of the distinction between thoughts and actions when he avows, "I almost never encountered any censor of my opinions who did not appear to me to be either less rigorous or less judicial than myself." [39]

It is germane to inquire why Laporte denies that Descartes dissembled his opinions about the Copernican theory, especially in view of that commentator's well-known scrupulous regard for the letter of the text. Unfortunately, despite his usual thoroughness, Laporte does not consider the passage just discussed. He fixes his attention instead on the correspondence about this matter, which is written mainly to Mersenne. Laporte discovers in the letters an intellectual and a religious scruple about the Copernican theory. The former arises from Descartes's declaration of intention to "render an entire obedience to the Church," and other statements to similar effect.[40] Yet Laporte also quotes numerous passages in which Descartes states that he did not regard the prohibition of the Copernican hypothesis as an article of faith; that on the contrary he saw the whole affair as an ugly attempt by the Aristotelian Jesuits to "abuse the authority of the Church to exercise their passions." It would seem therefore, that far from harboring a religious scruple because of the Jesuit-dominated Inquisition, Descartes maintains that the spiritual authority of the Church has not yet been committed on the question. Laporte urges, however, that the convocation of a Council was in those days generally expected, and that Descartes's scruples are based on the anticipation that the Council might rule against the Copernican theory.[41] This argument is strange because Descartes, as Laporte knows, is of the contrary opinion; he hopes, cautiously, that the controversy will be resolved in favor of the Copernican theory, even as the controversy over the antipodes was. Laporte, therefore, does not succeed in showing what Descartes's religious scruple was. It follows that the statements which Laporte took to reflect such a scruple—his resolutions to render entire obedience to the Church, etc.—have no other sense than the one that he denies.

The alleged intellectual scruple is so thin that it deserves mention only as an illustration of the straits to which one is reduced if he attempts to deny completely the dissimulation thesis. The scruple is said to be expressed in Descartes's assertion that if his own opinions cannot be approved without controversy, he has no desire to publish them. Laporte takes this to mean that since Descartes believed his principles to be clear and distinct, and therefore capable of commanding universal agreement, controversy must signify a reason for doubt.[42] Yet in the letters Laporte quotes to support this view, Descartes clearly states that the opponents of the Copernican theory are moved by passion and prejudice; and if Laporte had consulted Discourse VI, not to mention the letter to Dinet, he would have observed that Descartes anticipates determined opposition to his clear and distinct principles.*

In addition to the objective question whether Descartes dissembled his opinions, there is in the secondary literature a certain moral repugnance to that practice which seems to influence the discussion of the question. The complaint is made that to accept such an interpretation commits one to the view that Descartes was a coward, a Tartuffe, a man who had not the courage of his convictions. That judgment seems unduly harsh. Even in our times, in the atmosphere of toleration, C. S. Peirce observed that "the greatest intellectual benefactors of

---

* As for the evidence that Laporte and others adduce to prove that Descartes sought a middle way between the ecclesiastical position and the Copernican theory, see Appendix A.

mankind never dared, and dare not now, to utter the whole of their thought; and so a shade of *prima facie* doubt is cast upon every proposition which is considered essential to the security of society." Even so, this question too may be placed on an objective level by consulting Descartes's own ethical evaluation of the practice of dissimulation. Let us consider his most emphatic denunciation of the practice. It is found in a communication to Regius, who related to Descartes the opinion of his acquaintances that in the *Meditations* the master had espoused views that he did not truly believe. In response Descartes wrote:

> Those who suspect me of writing in a manner contrary to my views do me the greatest injustice. If I knew who they were, I could not help considering them my enemies. I admit that there are certain times when it is prudent to be silent and not to spread abroad all that one thinks. But only a vile and dishonest man would, without strong pressure, write something contrary to his own opinions and try to persuade others of it.[43]

Commenting on this passage, L. J. Beck remarks that while it is "not without its twists and ambiguities," he takes it to mean that Descartes did not conceal anything. The twists and ambiguities require examination. Descartes admits that the duty to truthfulness is sometimes secondary to the prudence of remaining silent. This statement is given only to a private correspondent, but could Descartes's readers have known that he held this view? Not to repeat what has been said already about the case of Galileo, in the midst of the statement of his provisional morality in the *Discourse,* Descartes remarks, "In order to ascertain [what the real opinions of men were] I should observe what they did rather than what they said, not only because in the corrupt state of our manners there are few people who desire to say all that they believe. . . ."[44] It is difficult to tell, from this statement, whether the corruption consists in the sanctions against those who say what they believe, or in the disinclination to say what one believes, regardless of consequences. The ambiguity would seem to be settled, however, by a passage preceding the one cited, in which Descartes discusses the social implications of his doubt. He fears lest "turbulent and restless spirits" who are called "neither by birth nor fortune to the management of public affairs," should take his doubt as an occasion for public reform. "The simple resolve to strip oneself of all opinions and beliefs formerly received is not to be regarded as an example" that could be followed by those who lack "prudence."[45] It seems, then, nay, we are explicitly told, that the communication of the cornerstone of Cartesian thought, doubt, is governed by a prudence which looks to its public effects, including the "disadvantages" that might accrue to its author.

Prudence then, is not itself "corruption," as Kant teaches, but is the intellectual virtue that knows how to deal with corruption. There is no doubt that in Descartes, at any rate, this virtue takes the form of cunning that Kant so deplored. It is clearly expressed in a letter to Mersenne regarding the intention of the *Meditations*.

> But I think that there are many other things in them [besides their theological themes]; and I tell you, between ourselves, that these six Meditations contain all the foundations of my physics. But that must not be spread abroad, if you please; for those who follow Aristotle will find it more difficult to approve them. I hope that [my readers] will accustom themselves insensibly to my principles, and will come to recognize their truth, before perceiving that they destroy those of Aristotle.[46]

From this remark one would gather that in the *Meditations* Descartes pursues a certain rhetorical strategy to secure the approval of the scholastic philosophers of the day to a philosophy fundamentally opposed to their own; and the success of this strategy requires prudent silence about its character and aims. Actually Descartes is quite voluble about the strategy in the *Discourse,* for he spells out his entire "battle plan" to potential recruits to his army.[47] But of this more later.

Keeping one's own counsel is one thing; to represent oneself as holding opinions he in fact does not, and to attempt to persuade others of them is something else again—a vile and dishonest act. However, not without qualification; it is vile only when one is not under "strong pressure." Presumably strong pressures, or the corruption of morals, might excuse a man for professing opinions he does not believe. Some have tried to show that Descartes had no cause to take refuge in this exceptive clause, by showing that in fact he was not in danger of persecution. Even if we granted the fact, which is dubious, it has no bearing on the present question, which is only whether Descartes believed that he was under strong pressure. Three quotations, which span the period of Descartes's publications, give some insight into his own appraisal of his circumstances in this regard. The first two were written to Mersenne, the second was told to young Burman in conversation.

> I allow myself to say that the Jesuits have assisted in the condemnation of Galileo; and the whole book of Father Sheiner [the *Rosa Ursinus*] shows very well that they are not his friends. But as several observations in this book furnish sufficient proof against the motions usually attributed to the sun, I cannot believe that Father Sheiner himself in his soul disbelieves the Copernican theory. This so astonishes me that I dare not write my opinion. For I

seek only repose and tranquillity of spirit, which are goods that cannot be possessed by those moved by animosity and ambition. . . . I think that I am little able to instruct others, principally those who, desiring to acquire some credit by false opinion, would perhaps be destroyed, if the truth were discovered.[48]

In this context Descartes reiterates his motto, *bene vixit, bene qui latuit* ("He lives well who is well hidden"). In 1641, on the eve of the publication of the *Meditations,* Descartes had not altered his opinion of the ecclesiastics. Writing again to Mersenne about the controversy over the Eucharist that broke out in the *Objections and Replies,* he says:

> I swear to you seriously that I believe what I have written. Therefore, I have not wanted to keep it hidden, in order that [I might] beat with their own arms those who mix Aristotle and the Bible, and who like to abuse the authority of the Church to exercise their passions, I mean those who have condemned Galileo, and who would like to condemn my opinions also, if they were able, in the same way.*

These battles were fought from the relative safety of Protestant Holland, where Descartes retired, as he noted in the *Discourse,* because its people are "more concerned with its own affairs than curious about those of others." Finally, regarding the rules of the "provisional morality" presented in the *Discourse,* Descartes told Burman: "The author does not gladly write of ethics, but because of pedagogues and the like he has prescribed them, for they would otherwise say that he is without religion and faith, and that by his method he seeks to overthrow them." [49]

These citations amply show that Descartes believed himself to be subject to serious pressures from men whose motives he suspected and whose passions he feared. Although much of the evidence presented thus far has been drawn from the correspondence, the same attitudes are amply present in the core writings. In his letter to Father Dinet, which was published with the second edition of the *Meditations,* Descartes addresses an appeal to the superior of Father Bourdin, whom he suspected of fomenting ill-will against him among the French Jesuits. The letter is full of accusations to this effect.[50] This lively phillipic only reiterates the more subdued, though unmistakable declarations of the *Discourse* regarding the anticipated clash between Cartesian philosophy and scholasticism. His-

---

* AT III, 349–50. Descartes was secretive about his thoughts on physics from his earliest years. When he first met Beeckman in Holland, he mentioned that he had never discussed his notions with anyone. (Gilson, 1930, 146).

torians may conclude after weighing the evidence that Descartes exaggerated the extent of the plots against him and the danger to his person. Certainly this is the opinion of his contemporaries, among whom was his first biographer, Baillet, whose work is one of the principal sources of Descartes's reputation as a somewhat timid man. Another source is Descartes himself, who wrote that he made "no other profession than cowardice," and who said in the *Passions* that "in a very unequal match, it is better to withdraw honorably or ask quarter, than to expose oneself brutally to certain death." [51] It appears that in those views which Descartes publicly and unambiguously espoused—the animal-machine hypothesis, the mechanistic universe, and so forth—he remained well within the limits of the tolerance of his day. As for the Copernican theory, the condemnation never was an article of faith, as Descartes well knew, and it appears probable that he might have advocated it even in France without suffering persecution. However, in acknowledging these probabilities, it is necessary to bear three things in mind. The first is that Descartes's own stout defense of himself and of the freedom of philosophy was doubtless a factor—it is impossible to say how important—in his vindication from such accusations and machinations as in fact were directed against him and in the discouragement of other opposition. But prior to the event, he could not be certain that his rhetoric would provide a successful shield, and Descartes is above all a man bent on certainty. Secondly, he was not interested merely in toleration of his person; he desired also that his philosophy be publicly acceptable. Given his views, this was a much more ambitious objective, and it no doubt accounts for the vehemence of his polemic. Finally, in appraising Descartes's relation to the opinion of the times, the historian must take as his primary evidence those views that Descartes stated clearly and unambiguously, rather than ambiguous statements that are perhaps intended to alert readers to views that he was too prudent to express unambiguously. If hints and indications of seriously heterodox views are scattered through his writings, Descartes would know that, and in defending himself would take precautions against their misuse by persons ill-disposed toward himself. Accordingly, he may have had far better reason to fear persecution than the historian is usually prepared to imagine. That is why Descartes's evaluation of the "pressures" under which he labored must take precedence over judgments by historians or by his contemporaries. His evaluation is indeed to some extent an index of his heterodoxy.

In his *Notae in programma,* Descartes interpreted the "program" of his former student Regius for its dissembled teaching.[52] Since I have elsewhere evaluated the significance of this text for the present question, I will present here only my conclusions. The *Notae* prove unhypothetically that Descartes was well aware of the art of politic writing and that he believed it amenable to nonarbitrary interpretation. In the course of his analysis, he states or implies several interpretive principles which he thinks are generally valid and which the commentator may therefore appropriate as a Cartesian hermeneutic. The reader will observe that most of them are implicit in the texts just examined. They are:

1. Dissembling writing is literally "double talk" because it presupposes that the author addresses two audiences simultaneously, one of which is mollified by the repetition of familiar prejudices, while the other are the "keen-witted" or "strong minds" for whom the truth is intended.

2. The domain in which dissimulation can be expected is determined by the received opinion of the day enjoying the authority of force or ostracism, namely, politics, religion, and scholastic philosophy.

3. Contradictions that arise from a clash between propositions drawn from reason and faith, respectively, are to be resolved in favor of reason. Contradictions that arise from a clash between traditional philosophic opinions and untraditional opinions are to be resolved in favor of the latter. Traditional philosophic terminology is suspect as being familiar bottles for new wine.

4. Contrary tendencies in Descartes's writings are produced by his intention to conciliate the Aristotelians while at the same time "destroying" the foundations of Aristotle's philosophy.

5. The authentic addressee is the man who "joins good sense with study."

Since dissembling speech thrives on ambiguity and nuance, it would be a serious error to apply these maxims in mechanical fashion. They stand somewhere between regulative principles and logical rules of inference. Although particular inferences can and ought to be drawn from them, the correctness of the inference should in each case be confirmed by the details of the text. Their use requires that the *esprit géométrique* be joined with the *esprit de finesse*. Caution must especially be taken in evaluating scholastic elements of Descartes's philosophy, since he surely exaggerates the extent of his break with Aristotle, although the rupture applies more to principles than to details. The subsequent treatment of the *Discourse* will show that the hermeneutics of dissimulation may be integrated with the hermeneutical rule of order.

The Antecedents of Cartesian Doubt

The most conspicuous sign of the subjectivity of Cartesian self-consciousness is the prominence Descartes gives to the "I." He adopted the first person standpoint in his initial publication, which is an autobiography of sorts. Without question he was the first to declare that *ego cogito,* that is, "my thinking," not reason, is the principle of philosophy; or rather, it may be said that he reinterprets reason as "I think."

As a species of philosophical self-consciousness, subjectivity bears a resemblance to antecedent interpretations of the nature and task of rational inquiry. Descartes was aware of this resemblance, and from time to time pointed out differences. His primary statement, which appropriately occurs in the Preface to the *Principles,* considers the philosophic tradition as a whole while also naming those philosophers with respect to whom his thinking has made an advance. After commending his philosophy as having at last consummated the ancient goal of philosophy, wisdom, he recalls previous efforts:

> The first and principal [philosophers] whose writing we possess, are Plato and Aristotle, between whom the only difference is that the former, following the steps of his master Socrates, ingenuously confessed that he had never been able to discover anything certain, and was content to set down things that seemed to him probable. . . . Aristotle, however, was less candid, and although he . . . possessed no other principles than [Plato's], he entirely changed the manner of retailing [*débiter*] them, and proposed them as true and certain although there is no appearance of his having ever held them to be such.[53]

The principal accessible philosophy of the past is that of Plato and Aristotle, which in the end reduces to Socratic skepticism. The cavalier treatment of Aristotle's attempt at wisdom, and the tacit dismissal of the Stoics and Epicureans, not to mention scholasticism, underlines, by exaggeration, the assertion that these "dogmatic" philosophies are so many unsuccessful attempts to achieve "certain" knowledge of first principles. From this broad perspective, it may be inferred that Descartes conceives his philosophy as having overcome the principal philosophic standpoint of the past—Socratic knowledge of ignorance, understood as doubt.* Especially in view of the prominence of doubt in Cartesian philosophy, it is regrettable that Descartes wrote no statement on Socratic philosophy. The spirit of confidence in the success of his own new beginning is doubtless a partial cause of his declared indifference to the past, whose thought, as he once expressed it, is "buried under the ruins of antiquity." For our pur-

---

* Descartes explicitly connects his own beginning with Socratic ignorance and the "uncertainty of the Pyrrhonists" in the *Search for Truth* (HR I, 314/AT X, 512). Also HR I, 43/AT X, 421.

poses, however, that past is significant as an aid to recovering Descartes's own beginning. A summary of the Socratic position will serve as a second best to the nonexistent statement from Descartes.

KNOWLEDGE OF IGNORANCE

Since self-consciousness is characteristic of all human beings, it is already present when philosophy arrives on the scene. The purport of this statement is empirical rather than dogmatic. Whoever is not demented recognizes in various ways—though not always in the same ways—that he is an individual different from his human and natural surroundings. Perhaps the two most important goads to self-consciousness in the natural life of man are death and praise or blame. For man's mortality brings his individuality into vivid if often transient focus, and so likewise his desire for good repute, or fear of ostracism. Like every human being, Socrates is quickened by these goads; in fact, no small part of his gadfly endeavors centers about them. Yet philosophy entirely alters this "natural" self-consciousness. Plato takes pains to exhibit this alteration, by showing Socrates' effect on his fellow Athenians, who are variously shocked, amazed, paralyzed, and discomfited by his interrogations.[54] What the Socratic dialectic reveals to his interlocutors that so affects them is their inability to give a consistent account of the most ordinary matters that seem evident and unproblematic. The shock and paralysis of this discovery stems from the recognition of an illusion in the least expected quarter—in that bedrock certainty untroubled by the least doubt. The dialogues represent a wide range of reactions to the recognition of the illusion of knowledge; in only a few cases is there any promise that the interlocutor might be led to philosophize as a consequence of his discovery. Specifically, there is no dialogue in which an interlocutor is led, step by step, from a particular question to the comprehensive ignorance of Socrates, even though the particular questions are plainly intended to mediate that result. It is instructive to observe that Descartes abandons Plato's reserve. In his one effort at dialogue, he represents Polyander ($=$ any man) as passing through the stages of doubt to the certainty of the Cogito.[55]

Polyander's artificially easy success in mastering the Cartesian doubt obliquely indicates the probable reason why Plato declined to represent the transition to Socratic ignorance. The rarity of Socrates himself is proof that it cannot be achieved by everyone. But the distinction between easy and difficult is external to the principal matter, which is the character of the transition. To enter upon the ground of Socratic ignorance, "natural" self-consciousness must be transposed into an entirely new plane. Socrates' questions are there as opportunities, invitations one might say, to that transposition; but they can be effective only if the interlocutor, or reader, apprehends the nature of his dilemma. Socrates' interlocutors, for the most part, neither entirely misapprehend it nor yet understand it. The surprise or amazement which accompanies their encounter with the problem brings them to the edge of the wanted transposition, for in that moment they are mindful of themselves in the required respect—as holding insupportable or unsupported views. But in almost every case the incipient recognition slips away because the mind's eye swings around to the wrong place; one becomes absorbed in solving the problem. Socrates does what he can to redirect the eye by bringing fresh objections to every solution propounded, thereby returning the interlocutor to the unsettled condition from which he might then set off aright. But always the result is the same. Whether out of embarrassment or from desire to extinguish their wonder through a plausible explanation that brings the return of certainty, they fail to recognize that the point of the *aporia* is not to settle a question, but to "turn around" their attention to themselves.* The recognition that what previously seemed evident to me is now unevident must be followed by an explicit recognition of the implicit knowledge that I hold, or held such and such a view; that I opined regarding the matter in question. Now the natural self-consciousness knows implicitly what it means to opine, as the very distinction between the words "opinion" and "knowledge" shows. The Greek word for opinion, *doxa,* means to see an aspect, to take a view. When I self-consciously opine, as I do when I select that word rather than "know," I mean to indicate that I recognize a contingency in what I take to be true; I recognize that a certain hiatus separates what I take to be true and the real disposition of things. I do not know that they are otherwise than I take them to be, for then I should know how they are; yet I recognize that some logical or informational distance separates my thinking from the actual disposition of things, and just the awareness of this distance I seek to express by saying that I have opined. The etymology of doxa, and the word "view," which is duplicated in the main European languages, shows the nature of the prephilosophic concept. From the experience of errors of sense, chiefly vision, we come to realize that seeing

---

* There was for antiquity a connection between "turning around the head" from the shadow images on the wall of the cave and the "purgation" of the conceit of wisdom through refutation that teaches modesty (see *Sophist,* 230 a-c). Aristotle says that philosophy began in wonder, and notes that whoever wonders and is perplexed thinks himself ignorant (*Metaphysics* 982 b17). But whereas Socrates wonders about his own ignorance, the *physicists,* of whom Aristotle speaks in this context, wondered about genesis. Compare this with the view of Epictetus for whom humility, understood as "consciousness of one's own weakness and want of power in regard to necessary things," is the beginning of philosophy (*Discourses,* II, ix).

is perspectival and that accordingly distinctions must be made between the way things sometimes appear and the way they really are when, for example, they are sensed close up by persons with sound organs.

These distinctions are only implicit in ordinary understanding. To give the above account is already to go beyond that understanding and to conceive what ordinary understanding only hazily notices. The self-consciousness intended by Socrates' questions requires that we conceive, that we bring to self-consciousness, these distinctions of the natural consciousness and generalize them. It is for the sake of the generalization that Socrates' problems are often paradoxes. The natural consciousness believes that only some things are opined. As for things "known," frequently its conviction is so assured that it hardly notices that an act of mind is involved at all, and for this reason in these cases it draws no distinction between its knowledge and the being of things it knows. Such is the status of the fundamental certainties of a people or culture. A *para-doxa,* however, lies "beyond belief" in the absolute sense that it never even occurs to us. By having recourse to the "unthinkable" and showing it to be plausible, Socrates' object is to show that both in opining and knowing the mind is necessarily compresent. To apprehend that necessity is to enter the domain of Socratic ignorance. For recognition of the necessary compresence of the mind in knowledge is to recognize the essential contingency of my "knowledge" of the world; for all I now know, the world may be quite otherwise than I imagined that I knew it to be. It is now evident that all "knowledge" has the essential character of opinion, in that knowledge requires the taking up of a position with respect to the nature and being of things.* I now require a reason for viewing it this way rather than that. Since the taking of position and finding of reasons is contingent, I recognize that the overwhelming natural experience of the fixity of the world was in some sense an illusion, for the world might be quite otherwise than I take it to be. The evidence of things now loses its weight, and there opens before us a hitherto unknown possibility— comprehensive inquiry into the nature of things. Socratic ignorance is thus nothing less than a whole culture of reason, which we today express in the degenerate and misleading term "open-mindedness." This self-consciousness,

---

* Perhaps one of Plato's reasons for adopting the dialogue form is that it makes the *personae* of philosophical discussions an indissoluble part of the subject matter. The same point is frequently made explicit within the dialogues by the importance attached to *ad hominem* arguments, the tracing of a doctrine to a particular man, or the conversion of a problem from a question of pure doctrine to a question that includes the person. E.g., the problem of knowledge becomes the problem of knowing what kind of man the sophist is; the problem of the political art becomes the problem of identifying the true statesman; and so on.

or some transformation of it, is the indispensable inner core of all philosophy. Its discovery and nurture against countless dangers of confusion and misunderstanding is an achievement of the first magnitude.*

To Descartes's mind, Socratic self-consciousness is skepticism. Apprehended exclusively in its universality, it is indeed the skepticism of the later Platonists such as the Academics.† Plato, by contrast, chooses to articulate Socratic ignorance through a remarkable blend of the universal and particular that helps obviate the tendency to apprehend them in isolation, and thus abstractly. The dialogues exhibit every universal—be it a "what" question, a theory of universals, or whatever—as tied to the particularity of the certainties, mistakes, experiences, etc., that engender the search for the universal. By this device Plato manages to keep before us the mundane sources that set inquiry in motion toward the universal; and conversely, he shows that precisely the transitory mundane particularity contains, however dimly perceived, the universal. For this reason, the dialogical representation of Socratic ignorance is not a picture of skepticism. Socratics become skeptics by fastening upon themselves, or the mind, exclusively as the medium of knowledge; since perception or reflection always mediates the apprehension of things, they draw the skeptical conclusion that it is impossible ever to know things as they are—all knowing is perspectival and conditioned. True to its self-consciousness, skepticism tends toward solipsism and in its later development seeks literary modes, such as the internal monologue, appropriate to its inwardness. Socrates, however, does not draw the skeptical conclusion because apprehension that we opine is not *eo ipso* knowledge that opinion has not reached the truth; for all we know the perspectivity revealed by the fact of opining may be the correct perspective. Socrates is prepared to recognize "right opinion," a category unknown to skeptics.

The dialogical representation preserves the difference between skepticism and ignorance. The dialogue imitates the actual relation between any con-

---

* For an interpretation of the bearing of the *Charmides* on what is said here about the character of Socratic ignorance, see Appendix B.

† The Skeptics count the Academics as a third school between skepticism and dogmatism because, rather than suspending judgment, they assert that the truth cannot be known (Sex. Emp., *Outlines,* I, 1–4, 226–34). One may say that the Academics dogmatically assert the skeptical view, whereas Socrates aporetically asserts the dogmatic view. As for the difference between the Skeptics and Socrates, the former suspend judgment about whether we know that we are ignorant (Cicero, *Academica,* II, 73–74). The peculiar dogmatic skepticism of the Academics is probably explained by the fact that the school arose as a negative response to the Stoic claim to have discovered an infallible criterion of truth, namely, the firm and constant judgment (Brochard, 1932, 96–97).

versational pair. Each is an individual with opinions emanating from his own
perspective, and neither knows the thought of the other except insofar as it
is revealed through discourse. Upon some things they agree; others are dis-
puted, although in both cases there is agreement on what is meant. Since
agreement presupposes apprehensions common to them both, it is evidence
that the perspectivity of opinion does not exclude its reaching, however feebly,
to things themselves.

SOCRATES AND PROTAGORAS

Plato devoted the *Theaetetus* to distinguishing Socratic ignorance from the wisdom of Protagoras. That man is the measure of all things is Protagoras's
epigrammatic summary of the thesis that "each thing is as it appears to him
who perceives it." Protagoras's position seems to be the opposite of skepticism,
since what he asserts is not that the truth of things cannot be known, but
rather that it is impossible to err. But the articulation of this thesis by the
argument of the dialogue confirms the opinion of ancient and modern authorities that Protagoras was one of the originators of skepticism.*

It is of the greatest moment that Protagoras, as interpreted by Socrates,
grounds his thesis on a theory of sensation, which in turn requires a comprehensive physics: the ancient physicists are the grandfathers of his argument.† The argument is visibly an attempt to come to grips with the paradoxes
of motion and rest, being and becoming, that were provoked by the attempt
to conceive all things as in motion, having their genesis and dissolution from
the movement of abiding elements. Since the whole thrust of Protagoras's
theory is to identify perception (more exactly, sensation) with true being, he
is evidently moved by the paradoxes of the disproportion between true being
(*physis*) and appearance, as explained by the physicists, a disproportion that
is particularly disturbing since the physicists typically claim no other evidence

---

* Brochard points out (1932, 14–15) that Gorgias's thesis that "nothing is true," while apparently the opposite of Protagoras's position, is an equivalent statement of it. This is also
noted by Sex. Emp. *Adv. Log.* I, 65. Since Plato and the Sophists assimilate the distinction between appearance and reality as it was drawn by Parmenides—namely the truth of things that
can be gathered in speech—it is understandable that throughout antiquity the Platonic writings
inspire skeptical outgrowths, such as the New Academy or Ciceronian probabilism, as Brochard
(1932, 93–96) indicates.

† Sex. Emp. is willing to number Protagoras among the Skeptics, except for his adoption of
the Heraclitan doctrine of change, which causes him to make positive assertions about the reality
which generates appearances, whereas the Skeptics abstain from judging the "hypokeimenon"
(*Outlines* I, 219). For the bearing of this fact on current debates about the continuity and difference between ancient and modern self-consciousness, see Appendix B. For the relation of
Protagoras to the pre-Socratics, see Boeder, 1966, 72–76.

for their theories than sensation. Protagoras, or certain unidentified "others," attempted the ingenious solution of retaining the theory of flux while denying the existence of any abiding elements underlying it.[56] There are two kinds of motions, active and passive, which, upon meeting, produce the thing perceived and the perception. Neither the perception nor the perceived thing exists in itself, but only each for and with the other; where nothing is perceived, nothing exists, and conversely, whatever is perceived, exists. "Then my perception is true for me, since its object at any moment is my reality, and I am, as Protagoras says, a judge of what is for me, that it is, and of what is not, that it is not."[57] The denial of any cleavage at all between thinking and being eliminates the distinction between appearance and reality, and therewith the difficult problem of the manner of being of appearance, or the problem of how we might think "what is not."

In view of the manifold vulnerability of this thesis, Plato's, or Socrates' point of attack must hold special significance. He begins with an *ad hominem* argument that asks why Protagoras claims that man, rather than other sentient creatures, is the measure of all things: "There would have been something magnificent in so disdainful an opening, telling us, while we were admiring him for his wisdom more than mortal, that he was in truth no wiser than a tadpole, to say nothing of any other human being."[58] The argument is psychologically shrewd and logically complex. As is so frequently the case in the dialogues, Socrates uses the passions, here self-esteem, as a means of reminding his interlocutors of something important they have overlooked. Since animals do not speak, they make no claim to wisdom and therefore do not merit the attention of a man in search of wisdom; this Protagoras overlooks when he places the being of man in what man shares with the animals. By his mistaken division, which presupposes discursive thought, Protagoras provides us with counterexamples to his thesis that knowledge is perception and that error is impossible.

The ad hominem argument anticipates the main lines of the reductio ad absurdum that follows it. Just as Protagoras is unclear whether man or animal is the measure of all things, so also he is unclear whether *each* perceiver is the measure, or whether I, as perceiver, am the measure; or better, Protagoras sees no contradiction in asserting that each is unto himself *the* measure. Socrates' reductio argument brings the contradiction into daylight. If each is the measure, even those who deny Protagoras's thesis measure as truly as himself; indeed, their measure is absolutely true for them. But Protagoras cannot admit that those who say that some men are wiser than others, or who say that they sometimes err, are right, for the object of his thesis is to deny just this, not only for himself but for all men. The fundamental contradiction in which Protagoras is trapped is his assertion, on the one hand, that truth lies in the particular apprehensions of each man, and the universality of his thesis. In asserting that each is the measure, Protagoras at once moves beyond the particularity of his own perceptions to gather in a multitude of particulars in the universality of a general thesis supported by an explanation. The possibility of the thesis, and its support, is at odds with what is asserted by the thesis.

By seizing upon the clash between what is true for Protagoras and what others believe to be true, Socrates reminds us of the necessity to acknowledge the distinction between what appears to us and what is in reality, i.e., between opinion and knowledge. To sustain and nourish this distinction is the *deed* of Socratic ignorance. Interpreting Protagoras's position in light of the skeptics, we may say that reality, as distinguished from appearance, from my perceiving or opining, recedes into inaccessibility since every claim to knowledge falls back within the sphere of my viewing.* The dialogical representation, however, rescues us from this extremity by exhibiting the fact that we cannot escape recognizing others as measures for ourselves. Upon being called out of my particularity by the claims of others and into a discourse, i.e., a reflection upon the truth, I further recognize that I and others measure ourselves against the things themselves. I cannot account for the fact of my viewing, nor even the clash of my views with those of others, except by referring that viewing to the things; we must acquiesce in the purport of opinion to have reached things themselves,

---

* The skeptical "suspension of judgment" (*epoche*) is therefore quite different from the Socratic *aporia*. The Skeptics do not positively assert even that anything is "indeterminate" or "inapprehensible": they do not claim to know that they do not know. Their dialectic is bent upon the demand for a criterion of truth; but plainly, every purported criterion would be subject to the same objections that destroyed the others; hence they fall into the infinite regress of those who demand a proof for everything. "And even he who asserts that not all things are relative," Sex. Emp. writes, "confirms the relativity of all things, since by his arguments against us he shows that the very statement 'not all things are relative' is relative to ourselves, not universal." Skepticism, therefore, as Sex. Emp. is fond of saying, is like a purgative, for it carries away not only the obstruction, but also itself. The unacknowledged dogmatism of the Skeptics occurs in just the two places where Socrates makes a dogmatic claim. The distinction between appearance and reality is essential to the skeptical enterprise, but it functions only as a *Meinung*, a would-be, that supports ever more dialectical indecisiveness. Socrates, however, seems to recognise that the distinction cannot be drawn except on the assumption that something is known. Secondly, the Skeptics claim to know the mental condition of doubt, as the precondition of any questioning, yet this knowledge too is annulled by doubt, since the mind is among the "inapprehensible things." One may say that they experience but do not conceive their perplexity. In this connection, it is instructive to note that Sex. Emp. is unsure whether he should classify Plato as a dogmatist or Skeptic. For the passages referred to in the preceding remarks, see *Outlines*, I, 19–20, 22, 59, 98–99, 139, 170–72, 191, 196, 215, 221–24; II, 74–75, 188. See also Cicero, *Academica*, II, 73–74.

however partial and encumbered by error opinion may be. Opinion accordingly is both prephilosophic knowledge become derelict, and the solid base from which rational inquiry begins.

We may easily imagine that Descartes's reduction of the philosophy of the past to Socratic skepticism is partly a jest at the expense of his Aristotelian contemporaries. Its deeper element, however, is that Descartes has no choice but to situate the Socratic standpoint within the horizon of those two great poles of his thinking, doubt and certainty. The category of true opinion, essential to Socratic ignorance, is missing from his thinking, or perhaps it should be said that it is replaced by the notion of prejudice. Accordingly, his skeptical interpretation of Socratic self-consciousness may be regarded as his first significant departure from the Socratic position on the way to his own standpoint.

But this first step is made within the horizon of ancient skepticism, which is therefore not novel. Our purpose in discussing Plato's polemic with Protagoras was not only to distinguish Socratic ignorance from skepticism, but also to reveal Descartes's affiliation with the skeptical tradition. This connection is not easy to make by study of later Skeptics who have already formed skepticism into a system whose origins are not clear. The value of the Protagorean theory is that it shows the origin of the problem of the subjectivity of sensations, and its connection with the Platonic view of the relation between being and truth. The perspectivity of sensation provided the skeptical tradition with its basis for distinguishing the phenomenal from the real, and consequently oriented its inquiry into the accessibility of the real to human thought. The Protagorean theory shows further that the problem of sensation arises by reflection upon pre-Socratic physics, and its theory of the genesis of sensations in particular. But this origin is obscured in later Skeptics, who make no assertions about the genesis of sensations because it would compel them to make assertions about the inaccessible real (nature), or the *hypokeimenon.* The Skeptics, in other words, take their concept of "appearance" as though it were a given, whereas it is an unacknowledged inheritance from antecedent physical theories. Cartesian skepticism, as portrayed in the *Meditations,* is also based on an antecedent physical theory (his own *Dioptric*), which is obscured in his presentation of the doubt. There is no difference between Cartesian consciousness of things as "thoughts" or "ideas" and the ancient skeptical "phenomenon." It is not true, therefore, that Cartesian doubt is more radical than ancient skepticism.[59] As Descartes himself stressed, it is not his doubt that is new, but his defeating doubt finally, decisively, by the establishment of science. This combination of skepticism and science engenders a specifically new self-consciousness, which we call "subjectivity."

2   The Scope of Subjectivity

The Onset of Subjectivity in the *Discourse on Method*

The preceding examination of the order of Cartesian philosophy has established that the *Discourse* is the first member of a series whose object is to set forth wisdom or knowledge of all things derived from "true principles." The *Discourse* both initiates the acquisition of wisdom and portrays the whole course of its acquisition, especially with respect to its genesis and goal. The portrayal of the whole can also initiate the acquisition because the portrayal reveals one of the true principles, mind as self-consciousness or subjectivity. Accordingly, the *Discourse* must show how subjectivity functions to unify wisdom.

The most obvious connection between subjectivity and wisdom as certainty is the literary character of the *Discourse*. The literary "I" of Descartes's first person narration is the datum through which his principle manifests itself. It is therefore appropriate to begin the investigation with an examination of the literary features of the *Discourse*.

THE *Discourse* AS AUTOBIOGRAPHY

The *Discourse* is a "history, or if you please, a fable," whose topic is the discovery and fruitful use of a method for the conduct of reason. The appropriateness of this genre to the topic is initially problematic. It would seem that reason, or the power of distinguishing truth from falsehood, as Descartes defines it, is essentially universal, whereas history is of the particular, and fables hardly seem pertinent to the discovery of truth in the sciences. Yet Descartes chooses to present the method in the form of a somewhat fabulous history of the "paths I have followed, [setting forth] my life as in a picture so that everyone may judge of it for himself." [1] His apology for adopting this mode of presentation is directly related to the topic. In the opening statement he notes that the differences of opinion among men are due not so much to inequality of reason as to the circumstances that men conduct their thoughts in "diverse ways" and do not consider the same "objects," the implication being that judgment would be uniform if all considered the same object in the same way. Thanks to "good luck," Descartes has hit upon "ways" of conducting his thoughts so as to arrive at truth in the sciences. These discoveries have provided him "extreme satisfaction." Indeed, the way he has chosen is the most "excellent and important" possible for "man as man," i.e., for the reasonable man insofar as he is not enlightened by faith. But this sweeping claim, which is reminiscent of Aristotle's claim that the pursuit of wisdom is the highest human perfection, is followed at once by a caveat: "Nevertheless, it is possible that I deceive myself, and that what I take to be gold and diamonds is no more than copper and glass." * In order to keep acknowledgment of this possibility in the foreground, Descartes substitutes an autobiographical account of the method for a didactic account. In this way, it would seem, Descartes reconciles a didactic intention with becoming modesty. For, although he offers his own example as a model—those who wish to imitate his "way" will find all that they need to know in the *Discourse*—he does not presume to prescribe the way each should conduct "his reason." [2] Descartes thus acquiesces in the factual diversity of judgment even as he presents *the* method for the conduct of reason.

This explanation, however, does not exhaust Descartes's comments upon his chosen genre. The *Discourse* is intended as a popular writing. It is written in the vernacular, rather than in the Latin of the learned, not merely because he hopes to reach a wide audience, as he does, but because those who have "never studied" are better recipients of his philosophy than the learned; for the judgment of the latter is corrupted by the prejudices of scholasticism.[3] Descartes's repeated deprecation of his talents, his apparent assertion of the equality of reason, his founding of philosophy on "simple and easy" notions, is all part of the popularization of philosophy, but a popularization anchored in his transformation of the subject; he has discovered that the right method, or the labor of the conduct of reason, eliminates the dependency of science or philosophy on surpassing genius. The presentation of the method ought to be appropriate to the addressees, instructing by the use of example. The genre is suitable to captivating the popular imagination since "the charm of fables enlivens the mind and histories of memorable deeds exalt." The rhetorical effectiveness of this

---

* HR I, 83/DM 4. The challenges to the historical reliability of the *Discourse* that have issued from Espinas, Cantecor, Gadoffre, and others arise when the work is measured by the standard of objective history. But Descartes is writing to achieve certain purposes which constrain him to a somewhat fabulous history. He indeed alerts the reader to its inaccuracies (HR I, 84–85/DM 6–7). On the other hand, the dates, events, and achievements to which he refers are well authenticated. On this subject, see the judicious remarks of Gilson (DM 99–100) and Gouhier (1949, 24, 283–86).

manner of address was not lost on the *philosophes* who wrote the *Encyclo-pédie*. According to the author of the article on "Cartésianisme," Descartes emancipated his readers from prejudice by showing how he freed himself from that predicament. By this device, Descartes "prepared . . . minds to receive the new opinions that he proposed to establish. It appears that this manner of address is in large measure responsible for the revolution of which this philosopher is the author." [4]

From these considerations it might be concluded that the autobiographical form is selected merely as a means of making the history concrete, and that the history, in turn, is for the sake of popularization. In that case, the autobiographical form would be only accidentally related to the subject matter, the method. If this appraisal is correct, the "reason" for which the method is devised must be essentially independent of the autobiographical first person. The explanation of the use of the first person, however, runs counter to such an interpretation. While Descartes believes that he has discovered the method that leads to truth, neverthless the skeptical reservation that leads him to use the first person expresses the consciousness that the ways he has followed are his own ways, that the reason in question is his own reason. The particularization of reason by the possessive pronouns "my," "his," or "one's," occurs throughout the *Discourse,* beginning with the title, which speaks of the conduct of "sa raison." [5] Corresponding to Descartes's relativization of his judgments to himself is the criterion by which he would have the method judged by his readers: he wishes for each to judge it for himself. If the manner of address of the *Discourse* is largely responsible for the "revolution" Descartes purportedly fathered, perhaps it did so because the first person is a true expression of the nature of Cartesian reason. The whole meaning of enlightenment, Kant said, is the progressus of man from his minority, in which priests and monarchs do his thinking for him, to the maturity in which he thinks and acts for himself. The *Discourse* portrays such an emancipation, intended, moreover, as a model for imitation not merely by a few, but by all men who combine "good sense with study." [6] The consciousness that reason is "my reason" is the opening shot of the Enlightenment.

The initial statement on the nature of reason, whose basic simplicity is obscured by a multitude of terminological distinctions and by irony, confirms the foregoing analysis. Reason is good sense, or the judgmental power of distinguishing the true from the false. Descartes seems to identify his notion of reason with the scholastic conception that it is a form of a species. In fact, he says that he would "like to believe" that reason is found complete in each individual and that he would like to "follow the common opinion of the philosophers, who say that more and less occurs only among *accidents,* and not among *forms,* or natures, of the *individuals* of the same *species*." [7] However, later in the *Discourse* we learn that he "expressly assumed that there was in the world none of those forms or qualities which are so debated in the schools." [8] He would "like to believe" that reason is complete in each because it is the condition upon which men may be differentiated from the brutes, and hence a condition for belief in the immortality of the soul, which in turn is a necessary support for the virtue of "weak minds." Consequently when, immediately after simulating the scholastic view, Descartes writes "but I do not fear to say . . . ," he implies that the simulation was extracted by the constraints of orthodoxy. The implication is confirmed by the fact that his extensive "proof" of the difference between men and animals, given in *Discourse* V, does not once invoke the notion of reason as a form. The *Meditations* incorporate the repudiation of the scholastic conception when they expressly reject "rational" (form) "animal" (species) as that which "I am." *

The episodically simulated deviation from the authentic Cartesian notion of reason serves to bring out its true character by the contrast with the scholastic notion. Reason as the form of a species is a universal concept mediated by discursive reason. Reason as judgment is immediately known. A form cannot in any way be "conducted" or molded, whereas judgment manifestly can be. Knowledge of reason as judgment is accessible independently of consideration about whether it constitutes a *differentia* between men and animals, whereas the scholastic notion is not. The immediacy of reason is emphasized by the formula used in this context, "raison ou sens," which the *Meditations* duplicate by the formula "sentiendi vel cogitandi": as the faculty of sentience as such, reason is immediately cognizable. Finally, it is pertinent to mention in this connection the awkwardness that afflicts exposition of Descartes's thought. Scholarly convention sanctions the use of the term "the I," or "the self." Like Descartes's expression "one's reason," the convention evidently misrepresents the perspective of Cartesian thinking since it treats as an object the one "thing" in the Cartesian world that is not an object. Complete fidelity to the concept of Cartesian reason would oblige the commentator to adopt first person discourse himself.

Recognition that the autobiographical first person truly expresses reason as "my thinking" essentially unites it both with "history" and the method. The

* The primary and secondary texts assembled by Denissoff regarding the opening statement of the *Discourse* prove conclusively that it is ironical (Denissoff, 1970, 51–52).

classical tradition reflected in the scholastic definition of reason had refused the identification of reason with my reason. The self-consciousness upon which the Socratic beginning was based distinguishes between the mutability of Socrates and the immutability of reason. In opposition to the pre-Socratic tradition, Plato and Aristotle could conceive the divine reason to be the first cause of the whole. No such objective reason is to be found in the Cartesian cosmology, for his God-head is characterized above all by omnipotence and incomprehensibility. Having relinquished objective reason, nothing is left to him but particular reason—"my reason." Particular reason inheres in a particular man whose judgments are determined by his antecedents, or as Descartes put it, his inherited prejudices. In order to portray the ways or method he has followed, especially his auto-emancipation from prejudice, Descartes therefore appropriately chooses the historical or genetic treatment of his subject. For Descartes's auto-emancipation is achieved in part through the improbable discovery that his reason, properly understood, is immutable. The historical approach thus uncovers, in the midst of the flux of opinion, an immanent absolute.

In order to explain the paths that he has followed, Descartes thinks he must set forth his "life as in a picture." A "way" or "path" is the literal sense of *methodos*. Method in the broad sense as it is initially encountered in the *Discourse* therefore pertains to the whole of life. It can do so because method in the broad sense is the "conduct of reason": the scope of method is as broad as the scope of reason. It is the "way" of the life of reason. The phrase "conduct of reason" is ambiguous, implying both "reason's comportment" and "leading reason." Both senses are intended, and they have their root in reason as self-consciousness. The conduct of reason is Descartes's comportment toward himself. That comportment is one of direction or governance, for he adopts toward himself—his judgments—the posture of leading them in the direction of truth "in order to see clearly in [his] actions and to walk with confidence in this life." [9] The conduct of reason is comprehensive self-governance or self-control. It implies an identification of virtue with knowledge, which Descartes embraces when he writes that "it is sufficient to judge well in order to act well." [10] Descartes accordingly follows Socrates in the view that all the virtues are merely manifestations of a single virtue. For Descartes that virtue is not *phronesis* but generosity, which is the pride, the self-admiration of reason conscious of its mastery. This new philosophic virtue is integral to the transformation of philosophy into wisdom.

The root of the double meaning of the "conduct of reason" is the determination of reason as self-consciousness. In the next segment it will be shown how, according to Descartes's account of the historical genesis of the method, the guidance of reason arises from consciousness of its situation with respect to knowledge and ignorance. Eventually, we shall see that Descartes's new link of virtue with knowledge provides the unity of theory and practice upon which the coherence of the "parts" of philosophy or wisdom depend.

THE COMPORTMENT OF SELF-CONSCIOUSNESS

Descartes begins the account of the genesis of his philosophy with an appraisal of his education.

> I was nourished on letters since infancy, and because I was given to believe that, by their means, it was possible to acquire a clear and assured knowledge of all that is useful to life, I had an extreme desire to understand them. But as soon as I had completed the course of studies . . . I changed my opinion entirely. For I found myself embarrassed by so many doubts and errors that it seemed to me that the effort to instruct myself had no other effect than the increasing discovery of my ignorance.[11]

The result of his education is doubt, the first of three doubts that occur in the *Discourse*. Unlike the others which are deliberately instituted, this one occurs unintentionally or naturally. It arises from the disproportion between his desire for certain and useful knowledge, and the character of the scholastic heritage.

The criteria by which he judged his education, certainty and utility, do not themselves have a genesis. They are not said to result from reflection, but spring spontaneously from himself. Their specific character becomes clear by attending to the way they are employed as criteria for the critique of his education.

Certainty. Descartes initially encounters certainty as a paradigm rather than as a concept. He records that he was "delighted by mathematics because of the certainty and evidence of its demonstrations." [12] The dependence of certainty on the mathematical paradigm in effect equates the reasonable with the mathematical. This decisive move nevertheless occurs within the initial determination of reason as my judgmental thinking. This circumstance is revealed by the fact that truth is construed as certitude, as clarity and evidence, which is nothing else than a determination of empirical consciousness; for mathematical certitude is taken up as immediately given and as demanding and requiring no interrogation. That the immediacy of certainty—the expression is actually redundant—should enjoy such precedence is anticipated by the equivalence "raison ou sens."

The subjectivity of certainty is mitigated by its power to effect agreement.

Of all the traditional sciences, only mathematics has been able to sustain unanimity. In philosophy, on the other hand, despite its cultivation by the best minds over many centuries, there is "not a single thing that is not subject to dispute." [13] The incapacity of philosophy to achieve unanimity signifies the obscurity of its subject matter as conceived hitherto. As Descartes's appeal to the unanimity of the mathematicians shows, he takes unanimity as no less factually or empirically given than certainty. It is essentially unproblematic. There is, however, a reasoned link between certainty and unanimity:

> Whenever two men come to opposite decisions about the same matter, one of them at least must certainly be wrong, and apparently there is not even one of them who knows; for if the reasoning of the second were sound and clear, he would be able so to lay it before the other as finally to succeed in convincing his understanding also.[14]

In this and similar passages, Descartes is at his most sanguine in the expectations he entertains from the diversity of minds. He is by no means always so optimistic. Or rather it should be said that while the optimistic view endures as a conviction, it is complemented by an explanation of deviations from the standard: agreement would be forthcoming, but for the "corruption" of bon sens by prejudice. A perverted reason may refuse to assent to clear and distinct truths. This contingency raises difficulties about the adequacy of either certainty or unanimity as criteria, since perverted reason may equally well claim certainty and unanimity. The problem is especially acute in view of Descartes's claim that his philosophy is capable of producing "concord and amity," not merely among the expert, but among the generality of men as well. He contrasts it favorably with the received learning: "The controversies of the schools, by insensibly making those who practice them more captious and self-sufficient, are possibly the chief causes of the heresies and dissensions that now exercise the world." * Granted that Descartes anticipates that science will remain the preserve of a relatively small number, how can he fairly hope to produce unanimity among those who are not experts? The answer lies in the second criterion, utility.

Utility. In his subject-by-subject review of his studies, Descartes is careful to point out in each case its use. Poetry and history help cultivate sound judgment;

---

* HR I, 213/AT IX–2, 18. Descartes told Burman that "the monks have supplied the opportunity for all sects and heresies through their theology, i.e., their scholasticism, which above all must be exterminated" (AT V, 176). Gouhier (1924, 242) attempts bravely to explain this remark away.

rhetoric is worthy of esteem for its powers of persuasion; morality is instructive for the conduct of life; theology teaches the way to heaven; and philosophy, he says wittily, but also seriously, "teaches us to speak with an appearance of truth on all things, and causes us to be admired by the less learned." [15] These uses, however, are secondary compared with the utility of mathematics: "In mathematics there are the subtlest discoveries and inventions which may accomplish much, both in satisfying the curious, and in furthering all the arts, and in diminishing man's labor." [16] But he goes on to add that he did not at once "understand its true use, and, believing that it was of service only in the mechanical arts, I was astonished that, seeing how firm and solid was its basis, no loftier edifice had been reared thereon." Here we stand at the watershed where the traditional notion of a "literary" liberal education divides from what has come to be understood as education for service.* Descartes's esteem for mathematics and the mechanical arts is determined by his own wish to meliorate the harshness of the human condition, but his conception of their utility goes deeper. Liberal education looks to the cultivation of the mind, leaving the improvement of man's material circumstances to the practical arts. Classical authors did not conceive the possibility of the improvement of the arts on the scale that Bacon and Descartes anticipate. They thought that man's material circumstances were more or less fixed by nature, with all due acknowledgment of the region of latitude between the harshness of barbarism and the refinements of civilization. Descartes's attention to the material conditions of life is not only governed by a reappraisal of the possibilities of melioration, but also by a reappraisal of the worth and status of the spirit vis-à-vis "the body." Speaking of the moral studies in his education, Descartes says, "I compared the [moral writings] of the ancient pagans to palaces most superb and magnificent, which are yet built on sand and mud alone. They praise the virtues most highly . . . , but they do not sufficiently teach us to become acquainted with them." † At the beginning of the *Passions* he remarks that "nothing in which the defective nature of the sciences which we have received from the ancients appears more clearly than in what they have written about the passions." [17] The root of this deficiency is the

---

* The *Dioptric* begins and ends with praise of artisans, for whom Descartes proposed a school late in his life. John of St. Thomas distinguishes the liberal from the mechancial arts in the following way: "External works, called 'things to be made,' are the matter of arts called 'mechanical,' because such works are more servile and subject to despotic government. But internal works are also to be set in order by art, and because these works are more free and less servile, the arts that rule them are called 'liberal' " (John of St. Thomas, 1955, 13). Descartes proposes in effect to refashion "internal works" so as to achieve the measure of control over them that is possible in the mechanical arts.

† HR I, 85/DM 7–8. In view of his dependency on the Stoics, this statement is exaggerated.

belief that the soul moves the body or, generally, that the mind can control the body. Belief in this premise is the basis of a morality based on "words," that is, morality based on persuasion, exhortation, and prescription. Descartes, however, is preoccupied not with exhortation but with medicine, for health is the "first good and the foundation for all other goods in this life." [18] Health can be the "foundation" of all goods only because, as he goes on to add, "the mind depends so much on the temperament and disposition of the bodily organs that, if it is possible to find a means of rendering men wiser and cleverer than they have hitherto been, I believe that it is in medicine that it must be sought." [19] Morals and the whole spiritual life of man generally must be reevaluated if the mind is not, as the Socratic tradition believed, the controlling principle in man. It is necessary to learn to apprehend the mind not only for what it is in itself, but also as a function of the "animal spirits." "Words," which have been the medium of philosophy hitherto, must be evaluated from the perspective of "works," or the material efficacy of things. "For it seemed to me that I might meet with much more truth in the reasonings that each man makes on matters that specially concern him, and the issue of which would very soon punish him if he made a wrong judgment, than in the case of those made by a man of letters in his study touching speculations which lead to no result, and which bring about no other consequences to himself excepting that he will be all the more vain the more they are removed from common sense." [20] Thoughts whose only reference is to other thoughts lack the control of a practical result to be achieved, and hence tend to be "vain" in more than one sense. Understood in its proper dimension, therefore, utility is not a happy but chance consequence desirable in philosophy; it is intimately related to Descartes's conception of certainty as rooted in art or techne. In addition, politically the concept of utility is even more advantageous for the achievement of Descartes's project in that it is able to produce conviction without being accompanied by understanding of causes. With respect to the program of popular enlightenment, it may be said with only some exaggeration that utility is to Descartes's "practical philosophy" what persuasion was to the "speculative philosophy" of antiquity. "Then I shall place before your eyes," Descartes wrote in the *Search for Truth,* "the works of man upon corporeal objects, and after having struck wonder into you by the sight of machines most powerful, and automata most rare, visions most specious, and tricks the most subtle that artifice can invent, I shall reveal to you secrets so simple that you will henceforth wonder at nothing in the works of our hands." [21] Unlike Socrates, the new wise man will be able to persuade the multitude, thanks to his power to work wonders almost like God.

It is, of course, untrue that the "speculative philosophy" of antiquity despised or ignored utility; it made utility thematic at the moral and theoretical levels, and accorded it a place of respectability in human action. The thinking of antiquity on utility appears "useless" only when viewed against the enormous extension of the scope achieved through the notion of technical control of nature and its consequences for the melioration of the human condition. The error of antiquity was its failure to appreciate the possibilities of such control. But the extension of the scope of the practical arts presupposes a specific conception of nature and promotes a fundamental change of attitude toward the world as well as a new estimate of human power. From this point of view, the ancient appreciation of means and ends is mere child's play.*

SUMMARY: OLD AND NEW FOUNDATIONS

Descartes's doubt of received learning is a function of the disproportion between his desire for clear and certain useful knowledge and the vanity of scholastic learning. Since certainty and utility are not doubted but instead reveal the doubtful as doubtful, they are constructive parts of the new foundations.

The foundation metaphor occurs three times in *Discourse* I. Having reviewed letters, he comes at last to the sciences, meaning primarily the natural sciences as they were inherited from Aristotle. Of them he remarks that "inasmuch as they derive their principles from philosophy, I judged that one could have built nothing solid on foundations so infirm." [22] The context indicates that "philosophy" means roughly the subjects treated in Aristotle's *Metaphysics* and *Posterior Analytics*. Rather than rejecting the notion that the sciences require a foundation, he indicates that it must be sought from mathematics: he was astonished that "seeing how firm and solid was its basis, no loftier edifice had been raised thereupon." [23] This foundation is indeed appropriated in *Discourse* II.

Descartes also alludes to foundations in his remark on the morals of antiquity. The importance of morals is signified by their juxtaposition with mathematics, which would seem to indicate the need for a new foundation of morals that is in some way related to or derived from mathematics. But Descartes's

---

* Laberthonnière seems to have been the first to recognize the importance of utility and technical mastery in Descartes's thinking. See Laberthonnière, 1935, II, 15–45. More recently it has been stressed by Alquié, who nonetheless disputes his appraisal of its place in Descartes's thought; for Alquié argues that Descartes passed beyond the conquest of nature to the horizon of transcendence or metaphysics (Alquié, 1950, 321–26). Röd argues that, on the contrary, Descartes's metaphysical interest was dictated by the same longing for certainty that produced his interest in technical mastery (Röd, 1964, 27–34, 51, 185–95).

treatment of morality in the *Discourse,* as elsewhere, is muted in deference to the opinions of the "pedagogues" and of his "censors." The precaution is most visible in the complete disjunction between morality and religion. The latter is styled the "way to heaven," which concerns us only as a future event, and concerns reason not at all because salvation depends on "assistance from heaven" rather than the efforts of study.* It seems at first that perhaps this unusually crude portrayal of religion expresses a certain malice; yet it accords with the single-minded "extreme desire" for what is useful in "this life." Even so, Descartes's endeavor to popularize wisdom through general enlightenment compels him to consider the effect of religion on public morality.

Although Descartes's suppression of discussion of his religious antecedents leaves a serious lacuna in his account of the desire for security and utility, nevertheless the connection of that desire with the comportment of reason is clear in its broad lines. Descartes after a fashion repeats Socrates' calling philosophy down from the clouds. He wants to plant truth and goodness squarely within the stress and adversity of human existence. His longing is not for serenity, nor for transfiguration, nor for sanctification, but for security.† The longing springs up when the mind returns from its diffusion in imaginary spiritualizations of itself as a "form" or "immortal soul" to the banal but compelling fact that it is I who exist. It is the comportment of reason that seeks security in "unshakable foundations." This self-consciousness, as the unity of philosophy, should provide the key to the unity of theory and practice.

The New Foundation

Having concluded that there was in the world no teaching such as he desired, Descartes recounts the thoughts of his day in the *poêle* when he laid new foundations by turning to himself. Comparison of the dates supplied by the *Discourse* with the posthumous papers fixes the date of this reflection as probably November 10, 1619, when Descartes believed that he had discovered a "marvellous science." ‡ The founding reflections divide into four parts. The first elab-

---

* Laberthonnière cites this passage to support his claim that, for Descartes, religion is extrinsic or "heteronomous" to the natural condition of man (Laberthonnière, 1935, II, 167).

† Security, no less than utility, is thematic in the philosophy of antiquity. It is significant that in the Socratic dialogue devoted to expounding the "good for man" (the *Philebus*) the preference of knowledge to pleasure depends upon its being solid, reliable, exact, symmetrical, in short, mathematical. Similarly, Aristotle describes his first principle, the principle of non-contradiction, as "unshakable." Finally, the Skeptics shun dogmatism because its fixity is illusion; firmness and tranquillity can be achieved only by the suspension of judgment.

‡ AT X, 179, 216. Although this science is not expressly identified in the early manuscripts, the Opuscula of 1619–21 contains the fragment: "Ut autem hujus scientiae fundamenta jaciam,

orates its plan. The second is a transitional section which considers the feasibility of the plan and which unleashes a doubt that clears the ground of old foundations. Then comes the method proper, which sets the new foundations in place. Finally the "provisional morality" is introduced. These segments will be considered in their order of occurrence.

THE PRECEDENCE OF TECHNE

The founding plan is unfolded through an elaborate metaphor whose leading idea is that "there is less perfection in works composed of several parts, and made by the hands of diverse masters, than those upon which one alone has worked." * The idea is explicated by brief comments on four arts. The first two mentioned, architecture and city planning, carry the initial reference to "works" and "hands" decidedly in the direction of the practical arts. The reflection thus seems to be an appraisal of the achievement of perfection, for which the practical arts illustrate both the nature of the material to be worked upon and the manner in which it is to be shaped. All commentary reiterates the supreme condition for perfection, which is that the plan of the work must be ordered and unitary, or issue from a single "master." An imperfect work, by contrast, is a planless accumulation: considering old cities it seems that "fortune rather than the will of men using reason has disposed them." [24] Mastery or perfection, then, is achieved by the power of art or techne, which is able to eliminate the operations of chance by imposing a single design.

The third and fourth examples mentioned are legislation and science. Good legislation requires that one "prudent legislator"—the examples are God and Lycurgus—give all the laws at once so that they tend toward the same end. The comment on science contrasts learning accumulated in books (*sciences de livres*) unfavorably with the simple judgments of bon sens about things immediately experienced. But bon sens is in turn contrasted unfavorably with an imaginary example of a man who escaped the deforming effects of "appetites and teachers" by having the use of reason from birth.

The sense of the third and fourth examples becomes clear only by reference to the subsequent transitional section in which the possibility and legitimacy

---

motus ubique linea repraesentabitur." The studies of Sirven and Gouhier lead to the conclusion that Descartes was at that time a "physicist without metaphysics" (Gouhier) who was not in sympathy with the poetry-philosophy of Bruno, Vanini, and other Renaissance figures. Kennington's thorough study of the *Olympica* comes to similar conclusions.

* HR I, 87/DM II. To my knowledge, only Gouhier and Kennington have attempted a systematic interpretation of this passage, and only Kennington has recognized its crucial significance for the understanding of Descartes's foundations (see Kennington, 1963, 381–83).

of the plan is discussed. Descartes appears to reject public reform as both illegitimate and impracticable, whereas the reform of his own thoughts lies within his province.[25] This shows that legislation and science define the initial scope of the founding plan. Since legislation is the moral art of greatest compass, the plan's scope includes the whole domain of theory and practice. Taken altogether, the foundational reflection contemplates the achievement of perfect mastery in theory and practice by reforming both in accordance with art. The initial reflection on utility and certainty has evidently been embodied in the founding plan.

The unity of the foundations can be brought to light only after the parts of the foundations are understood in their own terms. We shall first expound the relation between science and art within a discussion of the provisional morality and Stoicism; and all that in turn to the public reform announced in *Discourse* VI. At present a brief glimpse ahead will suffice. The reform of science eventuates in a "practical science" to replace the "speculative philosophy" of the schools.[26] That science knows natural effects as distinctly as artisans know their crafts because it has successfully imitated art. But because its object is the "vast and ample" power of nature, it will render us masters and possessors of nature.[27] The subsequent discussion of the impact of science on society shows that the plan for public reform, apparently abandoned in *Discourse* II, has been renewed.

THE CONTROL OF UNAIDED REASON

The first step toward the implementation of the plan is reform of the sciences. The plan calls for beginning from a clean slate, the obstacles to which are the received learning and prejudices developed since infancy. The broom is a new doubt instituted for a set purpose: "But as regards all the opinions which up to that time I had embraced, I thought that I could not do better than to try once for all to sweep them completely away, so that they might later be replaced, either by others which were better, or by the same when I had adjusted them to the level of reason." [28] The method proper makes its appearance at the conclusion of this all-destroying doubt. What he says about it is perhaps the most obscure part of the *Discourse* for most modern readers. And it must have been equally obscure to those of Descartes's contemporaries who were unacquainted with the mathematics of the day. In order to identify and comprehend the philosophic dimension of the method, it is necessary to restore the mathematical context.

It is apparent from the introduction of the method that Descartes is thinking in terms of contemporary mathematics: "Among the different branches of philosophy, I had in my younger days to a certain extent studied logic; and in those of mathematics, geometrical analysis and algebra—three arts or sciences which seemed as though they ought to contribute something to the design I had in view." [29] These three "arts or sciences" are then subjected to criticism. Besides the fact that logic is encumbered by many harmful "precepts," it is not an art of discovery. Geometry and algebra are too restricted in scope, and are also embarrassed by an abundance of complicated and obscure rules. In summary he says: "This made me think that some other method must be found, which, comprising the advantages of these three, is yet exempt from their faults." [30] Observe that logic, geometry, and algebra, previously called "arts or sciences," are now said to be "methods." Method in the narrow sense of the term is simply identical with mathematical science. Descartes conceives the nature and task of method in the broad sense in light of this fundamental identity: the rules or precepts for the direction of the mind are inspired by mathematical rules and methods. Furthermore, the science-method identity will prove to be the key to art-science identity. The thoroughgoing assertion of this threefold identity in the "other" method Descartes seeks is the key to the precedence that method acquired in his philosophy. Let us consider the method-science identity.

Method as Science. The reader is given to understand throughout the *Discourse* that the method extends to all things that reason can know, which is nothing less than the world. A methodological perspective on the world is already latent in the traditional mathematical natural sciences—astronomy, music, optics, and mechanics. What they all have in common, Descartes thinks, is "proportions in general," which may be detached from the particular objects in which they occur and studied separately by "pure mathematics." The new method is just the general science of proportions, for the development of which Descartes borrows "all that is best in geometrical analysis and algebra." [31]

In the fuller account of the mathematical origin of the method given in the *Regulae,* Descartes avers that the method he seeks was known, though imperfectly, by ancient mathematicians, especially Diophantus and Pappus:

We have sufficient evidence that the ancient geometricians made use of a certain analysis which they extended to the resolution of all problems, though they grudged the secret to posterity. In the present day there also flourishes a certain kind of arithmetic, called "algebra," which designs to effect, when dealing with numbers, what the ancients achieved in the matter of figures. These two sciences [arithmetic and geometry] are nothing else than the spontaneous fruit sprung from the inborn principles of the method here in question.*

In another passage, this method is identified as "precisely that science known by the barbarous name 'algebra'" if only it could be disentangled from a host of complicated rules. Such reflections recalled Descartes from "the particular studies of arithmetic and geometry to a general investigation of mathematics," the "true mathematics," or *"mathesis universalis."* † This mathematics is universal in a double sense: it links arithmetic and geometry by expounding the subject matter common to both, from which the particular questions of those disciplines spring. This subject matter is said to be "order and measure," which is elaborated by a general theory of proportions; and it is universal also in the sense that it exhausts the mathematical features of traditional "mathematical physics"—astronomy, optics, etc.—and it seems to promise the extension of the application of mathematics to physics from a few to all subjects.

The universal mathematics therefore fulfills the goal of inquiry announced by the *Regulae*. Descartes seeks "universal wisdom" or "good understanding" as sound judgment on all things. That ambitious end can be achieved on the condition that there is a comprehensive perspective from which the particular sciences can be grasped through a unity established by their "interconnection." The universal mathematics knows those connections as the "order and measure" that holds sway not only through mathematics but also through physics. The "other method," then, is the idea of a mathematical physics, whose principles and rules of application are set forth in outline by the *Regulae,* and whose concrete realization is attained in Descartes's mathematical and physical treatises. Although this assertion needs refining to take account of problems peculiar to the transition from mathematics to physical explanation, and to account for the nonscientific dimension of the method, nevertheless it represents the true tendency of the method.‡

---

* HR I, 10/AT X, 373. Viète had already claimed that his analytic art could solve all problems (Viète, 1968, 353).

† HR I, 13/AT X, 378. Although the *Discourse* does not mention the mathesis universalis, Descartes at one time contemplated titling that work "Project for a Universal Science Which Can Raise Our Nature to the Highest Degree of Perfection" (AT I, 399).

‡ Owing to these and other ambiguities, the identity of the mathesis universalis is subject to dispute. Liard was, to my knowledge, the first to argue that it is an "algèbre spécieuse" in the Viètan sense, whose achievement is the algebraic treatment of geometrical problems, which is carried out in the *Geometry* (Liard, 1888, 47, 50, 54). Klein's very thorough historical study confirms Liard's conclusion; the mathesis universalis, Klein writes, "corresponds completely" to the intention of Viète's "zetetic" (Klein, 1968, 183, 198, 206). In addition, Brunschvicg and

In order to show how the universal mathematics, as a general science of proportions or magnitudes, achieves "foundational" status in Cartesian philosophy, it will be helpful to examine briefly the historical antecedents that lead up to it. As Descartes points out, the expression "mathesis universalis" is of ancient origin; it goes back to Aristotle. Various commentators have pointed out the close connection in Aristotle's philosophy between the "common notions," the theory of proportionals, and first philosophy.[32] Both arithmetic and geometry make use of the common notions, but they do so *qua* numbers and lines. Similarly, various theorems about proportionals may be proved of numbers and lines, although they may be proved generally by reference to the generic property common to arithmetic and geometry. There is, or ought to be, a universal mathematics which attends to this property and which would link it with the common notions or axioms upon which the "universal treatment" of this property would presumably be based. But Aristotle assigns this investigation to the philosopher, because he conceives that it falls together with the philosophic investigation of the common notions and of the "being" of mathematical objects. Consequently, the metaphysical investigation of what the scholastics called the "principles of demonstration" was linked with the theory of proportionals, the development of which resulted in the algebra from which Descartes takes his point of departure. Thus, among the algebraists who immediately preceded Descartes, algebra is called the "queen of the sciences" and even "divine art." [33] Therefore, the tradition is pregnant with the suggestion that a properly executed *universal mathematics* would *fulfill* the goal of first philosophy, although in a way that dictates the rejection of key Aristotelian metaphysical principles. The nature of the continuity with the tradition, one may say, anticipates at the same time a sharp break with it. The break is signaled even in Descartes's most conventional definition of metaphysics, years after the composition of the *Regulae,* for it is said to be "perfect knowledge of all things

---

Klein have shown that Rules XII and XIV of the *Regulae* mark the transition from *mathesis pura et abstracta* to physics (Brunschvicg, 1912, 107–13; Klein, 1968, 206–10). L. J. Beck, on the other hand, opposes the identification of the mathesis universalis with the mathematics of the *Geometry* or, it would seem, with any mathematical science, except the "apprehension of . . . proportions and relations . . . [by] a pure act of the *vis cognoscens*" (Beck, 1952, 229; also 194–202). This view arises from an interpretation of pure understanding and imagination such that any use of imaginative aids places a science outside the realm of pure mathematics. Pierre Boutroux, who held the same view and opposed Liard's interpretation, concluded that the mathesis universalis is in principle unattainable (Boutroux, 1900, 24, 34). This conclusion is necessary on the premise that the operations of pure intellect are so entirely remote from imagination that they do not even use mathematical symbols. Although Descartes's manner of expression lends itself to such a reading, we shall argue that his misleading expression reflects an incomplete conception of the nature of symbolic thinking. See below, pp. 172–73.

that man can know . . . so that we must begin with the investigation of first causes, i.e. principles." *

The objective of the *Regulae* is not merely to expound the universal mathematics, but also to show that it is the beginning or foundation of science, by a methodological argument which establishes that this science exhausts all that the mind is able to know. "It ought not seem such a toilsome and difficult matter to define the limits of the mind (*ingenium*) that we immediately sense in ourselves (*quod in nobis ipsis sentimus*), when we often do not hesitate to judge things that are without us and quite foreign to us." [34] It is not toilsome to Descartes, as it was to Kant, because the whole project is contained in the doctrine of simple natures. This theory belongs to a general type that was stated in antiquity, notably in the *Theaetetus*. It has been advocated intermittently ever since, most recently in the form of logical atomism. Briefly, it claims that there are irreducible elements, simples, or atoms. The irreducibility shows itself epistemologically as the last residue of analysis; in the real order, the simples turn up as Epicurean atoms, Aristotelian elements, or Cartesian extension. The simples are the primordial stuff from which knowledge, or objects, are built up. Since they are first without qualification, they have no cause, nor any explanation, and in this sense they are "a-logical." But when the elements or simples are mixed together, they compose "complexes" that admit of explanation; and when all the elements are known, all the complexes can in principle be perfectly known by discovering how the elements are concatenated to produce the complexes.

Cartesian simples are real: they are "natures" or "things." † They are also simple to knowledge, although it is essential to his theory that they are not simple to knowledge in the same way that they are really simple. The union of these two orders of simplicity enables Descartes to state the limits of knowledge, and to found that claim not on some proto-transcendental deduction, but on certain knowledge of what there is for the mind to know.

Although the *Regulae* enumerate simple natures in discrepant ways, the discrepancies may be ignored at this point in order to concentrate attention on what is without doubt the primary enumeration, which announces that they

---

* HR I, 203–204/AT IX–2, 2–3. The stress on the objective of knowing all that man can know is repeated from the earliest to the latest writings. The "man" in question is man's reason. It is therefore distinguished from what is "above reason," i.e. theology, but also from the fruitless metaphysical speculations of the past.

† It has been debated whether simple natures are things or concepts. It seems that they are both, since Descartes distinguishes between the simple *in se* and for knowledge. See Beck, 1952, 72–73.

are "either spiritual or corporeal or at once spiritual and corporeal." [35] They are known as simple, that is, as "primary and existing per se, independent of others," by intuition. They impose themselves upon the mind and claim its recognition much as sense objects do: "In order to know simple natures, no pains need be taken, because they are sufficiently known by themselves (*qui per se sunt satis notae*)." [36] Descartes lays great stress on this point. We are to understand that simple natures are wholly known, without the slightest taint of falsity or incompleteness; he embraces the consequence that knowledge of them is immutable and infallible. Indeed, the main error that is made with respect to them is just the failure to recognize that they are completely known. This happens when definitions of simples are attempted, for that commits one to the fruitless and confusing attempt to explain self-evident things by something more evident. It must be understood that there is no *logos* of simples, no account of them which could render them more evident and even less "justify" them. It was Descartes's repeated complaint, in the *Regulae* and the later writings, that the scholastics obscured these notions by attempting definitions, for they are "not among those that can be acquired by study." [37] They are known, as the Preface to the *Principles* puts it, "without meditation."

The concatenation of simples into complexes provides simultaneously a theory of things and of thinking which Descartes asserts with great assurance. "We say, fifthly, that we cannot at any time understand anything except those simple natures and what may be called their intermixture or combination with each other." [38] If some natural phenomena, such as the magnet, contained something other than such natures, it would be "hopeless to expect that reasoning will ever make us grasp it; we should have to be furnished either with some new sense or with a divine intellect." * Science operates entirely with simples that can be known at the beginning of inquiry from common experience. It follows that "man has no way toward certain cognition open, except evident intuition and necessary deduction," which are the ways that simples and their combinations, respectively, are known.[39] The two operations of intuition and deduction, therefore, precisely delineate the nature and scope of human knowledge: "All human science consists in distinct perception of the way in which those simple natures combine to compose other things." [40] This means in turn that the deductive illation of simple natures (the ordo cognoscendi) is at the same time the unfolding of the real order of things (ordo essendi). The mind, when it thinks clearly, is like a mirror of corporeal nature or extension.

---

* HR I, 55/AT X, 439; also HR I, 47/AT X, 427. This statement is a paradigm of Descartes's methodological apriorism in science.

It is obvious that on this theory the first principles of science, which are expressly said to be "known by intuition alone," * are reason and extension. It is equally obvious that Descartes contemplates a science that consists entirely of *noesis.* It is the outcome of his determination to banish opinion from science; for Descartes there is no discursive movement from what is "first for us," i.e., sensation, to what is "first in nature," or the principles of things. Instead, science begins with what is first in nature. The only rupture in the otherwise uniform coincidence of the two orders is the need for analysis of experience to discover what "modes" of extension are operative in a given phenomenon, although this exception is by no means insignificant. Finally, it is obvious that such foundations are entirely self-sufficient, and could only be confused by any attempt to justify them.

The theory of simple natures as the foundation of science is the source of some of the most important features of Cartesian philosophy. Contrary to the sense of the divine warranty of clear and distinct ideas, in this theory the transition from certainty to truth is fundamentally unproblematic. The immutable intuition of extension, which we may have also in sense experience, is determined to truth by the real extension of body. This is why Descartes can collapse the ordo essendi into the ordo cognoscendi, even if he retains that distinction in the way just noted. In the same train of consequences, it follows that the principles of physics are "reduced to mathematics," as Descartes boasted; that the principles of physics are irrevisable, because they are based on infallible intuitions; and that it is possible to "deduce" the physical effects of the world "a priori," i.e., effect from cause.[41] Finally, it shows that Descartes's philosophy is poised at the threshold that separates traditional metaphysics from the modern orientation on epistemology. Descartes remains squarely in the precritical metaphysical tradition in the sense that he believes that the mind can know the world just as it is. The Aristotelian inquiry into being disappears from his philosophy, not because Aristotle's question is unanswerable, but because it is answered as soon as it is posed: we know intuitively that all things whatsoever are either corporeal or spiritual or a mixture of the two. To say that the essence of material things, or the world, is extension, is for Descartes merely to utter the identity statement that body is extension.

But in addition to the strong realist conviction embodied in the theory of simple natures, there are other tendencies to the opposite effect. One of them, which we shall discuss later, is the reservations Descartes expressed in connec-

---

* HR I, 8/AT X, 370. Beck (1952, 82) acknowledges that simple natures are the ultimate principles of explanation, but does not draw the conclusion that seems evident.

tion with the necessity for the use of hypotheses in science. The other is a latent secondary argument for the simple natures and, in general, the methodological foundation of science, which is insinuated throughout the *Regulae*. It is that if just these simple natures (extension and the mind) are all that we *can* know clearly and distinctly, then even if there were some other nature, it must fall outside the reach of human knowledge; consequently, an adequate survey of the principles of knowledge renders the traditional ontological investigation superfluous. It is insinuated rather than argued because Descartes recognizes that if there were some unknowable cause operative in the world, explanation of the phenomena it influenced would be impossible; consequently, the utility of the investigation of what the mind is able to know presupposes that it is able to know all there is to know. Descartes expressed this thought humorously to his critic Froidmont: "I never expressly denied any of those things . . . that others imagine to be in bodies; but my gross and rustic philosophy is content with few things." [42]

Some authors have thought that the theory of simple natures disappears from Descartes's later philosophy, to be replaced by a substance doctrine of mind and body. These substances, moreover, seem to lose their evidence as "simple and easy" beginnings, since Descartes doubts the existence of body and requires the laborious reflections of the *Meditations* to determine the "nature" of the mind. In this study it will be argued that Descartes changes his terminology without altering his conception. The substance doctrine depends almost entirely on the interpretation, given in Rule XIV, of the relation of the modes of extension to the real extension of body. What is wanting in the *Regulae* that is provided by the later writings is an analysis of the relation of mind to body, which would at the same time "confirm" its intuitive apprehension. The metaphysical "distinction" of the mind from body performs this analysis; and the *Meditations* attempt to show the necessity for the relatedness of mind to body, both in the ordo cognoscendi and the ordo essendi. Even the essentials of this argument are contained in Rule XII, where Descartes presents the first statement of the theory of corporeal imagination. As for the apparent obscurity of mind and body as implied by the metaphysical doubt, note that Descartes continues to claim that these ideas are the clearest and most distinct of all, and even that they may be acquired "without meditation." How this claim may be squared with the need for the *Meditations* will be discussed later.

Science as art. The science-art identity has its roots in the medieval concept of liberal arts, which itself is dependent upon Aristotle's *distinction* between science and art. Since the science-art identity implies a break with the classical notion of theory, and consequently entails a new notion of the relation between theory and practice, it is pertinent to examine the classical background.

The source for all scholastic discussions of this question is Aristotle's statement on the intellectual virtues in the *Nicomachean Ethics*. Scientific knowledge is characterized by necessity; therefore, Aristotle argues, the objects of scientific knowledge must be eternal, for otherwise they would be subject to the contingency of existence and could not be objects of unchangeable knowledge. Scientific knowledge, however, is the syllogistically established necessary connection between minor and major terms; therefore, science is a capacity (*hexis, habitus*) for demonstration. But art (techne) brings a product into existence. It is the capacity to produce its product according to the rule of "right reason." In general, the object of science is nature, which we know but do not make, whereas the object of art is a contingent existent, which we make but do not in the strictest sense know.[43]

There are various problems in Aristotle's distinctions. Most conspicuous to the medievals was that the capacity for demonstration is a capacity for bringing forth a product, a "work of reason." St. Thomas wrote in explanation of the term "liberal arts" that "they not only involve knowledge but a certain work which is directly a product of reason itself; for example, producing a composition, syllogism or discourse, numbering, etc."[44] The difficulty of drawing a viable distinction between the capacity of science and art became especially evident to the logicians. Syllogistic logic meets all the conditions that qualify art: it directs a process toward a work, namely, in "perfecting the speculative power by artificial logic"; it sets its work in order by rules, i.e., it brings forth its product not by chance but from knowledge; and its product embodies truth in a work. The scholastic Aristotelians, then, continue to call logic theoretical, but they have altered the sense of the term. The transformation went farthest in the logic of Fonseca and Toletus, whose texts Descartes used at La Flèche. For them logic is not about concepts, judgments, and inferences, but about functions of knowledge, that is, about conceiving, judging, and inferring; hence their idea of logic as *directio ingenii,* which provides Descartes his point of departure.[45]

Descartes defines method as "certain and easy rules such that if they are accurately observed . . . one will always increase his knowledge and so arrive at true cognition of all that does not surpass his powers."[46] He complains that hitherto there has been no method for the investigation of truth. Each man has struck out along uncharted paths, occasionally hitting upon some truth by chance; but for the most part such unregulated inquiries serve rather to obscure the natural light than to increase it. What is wanted is an *art* of discovery, i.e., a set of rules that will enable the mind to discover truths routinely. Methodical procedure requires that we move from what is known with certainty to what is unknown; we must begin with the "simple and easy," and only later attack difficult problems. The whole difference between the clear and the obscure, Descartes advises, "lies in the route taken." The great power of the arts, even such humble arts as weaving, is that "nothing in [them] remains hidden, and they are wholly adjusted to the capacity of human cognition, [so] that they reveal to us with the greatest distinctness, innumerable orderly systems, all different from each other, but nonetheless conforming to rule. In the proper observance of these systems of order consists the whole of human sagacity." [47] Contrary to Aristotle, the artifact is perfectly known, not with respect to its "form," but with respect to its genesis; and it is known because it is produced according to rules—the technical analog of laws—which are themselves known because men have made them.

There is no disagreement from Descartes with the scholastics and Aristotle that an art is possessed only when it has been assimilated as a skill. It is the sense of numerous passages in which Descartes advises his readers to "accustom" themselves to clear thinking by exercising with simple and easy problems whose solutions are known; to practice in making enumerations and deductions; and above all, to learn the correct use of those "instruments" of our knowledge—understanding, imagination, sensation, and memory. To illustrate the results of the technical capacity, Descartes directs attention to the capacity of artisans to distinguish objects of extreme minuteness and to direct their eyesight in an orderly and successive way.[48] He who would master the universal mathematics must learn to imitate the artisan; "unaided" reason is as impotent before nature, or mathematics, as the amateur is before the expert.

The endeavor to reduce science to art leads to Descartes's deprecations of "lofty and serious" studies and to his esteem for the useful. "It is a common failing that mortals," he writes, "deem the more difficult the fairer; and they often think that they have learned nothing when they see a very clear and simple cause for a fact, while at the same time they are lost in admiration of certain sublime and profound philosophical explanations even though these, for the most part, are based upon foundations which no one has adequately surveyed—a mental disorder which prizes the darkness higher than the light." *

---

* HR I, 8/AT X, 370. It is in this connection that Descartes's criticism of excessive curiosity ought to be understood. See HR I, 307–308/AT X, 501–502; *Passions*, §§ 73, 75–76.

This "disorder" is endemic to a large part of traditional philosophy. The preference Descartes blames was expressed in St. Thomas's statement that "the slenderest acquaintance with the highest things is more desirable than certain knowledge of the lower." [49] Descartes replaces the distinction between "higher" and "lower" knowledge with the distinction between simple and complex constituents, all of which are on the same "level of reason." The grandeur of methodological first philosophy lies in its utility for knowing all else, rather than in the sublimity of its objects. The method, which opens the path to knowledge, is the most useful thing of all.

The precedence of utility in Descartes's thought is rooted in the identification of science with art. The "rule-governed" character of art makes it possible to distinguish a means-end relation between any two steps in the technical process. Indeed, it is the business of art to order its work strictly according to successive steps, each of which is instrumental to the next. Utility as a criterion of judgment of artistic production means nothing else than the invention and good use of instruments to secure desired effects. When this conception is incorporated into science by reducing it to art, utility becomes a criterion for the evaluation of thinking. The powers of the soul are appraised as instruments, and reason itself is the "universal instrument." [50] The same is true of each thought or idea, even as the steps of a deduction are each instrumental to the next. It follows that the utility criterion will declare that ideas which are not instrumental—which have no "effect"—also have no place in knowledge. The interpretation of knowledge as art is obviously well suited to the interpretation of the world as a machine. Corresponding to the instrumentally ordered systems of ideas are the instrumentally ordered gears and levers of God's great artifact. Just as a master artisan would not construct a machine in which there were gears that idled permanently, so in the construction of science, noninstrumental thoughts are "vain."

There is perhaps no better illustration of the import of the conception of science as art than in the transition from classical to modern mathematics, of which Cartesian mathematics forms a part. In his outstanding study of this question, Jacob Klein has shown that, whereas for ancient mathematicians the subject matter of their science could not be understood apart from an ontologically determined concept of the "being" of mathematical objects, the modern algebraists determine the subject matter by reference to its computational properties. But since the discovery of computational procedures is wholly immanent to mathematics whereas the investigation of the "nature" of mathematical objects requires a "higher" and prior science, the new orientation emancipates mathematics from metaphysics. Mathematics is now understood to be self-contained, self-sufficient, and independent of other "foundations." *

Descartes's awareness that his conception of science consituted a break with the Aristotelian notion is sufficiently clear from the repeated references to his philosophy as practical rather than theoretical or speculative. The designation is misleading because Cartesian science is neither theoretical nor practical in the Aristotelian sense; rather, it combines both. The manner of the combination is explicated by the identification of science with art, and by the linkage forged in mathematical physics of the intellectual with the mechanical arts.

Empirical Consciousness and Self-Consciousness. To evaluate the philosophical position attained in the *Regulae,* it will be helpful to compare it with the theory of demonstration Aristotle set forth in the *Posterior Analytics.* Both believe that the beginning of science must be absolute, i.e., an unshakable certainty about irrevisable truths. The beginning is made with "basic truths" that are "already known" because they are available to knowledge always. For Aristotle the beginnings are common notions of axioms, plus the principles proper to each genus of things; for Descartes they are the simple natures and the common notions. In both cases the beginnings are known intuitively, although the nature of intuition is differently interpreted by them. Both thinkers orient their appraisals of science by what they take to be science in fact: arithmetic and geometry, syllogistic logic (which Descartes recognizes but thinks useless), and the mathematical physical sciences—optics, astronomy, mechanics, music. Both arrive at their theory of science by reference to these received sciences; it is knowledge that "cannot be otherwise," or necessary truth. Both accordingly say that scientific demonstration is deductive, although for Aristotle deduction is syllogistic, whereas for Descartes it is the illation of simple natures. In both cases, the theory of demonstration reciprocally assumes and entails the "ontology" characteristic of their philosophies. For Descartes, natural science is universal because it has only one object, extension; for Aristotle, there are irreducible differences, or genera, although in each genus the formal object of science—the "whatness" of a thing—recurs.[51]

The great difference between the Aristotelian and Cartesian methodology is that for Descartes, mind is a principle of science. The mind in question is not a *nous* abstracted from any particular identity, but empirical conscious-

---

* Natorp observed that the "principles of the method are independent of this metaphysics" (Natorp, 1896, 425). Heimsoeth (1912, 87–93) and Alquié (1950, 56) hold similar views.

ness. Certainly the Aristotelian root of this transformation is the identification of science with a "capacity." Thanks to the medieval tradition, Descartes recognizes that the identification implies that the methodological reflection must therefore be an assessment of the "powers" of the mind from which the scientific capacity springs; and that the assessment must determine what the mind is able to know. Yet the reflection is the mind's assay of itself; consequently, the mind as a first principle means, specifically, self-consciousness as a first principle.

However, when Descartes asserts that the mind is a simple nature and a principle, it is unclear whether he means self-consciousness or empirical consciousness, the latter indicating immediate certainty both in intuition and deduction that, according to the methodological or self-conscious reflection, characterizes the scientific capacity. In the attitude of immediate certainty or empirical consciousness, the mind is not self-conscious but conscious of the objects of which it has certain knowledge. Descartes does not explicitly draw this distinction because he claims immediate certainty of the mind, i.e., the mind itself is among the objects of which immediate certainty is possible. This claim is indeed integral to the claim that the method is itself science, which is to say that certainty about the mind's powers has purportedly the same status as certainty of mathematical objects. Yet this is not so; the *Regulae* do not meet the criterion of science that they set. To express this state of affairs in contemporary terms: the *Regulae* expound an "object language," the universal mathematics; but in order to do so, it has recourse to a "metalanguage" (the self-conscious reflection) which determines that the object language (empirical consciousness' certainty) *is* science. This ambiguity reappears in the *Meditations* in the problem that, on the one hand, mind and body can be known "without meditation," but only after an elaborate meditation. The ambiguity will prove to be fatal to the projected unshakable foundations of science. Let it be stressed here that the self-conscious "metalanguage" of the *Regulae* generates not immediate certainty itself, which is factually given in the capacity for mathematical certainty, but the concept of science as immediate certainty. Otherwise expressed, the theory of simple natures that founds the concept of immediate certainty is expressed in the "metalanguage" of the *Regulae,* whereas direct knowledge of those natures is expressed in the "object language" of empirical consciousness.

The distinction between methodological self-consciousness and empirical consciousness provides an exposition of the previous assertion that "method," in the *Discourse,* is ambiguous, with both a broad meaning which spans the entire work, and a narrow meaning which is expounded in a portion of the work. Mind as a simple nature, as empirical consciousness, fulfills the aim to reduce all knowledge to a "single level of reason." However, the empirical consciousness with which Descartes begins in the *Discourse*—the "uninterpreted" autobiographical first person—is not the same as the empirical consciousness which emerges through the methodological reflection. The initial "I" is now split into a self-consciousness, and an empirical consciousness conceived as the "level of reason." The method treats inborn, unaided reason like a raw material or an elemental force, whose powers require assessment. The result is the institution of rules for the direction and development of the initially rude and random capacity. The rules are operative as *acquired habits* that regulate and direct the capacity, and thus extend its powers. In this sense, empirical consciousness can be said to be produced by refinement of the native capacity, even as an athletic skill is the product of training. This aspect of the method will assume greater prominence in the discussion of the obstacle to the accessibility of the world posed by sense prejudice. In this moment, empirical consciousness will be posited in the mode of idealism as immediate knowledge of thoughts only, which is that interpretation of the cognitive relation which vindicates the "realism" of science while eliminating sense qualities as "subjective."

In conclusion, it should be pointed out that the difference between methodological self-consciousness and empirical consciousness as the scientific capacity shows that Cartesian consciousness contains within itself the seeds of its own diremption. The methodological reflection effectively identifies reason with the technical capacity of the strictest kind—mathematics. But the methodological reflection is not itself an art and cannot be converted to one, even if the art of thinking issues from it. Consequently, from the point of view of the scientific capacity, the self-conscious reflection is defective, uncertain, and unreliable. The scientifically oriented wings of contemporary philosophy could be said to reject the Cartesian principle that consciousness is the beginning of philosophy just in virtue of consistent application of the capacity that the Cartesian principle engenders. On the other hand, self-consciousness remains available, and remains the only way to self-comprehension. The "crisis of science" of which Husserl spoke, the crisis of reason that is widely discussed, and finally the division of contemporary philosophy into two great camps, might be profitably considered in the perspective of this dualism.

THE MORAL FOUNDATION

The provisional morality is something of an anomaly in the context of the foundations. The founding design stipulates reform of the sciences and of morals or "legislation." The first reform is achieved by the methodological reflection, but there is no corresponding reflection upon morals. Instead, Descartes presents his provisional morality as a temporary dwelling to be occupied while the new structure is abuilding.

If it is the *Passions* which present the "most perfect morality," it seems doubtful that moral foundations could at this point be laid, since the key to the virtues, generosity, presupposes physics, which is not yet available. The presentation of a "provisional morality" thus seems consistent with the stated conditions of the definitive morality. The exegetical difficulty of following this serial order is that the morality of the *Passions* is not related by that work to theory, with the result that from it alone we cannot discern the unity of theory and practice postulated by the founding design. Furthermore, the maxims offered as provisional in the *Discourse* reappear, in expanded form, in the *Passions* as principal parts of the moral doctrine, which indicates that they proved to be of permanent value upon examination in the light of what can be learned from physics about control of the passions.* Conversely, Descartes's exposition of the characteristics of generosity is evidently transferable to the *Discourse,* without entering into the physics of the mind's relation to the body. It is therefore appropriate to expound the moral foundation at this point, making use of the *Passions* to preserve continuity of treatment, but especially to establish the connection between theory and practice.

The Unity of Theory and Practice. The unity of theory and practice is the method itself understood as the mind's comportment toward itself, as a self-consciousness whose content is self-mastery or the self-governance of reason, and whose objective is security through certitude. Descartes requires the entire *Discourse* to reveal the path that constitutes this self-consciousness, since he is conscious of himself in relation to the world. The method is the "way"

---

* The correspondence on morals returns repeatedly to the maxims of the provisional morality; see especially the Letter to Elizabeth, AT IV, 263–64. Both Gilson (DM, 230) and Alquié (1950, 339) state that Descartes's definitive morality is the same as his provisional morality, which is to say that morality remains incomplete because, as Alquié argues, in the Cartesian scheme of things man himself is "provisional." Röd argues that the whole objective of Cartesian theoretical philosophy is a rationally grounded practice, i.e., a definitive morality (Röd, 1964, 43, 50–51, 210ff.). These views more or less reflect the ambivalence of Descartes's retention of the classical view that the sage can attain the sovereign good in a complete manner while yet projecting a "perfect morality" of the future.

of reason. Descartes consequently espouses a version of the thesis that virtue is knowledge; but it descends to him from Socrates through the Stoics.*

The third maxim of the provisional morality is an abbreviated statement of a fundamental moral principle of the Stoics, which is restated in the *Passions.* "My third maxim was . . . to accustom myself to believe that there is nothing entirely within our power but our thoughts." † This distinction between what is and is not within our power is the necessary antecedent to the definition of generosity as the consciousness that "nothing truly pertains to [us] but this free disposition of [our] will." [52] Descartes takes his inspiration from the part of tradition that placed the greatest emphasis on power and mastery. The Stoics teach that adversity does not consist in the so-called "evils of life," but in a wrong attitude toward passions and desires. Accordingly, the way to freedom is to "conquer myself rather than fortune, and to alter my desires rather than change the order of the world."

In view of his project for the mastery of nature, it seems strange, as various commentators have noted, that Descartes could adopt this position even provisionally. Yet resignation reappears in the *Passions,* and ultimately it signifies a basic inconsistency in Descartes's moral position. But before we reach that point, it is possible to understand, by examination of the teaching of the Stoics, how they and Descartes perform the metamorphosis from complete submission to domination.

The Stoic ethical horizon differs fundamentally from that of Plato or Aristotle. The latter comprehend the ethical primarily in the context of the social and political affairs of men. The Stoics, however, begin and end their ethical understanding in the horizon of nature as a whole or providence.‡ The Stoics seek to discern the necessities of nature, including a particular man's nature (his daimon); for they escape the empire of necessity, not by overthrowing it, but by willing it, i.e., by "following nature" or by "attaching oneself to God." § In the words of Cleanthes, which became canon for the

---

* Owing to Descartes's general reticence about his sources, it is difficult to know what writings were familiar to him, especially since Stoic doctrine is diffused through a great variety of authors. Mesnard has noted an almost literal agreement between certain passages of the *Passions,* especially the section on Fate and Providence, and Sieur de Vair's *La philosophie morale de Stoiques,* published in 1614 (Mesnard, 1936, 162). For an outstanding speculative reconstruction of the historical roots of Cartesian generosity, see Krüger, 1933, 260–70.

† HR I, 97/DM 25. To an unknown correspondent, Descartes defended the Stoic paradox "as a truth no one ought to deny." It does not mean that external things are in no wise in our power, but that they are in our power "only insofar as they follow from our thoughts" (AT II, 36).

‡ This standpoint has been stressed by Alquié (1950, 345), and expounded by Krüger (1933, 228–40) in a manner upon which it is difficult to improve.

§ Epictetus, *Discourses,* II, vii; I, i; Pohlenz, 1950, 93–99. Cartesian "love of God" is defined

Stoics, "Lead me, O Zeus, and lead me Destiny / Whither ordained is by your decree." Descartes adopts this horizon as the perspective of ethics. The immediate relation is to God, nature, or providence, and only secondarily to other men. Generosity is essentially dependent on a teaching regarding the relation between the will and nature or providence, which provides the chief benefit of ethics, a "sovereign remedy for the disorders of the passions."[53] An element of that teaching is present in the third maxim. The Stoic rule prevents Descartes from "desiring anything in the future beyond what I could acquire, thus rendering me content." *

Just as Stoic ethics is inseparable from physics, so is ethics inseparable from logic. This unity is visible in three characteristic theses. (1) The primary task of the philosopher is to test and distinguish perceptions, and to make use of none which is untested. (2) The essence of the good is the power of dealing rightly with perceptions. (3) Reason is the faculty that deals with perceptions.[54] These theses assume and interpret the claim that our thoughts are the one and only thing over which we can achieve sovereign dominion. The Stoics analyze sensation into the perception and assent.[55] The perception, which is passively received, lies outside our power; assent or judgment we join to the perception, and that is within our power. Logic and ethics thus center upon "dealing well" with perception, i.e., making true judgments, which is "right reason." True judgment requires that we distinguish between perceptions that do not merit assent or credence and those that do. Trustworthy perceptions are perceived to be such by their own nature—they are characterized by "vivacity," or in Descartes's terminology "clarity and distinctness." Trustworthy perceptions are thus "comprehensible" properly speaking. Of them only are "firm and constant judgments" possible. Defective perceptions are unstable and changeable. They invite assent that is precipitous and cast the mind into ignorance, opinion, and doubt. Firm judgments are the foundation of "willing to get and willing to avoid" that is stable. Descartes signifies his appropriation of this doctrine when he writes that "firm and determinate judgments . . . of good and evil" are the soul's "proper arms" in combat with the passions.[56] Such stability is the condition of ethical freedom, which for the Stoics means doing what one will, without let or hindrance.[57] Non-philoso-

---

by this Stoic attitude, for he says that Stoicism is "the wisdom of acquiescing to the order of things," while Christian wisdom is "submitting to the will of God" (AT IV, 292; also AT IV, 608).

* Observe that the "way to heaven" depends upon "extraordinary assistance from heaven" that is "above reason" (HR I, 85/DM 8).

phers pursue freedom by following their appetites, which soon reduce them to the condition of a "slave." But because they comprehend the universal necessity, or providence, that permeates all things, the Stoics teach that freedom is attained by desiring what one wills, and willing what one gets. By "following nature" or fatality, the Stoics achieve the harmony of conduct and conviction that makes a man rich though poor, free though a legal slave. The second maxim of the provisional morality draws out some of the conclusions: "And this [practice of always following firm and resolute judgments] was sufficient to deliver me from all the penitence and remorse which usually agitate the consciences of those weak and vacillating minds who . . . keep changing their procedure, and practice as good, things that they afterwards judge to be evil." [58]

Stoic philosophy begins with consciousness of one's weakness and impotence with regard to necessary things. Epictetus treats this beginning as though it were Socrates': philosophy begins with the humiliating discovery that we do not know what is good for us. But whereas Socrates, beginning with opinion as opinion, retains the ambiguity between thought and world and hence does not make the distinction between self and world primary, just this distinction characterizes the Stoics. Philosophy begins with thought as that which is within our power and hence properly our own. Nature, providence, or the world is fundamentally heterogeneous to thought. This beginning culminates in the perfect possession of what is one's own, the tranquillity acquired in the way just described. It is here that the metamorphosis from complete submission to domination occurs in Stoic thought. Tranquillity, because it depends only on ourselves, i.e., our thoughts, is a possession so absolute that "not even Zeus himself can conquer it," or as Descartes put it in the third maxim, the Stoics "rival their gods in happiness." * The Cartesian transition to the mastery of nature occurs by expansion of the Stoic position. Acknowledging his "impotence" or unfulfilled desire for useful and certain knowledge, he recognizes that "dealing well" with perceptions requires the establishment of a methodologically produced self-relation. Our natural situation with respect to knowledge is the entrapment of reason in prejudice. This natural relation toward the world, which extracts assent to the external existence of objects that are only modifications of the *sensus communis,* must be revised in the process of

---

* HR I, 97/DM 26. The extreme piety of Stoic submission to providence culminates in the liberation of the sage from its power. It might be said that the mastery of nature is Stoicism turned outward and optimistic. See Epictetus, *Discourses,* I, i, vi, xii; Trendelenburg, 1855, II, 162–79; Laberthonnière, 1935, I, 30–31.

establishing a new cognitive relation to the world. The reorientation depends upon withholding assent and constructing rules for the direction of cognition, which thereby frees reason from its bondage to prejudice. The exercise of freedom to control assent thus empowers reason to control the world through a methodologically determined mathematical physics.

Implicit in the relations between self-consciousness, freedom, and mastery is the unity of theory and practice in Cartesian philosophy. Cartesian self-consciousness is not given, but produced by will or reason's self-assertion in the resolution to assume self-control. The conduct of reason defeats prejudice and controls cognition specifically by the reinterpretation of theory in terms of art. But the method eventuates in the control of nature, thanks to its interpretation under a paradigm of art, the machine. Consequently, reason's self-control, or its methodological self-consciousness, empowers its control of the world, a control which satisfies the longing for certainty and utility, i.e., security.

To assert the unity of theory and practice is not to suggest that they are amalgamated, but to relate them through self-consciousness. The characteristics of self-consciousness in theory and moral practice are different, even though there are points of intersection, especially in the argument to the Cogito. Its attributes in the theoretical mode will be examined later.

The Private Man. By discussing the moral foundations under the rubric "the private man," our intention is to stress its undidactic and personal character. Descartes's maxims give the impression of having been chosen to suit his circumstances and the eccentricities of his person. Yet for all its implausibility, it is offered as a model for imitation. It can be a model because the moral foundation institutes a secular individualism that is integral to the constitution of subjectivity.

If the self-conduct of reason, based on the distinction between what is and is not within our power, is Descartes's initial principle, its moral application should stress the repossession of our thoughts as that which is properly "our own." Such is the result of the methodical doubt, for it frees his thoughts from the clutches of prejudice, both natural and conventional. His moral nakedness after the doubt is made explicit by the need to institute a provisional morality. The first maxim shows how Descartes attaches himself to the social order so as to preserve the fundamental loyalty to himself that was won by the doubt. Indeed, his morality is provisional only with respect to the tentative nature of his relation to the social order, although this tentativeness is itself permanent.

The maxim begins with a resolve to adhere to the religion of his birth and to obey the laws and customs of his country. Since this maxim brings Descartes full circle to his state prior to the doubt, it might be said that it shows all too clearly how artificial and ineffective the doubt really was. Yet the return home from the Odyssey of doubt was anticipated when he noted that in sweeping away all his beliefs, he might later either replace them or reappropriate them, after they had been "adjusted to the level of reason." [59] The moral adjustment is suggested in a Montaigne-inspired skeptical passage which observes that the beliefs and customs of men are a function of the tribe or nation into which they are born: their most fervent attachment to the most venerable beliefs is merely an error of perspective. Descartes's reattachment to his old opinions has corrected this error; it is based on the consideration that, given the accidents of his birth, it was "most useful" to harmonize his conduct "with the opinions of those with whom [he] had to live." [60] This rule of expediency is reiterated when he decides not to bind himself by "promises which limit in some degree our liberty" and when he declares it "a serious sin against good sense if, because I approved of something at one time, I was obliged to regard it similarly later . . . after I ceased to regard it in a favorable light." [61] The rule thus sanctions outward orthodoxy, including the religious fideism and political "conservatism" so frequently attributed to him, but his outward attachment is merely a means to preserve his primary loyalty to himself, i.e., his freedom of thought. In this perspective, too, Cartesian expediency should be distinguished from a variety of related types, from Socratic *phronesis* to Machiavellian *raison d'état*. The "selfishness" to which his expediency is in service is not morally objectionable because it does no man injury; Descartes merely claims for himself "liberty of conscience." But to say "merely" is to take the main point for granted. While Socrates' opinions were surely heterodox, he nevertheless defended the social requirement that he conform to received opinion. That Descartes shares a measure of agreement with this view is clear from his disapproval of "turbulent and restless spirits" who interfere in public affairs and from his caution that his own doubt is "not an example that each man should follow." [62] Yet in that modern parallel to the crime of Socrates, Galileo's recantation, Descartes did not seize the occasion to restate Socrates' argument for the suppression of heterodoxy. The skepticism of the *Discourse* indeed tends altogether to undermine the hold of authority on opinion, as Gerhard Krüger saw when he wrote that "Descartes loudly declaims that he wants to 'reform' only his own thoughts, not at all those of the public . . . but when one considers what he actually does by 'cautiously' *publishing* his method, then it is precisely what he denies doing." [63] What is no less important, this "subversion" of the subordination of opinion to social requirements is accompanied by a more or less explicit justification of private opinion against public regulation, although it remains just beneath the surface, because it appeals to the commonly received premise that each man has a right to his own property. Descartes's procedure is to show men that their thoughts can be their own—the consequences follow of themselves. Its meaning in the social context is that the attachment of men to religion and state is rightfully secondary and instrumental to allegiance to their own credence.*

The evidence is abundant that Descartes's self-isolation was occasioned by the enforcement of religious orthodoxy.† Similarly, the morality of "generosity" seems to be those "proper arms of the soul" chosen for their suitability to guard his independence against the doubts of conscience; for generosity is a teaching about good conscience.

Generosity, in its ethical content, consists only in the "good opinion we have of ourselves" for having made good use of our free will, which is the only thing that "truly pertains to [us]." [64] Descartes's orientation is apparent in this definition—he can speak of practice only in terms of thought. Good use of the will consists in a "firm and constant resolution . . . to undertake and execute all the things [one] judges best." [65] The indifference of this ethic to specifying what are good and evil acts accords with the expediency of the first maxim. They cannot be specified because the thing of chief importance is that a man's actions follow from the free exercise of his own will. The content of the teaching consists in explaining what this means.

Ethics are the "arms" by which the "disorders of the passions" may be remedied, for they are the obstacle to freedom. The disorders are irresolution, vicious humility, weak-mindedness, repentance, and remorse, all of which stem from two causes: wavering opinions about good and evil, which cause us to condemn as evil what we once practiced as good, thereby engendering bad conscience; and inability to make ourselves wholly self-sufficient, i.e., to free ourselves from dependency on others, especially upon "Fortune." These faults may be remedied by the proper exercise of will, which is "resolute" judgments of good and evil that we make by using our own reason exclusively. Having

---

* Since Hegel observed the similarities between Christian theology and philosophical subjectivity, various attempts have been made to relate them. There can be little doubt that especially the Augustinian theological tradition, with its emphasis upon the *reditus in seipsum*, facilitated the reception of the Cartesian principle. We have not treated the question of Descartes's dependency upon Augustine because its complexity would carry us too far from the texts. But that Descartes in some sense stands in this tradition is obvious.

† This point is made in the *Discourse* (HR I, 100/DM 31) to explain his moving to Holland. In a letter to Balzac, written shortly after his move, he praises the freedom and anonymity that he enjoys in Amsterdam (AT I, 203–04).

done this we know that we have done our best, even if our judgments should turn out to be very bad. By embracing this doctrine, the virtuous man enjoys "tranquillity and repose of conscience," which is the "sweetest of all the joys, because it depends only upon ourselves." [66] The specific quality of this tranquillity is a "good opinion of ourselves" or the self-admiration produced by recognition that nothing is more wonderful than the soul that has achieved self-conscious mastery. The "individualism" Descartes espouses is accompanied by an appropriate "egoism."

The Diffident Benefactor. The reform of "legislation" projected by the founding plan seems to be rejected in the immediately subsequent reflection, on the consideration that it is illegitimate and impossible for a "private individual" to overturn "all foundations" of a state.[67] Yet in *Discourse* VI, Descartes confronts his readers with a public work of enormous dimensions, the mastery of nature. The possibility and legitimacy of this reform are explicitly asserted: "But when I acquired some general notions of physics . . . I observed to what point they might lead us . . . , and I believed that I could not keep them concealed without greatly sinning against the law which obliges us to procure . . . the general good of all men." [68] His new "legislation" is not directly political; like the law of the New Testament, it may be introduced by a private individual. The new law is the politics of man's auto-emancipation from his enslavement to nature: it is the politics of progress.[69]

In the legislative portion of the foundation, as with the moral foundation, Descartes uses literary devices to indicate his meaning indirectly. His grand design, for example, is proposed in the unlikely context of a discussion of his reasons for publishing his philosophy. Owing to the difficulties he must meet in order for his plan to succeed, the persistence of the autobiographical form gives him a spectacular rhetorical advantage, and indeed creates the public posture that was to be appropriated by the rhetoric of the Enlightenment. Descartes represents himself as wishing to "lose no opportunity of benefiting the public" by the generosity, or *humanité,* of a gift that will vastly ameliorate the human condition. He describes the fruits of science in brief but unforgettably stirring words:

[The mastery of nature] is not merely desirable for the invention of an infinity of machines that will enable us to enjoy without pain the fruits of the earth and all the good things to be found there, but also principally for the preservation of health, which is without doubt the first good and the foundation of all other goods of this life.[70]

However, he is prevented from publishing his physics by the learned of the day, whose opposition would, in his euphemism, "rob him of his leisure." He is thus the embattled public benefactor thwarted by the ignorance and obscurantism of the learned, who happen to be also the principal guardians of religion and morals. This rhetoric seems clearly designed to weld the self-interest and the indignation of the multitude into a powerful force that will "overturn" those states and institutions that attempt to frustrate the public work that Descartes would set in motion. It easily translates into the Enlightenment battle for science and *humanité* against the dark powers of superstition and despotism.

Although the thoroughly secular nature of the project has been frequently remarked, Descartes's presentation of it nevertheless draws upon affinities with Christian doctrine. One of the most striking, which Bacon had already exploited, is the kinship between the scientist's generosity and charity. Descartes understands the roots of these virtues to be polar opposites; nevertheless, popular fancy could easily mistake generosity for a kind of charity, especially since the fruits of science extend to "all men": his project incorporates the moral and evangelical lesson of the New Testament. There is a further resemblance in what might be styled the "secular eschatology" of the Cartesian project, a resemblance that is most pronounced when one considers the genre of the *Discourse* as "fable." It is the tale of a man who by quiet but Herculean labors has seized the truth; he now stands before his fellow men calling them to a momentous undertaking that will require great expenditure, wide public support, and the effort of "many hands" over a period of "centuries." It must have occurred to Descartes that if men could be induced to support a large number of priests in the hope of their future salvation, they might be inspired to support the leisure and expenditures of a cadre of scientists, provided that they were suitably edified by a myth. Certainly the *Discourse* has the elements of a great myth. Its brief description of man's future state is just sufficient to suggest a utopian condition reminiscent of the Garden of Eden, but with man's dependence on God's bounty and prohibitions replaced by efficient workmanship of machines. This chiliastic orientation on the remote future is thus correctly proportioned to occupy the place prepared by centuries of religious instruction. Nor does the myth neglect that all-important ingredient, the hero. The enormous dimensions achieved by the modest and diffident scholar as the fable of his conquest of the world unfolds is surely suited to inspire the edifying belief that there is no evil for which nature, orchestrated by man, has not provided the remedy.* Since direct evidence is wanting, it is not certain that Descartes intended all these features. But reflecting upon what is said in the *Discourse* on poetry, history, and rhetoric, and considering Descartes's clearly stated aim to appeal to the "unlearned" public, its plausibility must be acknowledged. The myth failed, no doubt partly because Descartes was not Newton, and partly because, in his eagerness for recognition, he forgot that gods do not write books, especially about themselves. But elements of it survived, or were reborn many times, with new heroes and altered plots, until faith in progress was transformed into an unshakable conviction.

To say that Descartes wished to perpetuate a myth does not imply that he did not believe its essential elements. There is no evidence that he had more definite views on the future than are stated in the *Discourse*. Perhaps he was content with the projections of Bacon's *New Atlantis*. That he took seriously the possibilities afforded by medicine is plain from his misplaced confidence that the results of his own studies would enable him to extend his life beyond a hundred years; his opinion illustrates the peculiar effect that the open scientific horizon has upon imagination. Finally, the alternation of the Cartesian "I" between becoming modesty and the heroic pretensions of a Promethean benefactor is more than a personal idiosyncrasy. Descartes portrays a new type of hero: the private man, the scholar or scientist, who is preoccupied with his own thoughts. He does not appeal to popular awe of the saint nor to admiration of the great political figure who restores justice. These two types are ethical examples because they act for a good greater than themselves; and the great models prove the authenticity of their motives by suffering or dying for a cause. Cartesian heroism, however, is based on the premise that there is nothing more valuable nor more admirable than one's own soul and his own private existence. From this perspective, the high drama of the traditional hero or saint assumes the aspect of vainglory or a somewhat foolish self-forgetfulness. The benefits bestowed by the new hero are commensurate with his character, for they enhance the private welfare of each without invading the privacy of any with moral admonitions and public requirements. His gifts are, so to speak, morally

---

* The heroic proportions in which Descartes portrays himself are related to, but not identical with, his amour propre. In addition to the *Discourse*, it is clearly present in the Letter to Dinet, the *Search for Truth,* and the letter from the unknown correspondent that Descartes used as the Preface to the *Passions.* The latter writing, in which the praise for Descartes's Promethean achievements passes all limits, may well have been composed by Descartes himself, as several passages of his responding letters suggest (AT XI, 323, 325).

neutral toward the individual. This model of the apolitical private man who nevertheless benefits his fellows more concretely than any morality, which the statesman recognizes as enlightened self-interest, is the basic content of Descartes's "legislation." Henceforth, the selflessness of Socrates and Galileo are admired, while Descartes is imitated.

The Problem of the Metaphysical Foundation

The completion of the provisional morality brings to a close the foundational reflections of the day in the poêle. But just as it appears that the foundations are complete, Descartes suddenly reverts to them in a new way. We learn that he conducted physical inquiries for nine years, while refraining from taking any "definite part in regard to the difficulties that the learned are wont to dispute, [nor had he] commenced to seek the foundations of any philosophy more certain than the vulgar." [71] There is no further explanation as to why still another foundation might be needed, except for the opening statement of the summary of metaphysics: "I do not know that I ought to tell you of the first meditations that I made, for they are so metaphysical and so unusual that they may perhaps not be to the taste of everyone. Nevertheless, in order that one may judge whether the foundations which I have laid are sufficiently firm, I find myself constrained in some manner to speak of them." [72] The laying of the second foundation engenders one of the most intractable problems in Cartesian philosophy—the problem of the relation of metaphysics to method and physics or, in general, the problem of the purpose and achievement of metaphysics. It is also the decisive problem for the evaluation of the achievement and intention of Cartesian philosophy. The objective of the present discussion is to state the full range of ambiguities that surround Descartes's metaphysical intention, showing that several prominent interpretations of that intention cannot be supported in view of the evidence to be presented and also that the *Meditations* must be evaluated in the perspective of Descartes's attempts to secure the reception of his innovating philosophy from a hostile audience and, in particular, that the requirement of order demands that the *Meditations* be approached directly from Cartesian physics.

THE REDUNDANCY OF THE TWO FOUNDATIONS

There is a basic discrepancy between Descartes's actual procedure in his physics and his subordination of physics to metaphysical principles.

In the *Discourse,* Descartes explains that he used his method for nine years to solve many problems in physics, samples of which are contained in the *Dioptric* and *Meteors*. That he has made the transition to physical investigations under the aegis of the method is evidenced by his statement that he was "careful to conduct all [his] thoughts according to the [method]." * Rule Three of the method is a rule of order according to which investigation must move consecutively from the simplest to more difficult questions. In particular, he notes that he treated physical questions mathematically by "detaching them from all principles of other sciences which [he] found insufficiently secure." [73] Therefore, during this nine year period (1620–29) Descartes seems to have thought his mathematical foundation adequate for science.

However, this order is altered by the metaphysical foundation. Upon discovering that the "first causes and principles" are "God and the soul," Descartes "deduces" the effects of the world using "no other principle than the infinite perfections of God." [74] This discrepancy faithfully mirrors the discrepancy of order in the Preface of the *Principles*.† The problem is that according to the genetic and methodological order, Descartes proceeds directly from his method to physics; the metaphysical principles to which physics is then subordinated are reached only by means of the doubt which overthrows sense evidence and "all the reasons formerly accepted as demonstrations," that is, both sense prejudice and the principle of the methodological foundation, extension. The latter is replaced by God, although the physics deduced is identical with that derived from the methodological foundation. The question remains why Descartes needs yet another doubt (the third in the *Discourse*) to overthrow foundations he has previously declared secure. Why is not the doubt an explicit critique of the methodological foundation, and, indeed, why does he not even allude to its existence in either the *Meditations'* or the *Discourse*'s account of metaphysics? Finally, what is the function of the metaphysical foundation?

The last question requires discussion along several avenues, but there is a primary datum for the point of departure—Descartes's statements of its func-

---

* This important fact has been frequently overlooked. Gueroult, for example, commenting on the order of philosophy as stated in this context, says that the first application of the rules of the method are "precisely to metaphysics" (Gueroult, 1962, 175).

† Above, p. 6. Recognition of this problem is not new. Already in 1661 Sobière declared that Cartesians were generally agreed upon the independence of physics from metaphysics (Balz, 1951, 71). The problem was brought to the attention of modern scholars by Liard, who forcefully argued that Descartes's physics rested exclusively on his method (Liard, 1882, 5, 89–110). Sebba credits Liard's study with profoundly influencing Lévy-Bruhl, Charles Adam, M. Blondel, Laberthonnière, and Gilson (Sebba, 1964, 46–47). The wave of scholarship that was led by Gouhier and culminated in Gueroult's *Descartes selon l'ordre des raisons* might be seen as an extended attempt to refute Liard, as indeed Alquié has remarked (Alquié, 1950, 9, 24).

tion when he characterizes metaphysics broadly in contrast to other parts of philosophy. They all agree that metaphysics discovers "first principles and causes," whose function is not to justify a previously existing science, but to initiate science as a deduction a priori, i.e., effect from cause.[75] But since the methodological foundation also initiates science, the discrepancy of the two orders reduces to an apparent redundancy of function.

METAPHYSICS AS THE BEGINNING OF PHILOSOPHY

This problem may be attacked by consulting the correspondence on the origin of metaphysics. It is first mentioned in 1630 when Descartes wrote Mersenne that he had devoted the previous nine months to a metaphysical study of the foundation of physics.[76] The date confirms the chronology of the *Discourse* and proves that Descartes came to the metaphysical foundation after he possessed a considerable body of physics. Although the nature of the foundational problem is not discussed, it is apparently theological since Descartes here announces his theory of God's creation of the "eternal" truths as the fruit of his metaphysical labors. It is difficult to extract inferences from this datum. The theory does not figure in *The World,* the writing closest in chronological proximity to the earliest metaphysical researches; nor in the *Discourse* summary of *The World,* nor in the *Meditations* or *Principles of Philosophy.* Descartes never explained how it founds science, if it does, nor how it can be reconciled with God's immutability, upon which he laid great stress. Nevertheless, most commentators have thought it a key metaphysical doctrine, even if there is little agreement about its interpretation. A cautious evaluation of the correspondence leaves us with the datum that the origin of metaphysics is in some way theological and connected with foundations, and in that confirms the *Discourse.*

A more promising approach is offered by discussions of the use of hypothesis that link achieved science to a foundational problem. In the *Discourse,* Descartes noted that his use of hypothesis in the *Dioptric* and *Meteors* might give occasion to objection, which he attempts to disarm in advance by appeal to the coherence of his hypothetical arguments, and by assurances that he possesses principles from which the hypotheses may be deduced. His anticipation was correct. In correspondence with Mersenne and the astronomer Morin on this question, Descartes took two positions. One of them was that he could satisfy the objections only by his metaphysics, which would establish the first principles from which he had deduced his assumptions.[77] This declaration seems to solve the problem of redundant foundations. Metaphysics does indeed initiate science although not genetically but only as deduced from first causes. It is therefore compatible with preexisting science, which presumably originates from the hypothetical procedures sanctioned by the method. The proposed metaphysical discharge of hypotheses may even be linked, conjecturally, with the creation of eternal truths. If the ultimate assumption of science is the uniformity of nature (theologically, the immutability of God), is it not challenged by the creation doctrine? If so, that doctrine would overthrow the methodological foundation, for perhaps nature's creator is a deceiver. But when we know God as he truly is, we know that his omnipotence entails his immutability, hence his "veracity."

This reconciliation does not so readily succeed. While Descartes does say that metaphysics eliminates his hypotheses, he continues in the same letter to explain why it is impossible to eliminate hypothesis from science.[78] This assertion is confirmed by *The World* and *Principles,* where, despite explicit appeal to God as principle, and the presence of the claim to an a priori deduction, the necessity for hypothesis is acknowledged. Moreover, in other letters of the same period on this subject, he says that the elimination of the hypothesis used in the *Dioptric* would require, not metaphysics, but "the complete course of my physics." [79] In any case, Descartes never achieved nor claimed to have achieved an a priori deduction entirely free from hypothesis, so that the metaphysical foundation cannot be interpreted as addressing this objective.

THE UTILITY OF METAPHYSICS

The first statement on metaphysics or "philosophy" occurs in *Discourse* I, where Descartes remarks that all the sciences depend on it, although he thinks that one "could have built nothing solid on foundations so infirm." Mathematics, which in *Discourse* I appears capable of supporting a much greater edifice than has been built upon it, is made the methodological foundation in *Discourse* II. At the conclusion of that *Discourse* Descartes writes that he "dared not undertake all at once [to solve every difficulty] that might present itself; for that would have been contrary to the order prescribed by the method. But having noticed that knowledge of these difficulties must depend on principles derived from philosophy, in which [he] as yet found nothing certain, [he] thought that it was necessary to establish certainty in it." [80] This task was laid aside because he was, he thought, not yet mature enough. Nevertheless, in *Discourse* III we find him engaging in physical investigation on the basis of method alone. Method alone sufficed, presumably, because Descartes believed that he had succeeded in founding physics on "no other principles than mathematics." * It

* *Prin.* II, § 64; HR II, 131/AT IX-1, 212; AT XI, 47; AT II, 268; AT III, 39. Observe that in DM Descartes says that he chose for principles of his physics knowledge "so natural to our minds that none could even feign ignorance of it" (HR I, 108/DM 43).

appears that Descartes, observing that "so many excellent men" had failed to establish anything certain in "philosophy," has excised it altogether. If so, the new foundation breaks radically with the past. The metaphysical foundation is pressed into a correspondingly awkward posture.

How very awkward it is becomes apparent from the one statement in the *Discourse* on its origin. Descartes explains that he had (from 1620 to 1629) taken "no part in the difficulties that the learned are accustomed to dispute, [nor had he] sought the foundation of any philosophy more certain than the vulgar." [81] The "foundation" meant here is metaphysical, for he attributes his diffidence to the fact that not even the most excellent men before him had succeeded. Descartes would "not have dared" undertake it himself, but for the embarrassing rumor that he already possessed a new philosophy. This circumstance caused him to do what, left to himself, he would not have dared, because "having a heart too good to will that I should be esteemed otherwise than I am, I thought it necessary to strive by every means to render myself worthy of [my] reputation." [82] No doubt more than one metaphysical treatise originated from similar motives, but rarely is it so candidly admitted. Unless this remark is dismissed as episodic sarcasm at the expense of the learned, it may be inferred that the metaphysical foundation was not dictated by some defect in the methodological foundation, but arises from Descartes's wish to ingratiate himself with the learned.

The remark cannot be dismissed as episodic because there is the imposing body of evidence linking the *Meditations* and its publication to Descartes's relations with the learned. The first mention of metaphysics to Mersenne (15 April 1630) is accompanied by the injunction to tell everyone about the doctrine of eternal truths, without attributing it to himself. On 25 November 1630, he explained to Mersenne that the "principal points" of the metaphysics upon which he was at work were to "prove the existence of God and this of our souls: when they are separated from the body, their immortality follows. For I am angered when I see that there are people so audacious and impudent that they fight against God." [83] These statements prove that the metaphysics was originally conceived as an apologetic writing whose pious intention could not but be approved by the scholastic theologians. The launching of the *Meditations* and its subsequent career in Descartes's lifetime is inseparable from this intention, which is so plainly marked in the text itself by the letter of dedication to the Sorbonne faculty, from whom he sought approval of the work. Hertling's detailed study of the intense diplomacy between Descartes and the theologians in regard to its publication reveals in vivid clarity the sometimes embarrassing lengths to which Descartes went to secure approval.* Gilson's study of the doctrine of freedom in the *Meditations* concluded that it is a "tissue of borrowings" from then current Oratorian and Jesuit positions, not to mention the "opportunism" with which Descartes appropriates doctrines from St. Thomas, St. Augustine, and other standard authors.[84] To Koyré it seemed that the *Meditations* are "not only a resurrection of Augustinian philosophy . . . but [are] profoundly imbued with the doctrine, methods, points of view, and even the prejudices of the scholastics." [85] Even the most generous readers find it difficult to acquit Descartes of some duplicity in these proceedings. He wrote Mersenne that he desired the approval of the Sorbonne because "it seems to me extremely able to serve my designs; for I tell you that this little work . . . contains all the principles of my physics." [86] Mersenne is cautioned not to mention this because he wanted the Sorbonne to pay attention to the work's theological themes, which should distract them from noticing that his principles "destroy those of Aristotle." These remarks throw light on a textual peculiarity of the *Meditations*. The Sorbonne letter commends the work for its pious intention to refute the atheists by proofs of the existence of God and the immortality of the soul. Nothing is said about the intention to found the sciences, which is broached only in the First Meditation, nor are these two plans ever explicitly connected, even as the *Discourse* disconnects the two foundations; it seems indeed that there is some tension between the apologetic and scientific intentions. The remarks to Mersenne prove that they were clearly distinct in his mind and that he understood the apologetic argument as an opportunity to persuade "insensibly" the theologians to approve his "foundations" before they realized that they destroyed those of Aristotle. This was the evidence that provoked Charles Adam to characterize metaphysics as a "flag to cover the goods." [87]

On analysis, the evidence regarding the two foundations suggests that the first principles of the metaphysical foundation are "God and the soul," while the first principles of the methodological foundation are reason and extension or mathematics. In order to secure the reception of his methodological foundation, Descartes seems to have fitted it out in the fashionable dress of the day by displacing extension with God in the foundation.† This reading is suggested by the evidence of the *Discourse*. After the summary of metaphysics, Descartes

---

*Hertling (n.d.) believed that his study was a corrective to the then dominant view that Descartes had severed his ties with scholasticism. He believed that by showing the contrary, he had helped restore recognition of Descartes's philosophical dependency upon scholasticism. What he proved instead was Descartes's heavy involvement in academic politics.

† For an interpretation of the metaphysics of the *Discourse* in conformity with this view, see Caton, 1970, 239–41.

writes that his physical investigations taught him "many truths more useful and more important than [he] had learned or hoped to learn." [88] This denigration is followed by the remark that he was moved to publish his metaphysics only after he recognized the utility of his physics.

The context will not permit us to interpret these remarks as appeals to popular prejudice. As was mentioned, *Discourse* VI explains the obstacles Descartes faces in publishing, the reasons why he decided at last to publish, and the measures he will take to secure the reception of his philosophy. The great obstacle is the opposition of the learned, who will oppose the "foundations of his physics," and rob Descartes of his leisure.* The opponents are characterized in language that a soldier might use to describe an enemy. The publication of his foundations will be like throwing open windows in the "dark cave" of obscure terminology and ill-conceived principles in which the "blind" take refuge "to fight without disadvantage against those who can see." [89] Descartes in fact likens himself to a general, who appraises the difficulties already overcome as "so many battles in which I have had fortune on my side"; success in the few remaining struggles will "bring [his] plans to completion." † The remaining struggles must be the fight for the legitimacy of the new foundations.

Since the identity of the enemy (the learned) and the contested terrain (foundations) are known, the battle plan can be inferred from these data. It is clear that Descartes cannot hope to win by the use of force; he must therefore use cunning and audacity. He will write a treatise on metaphysics whose objective is to neutralize the opposition by passing directly into the citadel (or cave) of the enemy under a flag of piety. For if the learned will oppose his foundations, they must oppose either reason and extension, or God and the soul. But clearly, the opposition of the schools will be raised by foundations that clash with the foundations of religion, as Descartes's own experience proved. But the foundations of religion are God and the soul, as the Sorbonne letter expressly declares. The learned are thus in accord with the metaphysical foundations; hence, Descartes must anticipate that they will oppose the methodological foundation, which must therefore be the genuine foundation. If this

---

* HR I, 123/DM 68. As late as 1640, Descartes was uncertain whether he would publish his physics in his lifetime, for he thought that he could not write the truth without stirring "the hatred of the learned" (AT III, 39; AT V, 112).

† Ibid. Bohatec (1912, 30) reports that it was a generally received opinion among the scholastics of the latter part of the 17th century that Descartes had "declared war" upon their philosophy. Protestants in particular believed that Descartes's philosophy was incompatible with their theology. For the list of the ten theses of Cartesian philosophy that were condemned at the University of Louvain, see Monchamp, 1886, 356–57. For a summary of later 17th century opinion of Descartes, see Daniel, 1694, 188ff.

opposition is not thwarted, the success of his grand design is imperiled. But the publication of his metaphysics will "extremely serve" his design to secure the reception of his philosophy, because it will confuse the assaulting troops by camouflaging their objective.*

It seems, then, that philosophy has but one foundation, which is the work of a single hand and not an accumulation of scholastic learning. If this is the case, the *Meditations,* at their deepest level, must be a recapitulation of the methodological foundation. Penetrating the scholastic facade that obscures it requires approaching the work according to the rule of order, that is, after physics; for it recapitulates the method after the fact of physics, especially optics and physiology. The optical theory of vision and the physiological theory of animal automatism are indispensable for grasping the true foundational problem.

* This intention has not altogether escaped notice. Maritain wrote that Descartes knew "the profound incompatibility of his philosophy with the whole authentic tradition of Christian wisdom. And I say—and this is much more serious—that it is a characteristic of Cartesian thought itself to be a masked thought." The mask is a product of the "double cloak" of science and apologetics in which Descartes presented his philosophy. Thanks to the apologetics, Cartesian science was received as compatible with faith, but it ultimately destroys faith (Maritain, 1945, 44).

3 Objectivity: Man as a Machine

> The foundation of Descartes's system rests on his theory of the pineal gland.
>
> Malebranche

> The fundamental principle of modern philosophy is the opinion concerning colors, sounds, tastes, smells, heat and cold; which it asserts to be nothing but impressions in the mind derived from the operation of external objects, and without any resemblance to the qualities of the objects.
>
> Hume

The Optical Bias of Cartesian Physics

In May of 1632 Descartes wrote to Mersenne that to discover the order of celestial motions is the "key and foundation of the highest and most perfect science of material things," since it would enable him to deduce all terrestrial effects.[1] Although Aristotelian science sanctioned no such deduction, it did ascribe to astronomy a privileged position among the sciences, on the ground that the most comprehensive effects must exhibit the most comprehensive principles. This notion, common to most of antiquity, was an important part of the scientific outlook that prevailed in Descartes's time, and it no doubt helps explain the enormous impact of the Copernican theory upon early modern scientific thought. Descartes, however, was unable to assimilate Kepler's profound discoveries, so that the key he sought eluded him. But he did not relinquish the notion of a privileged science that might provide such a key. When *The World* was completed in 1633, optics had displaced celestial mechanics as the key to nature, for the work bore the subtitle, *Treatise on Light.**

---

* Descartes remarked that a theory of planetary motion would require preliminary observations conducted along Baconian lines, and he feared that a system of celestial mechanics was perhaps "beyond the reach of the human mind" (AT I, 249). These remarks reveal almost total ignorance of Kepler's astronomical writings. Like Galileo, Descartes never realized that Kepler had proved that the planetary orbits are elliptical.

The first scientific treatises Descartes published, the *Dioptric* and *Meteors*, set forth an optical theory and applied it to an explanation of vision and of the color spectrum of the rainbow. The theory of vision is a physiological optics, which provides the theoretical and experimental foundation of the celebrated animal automatism hypothesis. Automatism is the point of departure for the treatise on the *Passions,* in which Descartes undertakes to explain the mind's union with the body. The prominence of optics and automatism in the published writings is even more pronounced in the correspondence and posthumous writings. These easily recognizable facts allow one to speak of the optical bias of Cartesian physics.

It is possible to trace virtually step-by-step the displacement of celestial mechanics by optics as the key and foundation of the sciences. Descartes's general physical laws are rules for the composition of the motion of percussing rigid bodies. Since the dynamics of percussing bodies had been amalgamated by the late medievals with optics as the standard model of the action of light, Cartesian physics is clearly an attempt to generalize an optical model.[2] This becomes yet more evident as the vicissitudes of Descartes's laws are traced through his physics. The vortex theory was unable to overcome the grave obstacles to the application of these rules to planetary motion; indeed, the rules did not yield the correct quantities even for percussing bodies until they were revised by Christian Huygens.[3] Descartes enjoyed more success applying the percussion concept to reflection and refraction, for it was the model he assumed in his proof that refractive properties follow the law of sines. Building upon the momentous optical studies of Kepler, he extended the demonstration of the formation of the retinal image to a theory of visual sensation and its aberrations. This success apparently prompted him to extend the optical model to the explanation of the other senses, so that ultimately it became the model for a general theory of sensation. The optical paradigm was transferred to the sense mechanism of the human automaton, where it plays the central role in the explanation of the nexus between sensation and locomotion, which is the core of the automatism hypothesis.

Despite this retreat from celestial mechanics, Descartes did not abandon the attempt to link his foundations with astronomy. The connection is provided by light. Descartes reasons that if this cosmic phenomenon can be explained in its optical and physiological context, then he must in some sense possess the key to the true cosmology, despite the want of a demonstrative celestial mechanics. Owing to this series of connections, optics became for him the primary link between the general laws of nature, celestial motions, and man, who is "the spectator of all." [4]

The precedence of optics goes yet deeper. The opening statement of *The World* announces a double perspective that unites Descartes's scientific and philosophical endeavors: "It is commonly believed that the ideas we have in our thoughts entirely resemble the objects from which they proceed . . . , but I observe, on the contrary, several experiences that ought to make us doubt it." [5] Descartes requires foundations for physics because he is animated by the notion that the relation between idea and object is the point at which ontology, or the principles of nature, intersects with epistemology, or the principles of knowledge. His optical studies are the framework in which Descartes works out his methodological answer to the ancient question of the relation between thinking and being. The high significance of these researches has occasionally been appreciated. Biologist Thomas Huxley wrote that Cartesian optics "is the physiological foundation of the doctrine of the relativity of knowledge, and a more or less complete idealism is a necessary consequence of it." * Specifically, optics either inspires or confirms three crucial Cartesian doctrines: that extension is the only property of matter; that we have immediate knowledge of ideas only; and that ideas are corporeal. The reciprocity and inseparability of the physical (ontological) and epistemological inquiries, which constitute the true Cartesian metaphysics, are reflected by the fact that Descartes always defended his physical principles by reference to his theory of sensation; and, conversely, he never attempted to state "what the mind is able to know" without reference to his physical first principle, extension. [6] We will argue that this point of intersection is the true axis of Cartesian dualism because it links physics together with metaphysics through a recapitulation of the method, whose objective is to exhibit thought and extension as the coordinate principles of science.

Animal automatism prepares the metaphysical link between reason and extension because it provides a critique of the traditional soul conception, thereby eliminating a potential third principle, and because its constructive function is to prepare the concept of thought. It leads to the replacement, in

* Huxley, 1897, 210. Contrary to the view of such early Cartesians as Malebranche and Leibniz, modern interpreters have been almost unanimous in their disregard of the philosophical import of the animal automatism hypothesis. The exceptions are Kemp Smith and A. G. A. Balz. In regard to it Smith wrote: "Hence the utter misrepresentation of the internal dialectic of Descartes's thought, if we start, as Descartes himself does, with the cogito ergo sum as the really ultimate element in his system. The cogito ergo sum is simply one consequence of the doctrine of representative perception, which is itself a consequence of his dualistic starting point" (Smith, 1902, 14).

the *Meditations,* of the traditional notion of man as rational animal with the definition of him as a thinking machine, or in the more elegant phrase that Leibniz borrowed from Spinoza, as a spiritual automaton.[7]

This bond between science and philosophy arises through a self-reflection that seeks to comprehend the status of the knower and his knowledge in the light of what he asserts the world to be. The subjectivity of the knower and the objectivity of the world are generated by one and the same reflection that "distinguishes" the mind from the body. This reflection, which from the perspective of the *Meditations* appears to occur in a moment and without reference to the world, in fact has its roots in animal automatism and physiological optics. The optical bias of Cartesian physics is therefore ultimately the optical bias of Cartesian metaphysics.

The Mechanistic Theory of Sensation

The great question at issue in the theory of vision is the nature of the relation between sensation and object. Descartes opposes the Aristotelian-scholastic view that sensations are images or copies of the objects which cause them and which the images depict. The fundamental assumption of the copy theory is that since sensations must resemble objects if we are to know them, the resemblance must be of the most perfect kind if we are to know them perfectly; and the most perfect resemblance would be a copy or picture.[8] Descartes objects that the proponents of this theory cannot show us how sensations "can be formed by these objects, received by the external sense organs, and transmitted by the nerves to the brain." [9] The received theory gives good assurances that resemblance exists, but it fails to explain the way it is physically achieved: it is an epistemology that dangles insecurely from an inadequate physics. Descartes contends, moreover, that the Aristotelians have not thought through the resemblance relation. A depicted copy is but one way in which one thing might represent another; but there are other modes of representation, such as language, in which the object has nothing in common with the representation. The question at issue is not fidelity of depiction as reproduction, but in general to find a means of representation such that "the mind [can] perceive all the diverse qualities of the objects to which [the representation] refers." [10] The motive of the criticism is clear. Once the problem of the relation between sensation and object is freed from a special interpretation and stated as a problem of correspondence of some kind, there is greater latitude for admissible types of physical explanation of the genesis of sensations. Since Descartes's only physical principle is extension, figured extension is the only real thing that sensations need represent; and he is certain that his theory of the formation of the retinal image will satisfy that requirement.

By emphasizing his differences with received opinion, Descartes obscures his agreements with tradition, and consequently also the extent to which his own orientation is shaped by the traditional problems. His relation to anteced-ents is especially significant in this case. The Aristotelian theory of vision is inseparable from Aristotle's concept of the soul and even his ontology. Optics developed only as a mathematical theory in antiquity, and was not applied successfully to the theory of vision until Ibn al-Haytham (d.c. 1039) discovered the inversion of the retinal image and produced an optical explanation of it based on the assumption that light was not instantaneously transmitted.[11] His *Optica* was translated into Latin in the 12th century, and became the foundation for all subsequent studies; Witelo and Kepler are directly depend-ent upon him. The new theory of vision had no important philosophical con-sequences until Descartes drew out its destructive implications for the Aris-totelian theory of sensation and joined it to his own theory of the soul.

CRITIQUE OF ARISTOTELIAN REALISM

Aristotle's theory is classic because it outlines the framework of basic distinc-tions and problems that any successful theory of sensation must meet. He draws the distinction between object, medium, sense organ, and sensation, and describes their most elementary relations. He distinguishes between the special (or external) senses and the central sense (*aisthetikon koinon* or *sensus communis*). Most of the Cartesian critique of scholastic psychology falls within this schema.

Sensation, according to Aristotle, is in general a change of state of the soul, produced by the object acting upon the sense organ through a medium. Visual sensations are of colored objects. The color acts on the transparent medium, air which, being continuous with the object and eye, is able to act upon the organ.[12] Aristotle does not hold the view, criticized by Descartes, that an image flies through the air from the object. Color imparts a mechanical or local mo-tion to the medium, which in turn affects the eye in the same way. Descartes is therefore in agreement with Aristotle that the immediate cause of sensation is a motion quite unlike the sensation, although Aristotle gives no description of the motion of the medium nor of the motions it induces in the eye—it is one of the strengths of Descartes's theory that it does so. Aristotle's next stage of the explanation, the translation of the organ's movement into a sensation, is equally obscure, but it is a much more significant obscurity. Here he holds that the soul, and specifically sensations, are incorporeal, although it is some-how acted upon by each motion of the organ; and this must be the case, other-wise the causal link between sensation and object would be broken. His ap-preciation of the importance of the link is signaled by his assigning sensations location in the organ. Still, his inability to explain how a corporeal organ acts upon an incorporeal soul is a saltus in the causal chain.* It is therefore an error to tax Descartes with the onus of having originated the mind-body problem.

Aristotle's distinction between the special senses and the common sense is dictated by the need to account for two evident facts. One is that there are five separate organs of sense—separate in location and distinct in regard to the qualities they perceive. Yet these qualities are experienced together, for the soul is able to compare them. Furthermore, although reflection can isolate the qualities in sensation, they do not appear to be what we primarily perceive, as if sensation were a summing of those qualities; rather, it seems that we perceive a thing or a whole (a *morphe* or *eidos aistheton*), such as a flower or a person. Consequently, Aristotle posits a unifying sensitive faculty, the cen-tral sense. But since the soul is the form or activity of the body, all its powers (reason excepted) must have a corresponding corporeal organ. Aristotle lo-cates the sensus communis in the heart.[13] This creates the difficulty that sensa-tion seems to be duplicated: it occurs once in the organ and again in the sensus communis. He attempts to meet this difficulty by proposing that while the sensitive soul is a unity, it nevertheless has parts, namely just the perceptions of the five organs.[14] However, since he is committed to the view that sensations have locations, the unity of the sensitive soul cannot be unity of place; he must therefore explain how the sensations of the separate organs are communicated to the sensus communis, i.e. how colors or distance can be perceived in the middle of the body.† Aristotle cannot meet the problem; Descartes meets it by denying that there is any sensation in the organs, and affirming that all sensation occurs at the seat of the sensus communis, the pineal gland. He can

---

* For Aristotle the problem is that whereas corporeal motions must "penetrate" to the soul and originate from it, yet the soul itself has no motion. The passions, which he thinks are both corporeal motions and psychic effects, prove to be particularly difficult for him. *De An.* 408 b1–30, 411 a1–15, 411 b5–20.

† *De Sen.* 448 b9–10, 17. Aristotle argues that the relationship between the unity of the sensus communis and the diversity of the organs can be understood as the relationship between a thing and its attributes. The argument is a serious piece of question-begging, since the adequacy of the metaphysics of thing and attribute is at stake; the analysis must be posed in causal-empirical terms rather than in logical formulations.

dare this solution because he rejects the copy theory and its implicit requirement that sensation is a direct intuition of the object.

Aristotle's account of the way in which sensations resemble objects can be
stated only by introducing his ontological terminology. Sensible things are
substances composed of form and matter. This holds for men and animals,
whose form is the soul and matter their bodies. The sensitive faculty or soul
is the form of each of the organs of sense; and to be such a form is just to be
the function (the *ergon* or *energeia*) of the respective organ, namely, sensing.
What the soul senses is the forms of objects "without their matter." * Since in
Aristotle's ontology the form or "what" of a thing constitutes its true being, to
perceive the form is to perceive the object as it really is; the soul is passive
toward objects. Aristotle thus holds not merely a copy theory but an identity
theory, for the reality (energeia) of the sensation and the object is the same,
though their being (*einai*), i.e. location, is different.† This identity is underscored by his denial that there are invisible magnitudes or imperceptible times,
whereas the existence of both is for Descartes a cardinal principle.

The significance of the Aristotelian analysis is the remarkable degree to
which its problems anticipate and recommend the Cartesian solution. Let us
consider three decisive points. The substance ontology is undermined by the
factual requirements of Aristotle's theory of sensation. Ontologically, a thing
is a single form or "what," which constitutes its true being, and it is distinguished from the accidents that accompany it. According to the theory of
sensation, the senses perceive only qualities, although ontologically the qualities are accidents.[15] Sensation therefore perceives only what is inessential to
the thing; consequently the ontological substance can be known only by a
discursively prepared noetic intuition. This problem is recognized when
Aristotle distinguishes between the sensible and the intelligible form or eidos.[16]
The distinction only emphasizes the intransigence of the problem. There is
no such thing as a single sensible form of an object; not only are the forms
divided into five modalities, perceived by double organs, but every sensation

---

* One of the principal problems of Aristotelian psychology and physics comes to a head in
this formulation. See Rosen, 1961, 134–35.

† *De An.* 407 a7; 425 b17 and Hick's commentary thereto; 429 a28; 432 a1; also Oehler, 1962,
193ff. Aristotle's identity theory is pressed by many difficulties. Sensation is passive with respect
to the object, but also the "activity" of the sense organs; yet its actuality in the latter sense
depends upon the sensation being wholly unlike the organ and entirely similar to the object;
therefore, it cannot be the actuality of the organ and of the object. Similarly, the object must
have two actualities—its own as a thing, and an infinite number insofar as it is perceived. An
organ that perceived itself, as happens in the case of Purkinje's vascular pattern, would be active
and passive with respect to itself at the same time. For a discussion of this peculiar and chal-
lenging phenomenon, see Linksz, II, 1952, 355–79.

of a quality is equally a sensation of a form, and there are infinitely many quality sensations. The facts of sensation are therefore quite at odds with the commonsensical view, which Aristotle wishes to save, that we experience things as unities. The ontological form or substance seems to disintegrate into an infinity of impressions, which leads straight to the view adopted by Descartes that the senses do not provide direct acquaintance with reality. It is the outcome of the problems that caused Aristotle to distinguish between the sensible form and the intelligible form known only by reason (nous).

The second problem is presented by the distinction between form and matter and the assertion that sensibility perceives the forms of things without their matter. Matter (*hyle*) is a general term denoting the materials out of which a substance is made, all of which reduce ultimately to the four elements: fire, earth, air, and water. If ontologically things are substances composed of form and matter then, according to the theory of sensation, only the formal part of the composite is known to sensation. Yet the elements themselves are subject to sensible experience, leading to the conclusion that they have sensible forms, but no ontological forms. This difficulty results from Aristotle's ontological use of the form-matter distinction, which subordinates material and efficient causality to the formal cause, or the essence of a thing; and his distinction between matter and body (*soma*), which he understands to be extension. The matter of all sensible things, including the elements, has body or extension as an ingredient. The ontological distinction between form and matter then reduces to the problem of the relation between a thing's essence and its extension, which Descartes dissolves by identifying the form with extension.[17] The epistemological problem of the unknowability of matter, based on the assumption that we sense only forms, is thereby transformed into the problem of how we know the form of extension, i.e. how sensations represent the extension of things, without being in the sense organ.

Finally, the problems which seem to motivate Aristotle's identification and differentiation of sensation and object are based on his affirmation that their reality (energeia) is the same, but their being (einai) is different. The fact that the sense organ is spatially remote from its object requires, among other things, the distinction between sensation and object and the subsequent attempt to explain the transmission of the form. But this distinction, necessary though it be, is not easily reconciled with immediate experience, for we do not experience two things, sensation and object, but only one. Immediate experience, or in Descartes's terminology, prejudice, leads us to believe that we directly apprehend external objects; but Aristotle has revised the beliefs of immediate experience far enough to recognize that the soul is in immediate contact only with the sense organ, and that consequently its immediate object is a sensation, i.e., the psychic result of a motion in the organ. He is therefore quite close to the idealist thesis that we have immediate knowledge of sensations only. The identity thesis is an attempt to bridge this yawning idealist chasm, with which Aristotle became acquainted by study of pre-Socratic physics. Once Descartes's optical theory of vision shows it to be untenable, the leap into the chasm becomes necessary, and so Descartes asserts an identity thesis of another kind.

DESCARTES'S THEORY OF VISION

The mathematical core of Descartes's physiological optics is the explanation of the formation of the retinal image. The explanation depends upon certain assumptions about the nature and propagation of light. It suffices to accept here the definition of the *Dioptric* that light is nothing else ". . . than a certain movement or action . . . which passes [from the luminous or reflecting body] through the medium of the air and other transparent bodies [to the eye]." * One of the models for this type of action is the communication of resistance from an object, touched with a stick, to the hand. The light source is like the object touched, the stick is the analog of the line of action, and the hand is like the eye; the action is communicated instantaneously. The lines of action are called rays of light, and they should "always be imagined to be perfectly straight" when they pass through a uniform medium.[18] Descartes supposes further, as Kepler had before him, that there is an infinity of such rays acting in all directions from each point on the luminous body.[19]

---

* Olscamp, 1965, 67/AT VI, 84. The nature of light and its propagation is one of the notable fruitful problems of Cartesian physics. Descartes believed that light is transmitted instantaneously through a material medium, the model for which is the communication of pressure through an incompressible medium. The theory is dictated by the reduction of the principles of physics to extension or space, and the subsequent need to posit a plenum (Koyré, 1939, III, 159–62; 1957, 101; Sabra, 1967, 62, 79). In 1634, Descartes acknowledged that if the instantaneous transmission of light could be disproved experimentally, "the whole of my philosophy would be shaken to its foundations" (AT I, 308). But in 1638, he asserted that the argument of the *Dioptric* is independent of a theory of the nature and propagation of light (AT II, 143–44). Perhaps he had recognized that his percussion model of refraction treated light as particulate and of finite variable velocity. The fundamental postulate of instantaneous transmission is that the minute bodies touching a light source have a "tendency to move" in all directions at once; but this tendency must be actual, as Christian Huygens pointed out by asking in what direction the pression of bodies would move if two eyes opened simultaneously from different directions. The pression model is also vexed by the difficulty that it cannot explain the communication of the spin of the particles through the medium, although the spin is required to explain the color spectrum. See Sabra, 1967, 46–68.

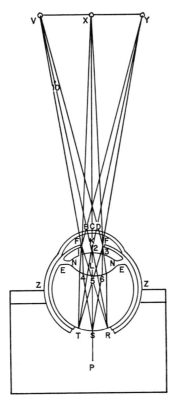

Figure 1. Camera obscura. The drawing is an adaptation of Descartes's original, which appears in AT VI, 191.

The formation of the retinal image is explained by reference to an experiment with a *camera obscura*. An animal eye with the sclera removed is placed in a dark room so that the aperture of the eye is the only source of light in the chamber. When the retina *RST* is observed from *P*, "you will see there, perhaps not without admiration and pleasure, a picture which will represent in natural perspective all the objects outside toward *VXY* . . . ," [20] but for the fact that the image is inverted. The optics of the phenomenon is this. *VXY* is a luminous body whose light acts along an infinite number of rays from all points on the body. *VXY* are three such points. The rays from *V* enter the pupil and reconverge at *R* according to the refractive properties of the cornea, humours, and lens, which has been mathematically defined by the law of sines. In general, for any point P on a light source whose rays pass into the eye, there will be a corresponding point P′ on the retina; and as all points P′ retain the relative positions toward one another that characterize the points P, the retinal image is topographically isomorphic with the object. This isomorphism is the fundamental fact upon which Descartes is able to reject the copy theory and set forth his own theory of sensations as representations of objects. In order to expound the representative relation, we must introduce new physical and physiological principles.

The rays consist of minute particles that have, in addition to their rectilinear motion, a rotary motion, whose velocity varies according to the surface properties of the object from which it emanates. The retina is composed of fibrous nerve endings that are differentially affected by the different rotational velocities. In the *Meteors,* Descartes shows that the supposition of these rotational properties will account for the color spectrum observed in the rainbow and prism.[21] He now applies this to vision. When the nerve endings of the retina are affected, the motion is transmitted through the optic nerve to the pineal gland (in a way explained below) where these motions translate into differences of color. The topography of the sensation, defined by color differences, therefore represents the topography of different motions striking the retina, which in turn is isomorphic with the topography of the object. In this way, Descartes completed the program, announced in *Regulae* XII, "to express all the differences of sensible things by an infinitude of figures."

The reasons for Descartes's unremitting criticism of prejudice and for his claim to have destroyed Aristotle's foundations gradually become clear by considering his comments on the imperfections of vision. He observes that this picture on the retina is painted by the activation of thousands of nerve endings—a painting in pointillism, as it were. Since there are not enough endings to receive each of the rays, not all points P can be registered. Such distributive nonperception is what "often makes it seem that a meadow which is painted in an infinity of altogether different colors will appear from a distance to be all white, or all blue." [22] We do not perceive forms or wholes of any kind, but a distribution of points whose representative fidelity is a function of distance.

How much the visual effigy is a function of physiology rather than the object is proved by the explanations of the perception of position, distance, size, and shape. It is a principle that we can "distinguish the parts of bodies we see only insofar as they differ somehow in their color." [23] The two-dimensional retina is incapable of registering three-dimensional space; hence we have no immediate perception of position or distance. Descartes explains estimations of distance by "natural geometry" or Kepler's telemetric triangle. Since two angles and a side suffice to determine another side, the distance along the axis of vision to the object can be computed as a side, the distance between the eyes taken as the base, and the angle of incidence of the rays on the base (i.e. the two retinas) as the given angles.[24] Although this computation occurs by a "simple act of imagination, nevertheless [it] implicitly contains a reasoning quite similar to that used by surveyors." * Berkeley's critique of the telemetric triangle was based partly on the absence of an explanation of how the imagination performs this feat. But it performs another that is equally astonishing. Optically, the size of the image decreases as the distance from the eye increases. If vision were purely optical, we should see as smaller those images which are smaller on the retina. But we accommodate our estimate of the size of objects to what we judge to be their distance from us, and therefore see familiar objects as constant in size despite their reduced size on the retina. The same is true of figure and shape, for although the retinal image "contains only ovals and diamonds, yet they cause us to see circles and squares." [25]

These remarkable discoveries, which are standard propositions of contemporary physiological optics, seem to show that vision is an acquired capacity, based on complicated inferences that are made presumably on the basis of comparing experiences through trial and error. But none of it is a conscious activity. The simple "act of imagination" is performed by animals as well as men and Descartes evidently means by it a brain activity, to which the *Dioptric* so often refers.†

Ferdinand Alquié has spoken eloquently of Cartesian metaphysics as a "de-realization of the world," a phrase which aptly describes the diremption that the perceived or prejudiced world undergoes. The diremption is not, of course, total; rather, Descartes has adjusted the senses "to the level of reason" by interpreting sensation as a representation. In the next segment, we shall explain how this optical epistemology is related to the "ontology" of first principles.

---

* Olscamp, 1965, 105/AT VI, 137–38. Stereopsis is still imperfectly understood. For a discussion of a model that uses the notion of topographic isomorphism between the retina and cortical image, see Linksz, 1952, II, 380–405.

† Descartes's explanation of vision on analogy to the blind man using sticks (the example is probably drawn from Lucretius, see AT II, 417) implies that vision is an acquired capacity, because sensations that at first seem "confused and obscure" become clear with "much practice" (ibid., 67/AT VI, 84). However, this involves judgment in the proper sense, which is not easily reconciled with a purely reflex account of vision. This problem is one of the points at which conscious "action" requires reconciliation with mechanism, both in the Cartesian system and in modern psychophysics.

OPTICAL EPISTEMOLOGY

One of Descartes's most important innovations is his rejection of the Aristotelian rule according to which knowledge of first principles is gathered by a stepwise advance from the sensed particular. That is, Descartes advances directly to first principles by his intuitive identification of matter with extension, and then descends by a priori deduction, thus simultaneously homogenizing nature and establishing mathematics as the "level of reason." This step is the foundation of physics. It is the "level of reason" which defines what the mind is able to know and entails the establishment of a new cognitive relation toward the world.

Descartes presents *The World* as a fable of a world "feigned at pleasure." [26] Opinion is nearly unanimous that this claim is a canard by which Descartes hoped to disarm opposition to his theories. [27] The evidence for this interpretation is abundant; among other things, one need only observe that the true world with which the fable is contrasted is nothing more than the prejudiced conceptions of the scholastics and of untutored sensibility. [28] Granting this, examination of Descartes's principles shows that *The World* is a scientific fabrication. The effort to "feign" a world in "fantasy" leads directly to the specification of the nature of the matter that will be found in the "new world." It ought to be something of which we cannot even "feign ignorance." [29] But extension meets this requirement, because "its idea is so comprised in all other things which our imagination is able to form, that it is necessary for you to conceive it, if you imagine anything whatever." [30] The subsequent exposition of the brain model will show that this necessity is founded upon the "corporeality" of imagination. In the present context, it enables Descartes to assert that knowledge of the concatenations of extension must exhaust all that is possible for the mind to conceive clearly. Since God is able to create all that we can in this manner imagine, and in the course of time must create it, only an imagined or fabled account of the world renders the world accessible. [31] For, having seized the first principle, it is then possible to deduce its effects. An imagined world, which is scientific because it embodies the rigor of mathematics and which is within our power to construct, thus displaces the true or sensed world as probative of what is. This displacement of the senses by mathematical imagination in the scientific writings fulfills the methodological institution of a new cognitive relation toward the world.

The ontological commitment of the fabulous physics, which hangs by the thread of what can be conceived clearly, is vindicated by its intersection with the theory of vision. The senses, indeed, must be used in science; but science requires invisible magnitudes, imperceptible times, unobservable straight lines and rigid bodies. Experience thus clashes with what imagination attributes to the world.[32] We require, then, a probative science of sensation that is able to evaluate what we should and should not demand from it. The *Dioptric* provides just such a science, and might have been subtitled "The Right Use of the Senses in Science." The theory of vision as a topographically isomorphic representation enables Descartes to comprehend sensibility from outside, i.e. objectively, or as he would say, by reason. Indeed, this objective grasp of experience is precisely what defines and confirms the subjectivity of experience taken immediately. In this way he acquires a binocular perspective of himself and the world, a dual perspective of objectivity and subjectivity that becomes increasingly pronounced as Descartes advances toward animal automatism.

The possibility of replacing the image-copy notion of sensation by representations mathematically conceived depends also upon Descartes's specific mathematical achievement. Aristotle as well as Descartes takes vision as his paradigm for sensation. The primary meaning of the word *eidos* is the looks of a thing; Aristotle transfers the meaning to all sensation through his theory. The looks of a thing is primarily its shape (*morphe*) and figure (*schema*). In Greek mathematics, shapes or figures cannot be reduced to magnitudes. To be sure, plane geometry does show relations obtaining among figures and with one and the same figure, but the figures themselves are irreducibly primitive. As Liard points out, however, the Cartesian universal mathematics accomplishes this reduction.[33] The algebraic treatment of geometric figures shows how a figure may result from the positions of the points that compose it, and these positions may be determined by numbers. This idea, fundamental to analytic geometry, depends upon the method of adding and subtracting lines, and upon the method of determining position by reference to Cartesian coordinates. By the introduction of variables, numbers themselves are replaced by letter designations that bring to number relations the same generality achieved by geometry when it abstracts from the magnitude of its figures. The result is a way of determining the properties of space, or figures, by computational methods that do not require the imagination or visual intuition of constructions, e.g. as "$x + y = 0$" determines a line.[34] The method abstracts no less from figure than from number, because it considers only proportions in general.[35]

To evaluate the import of these mathematical conceptions for the meaning of sensations as representations, consider that Descartes has successively as-simulated figure to number, and number to an anumerical, i.e., algebraic, method. Direct intuition of figure or line has been replaced by numerical relationships, and they in turn by algebraic relationships. Algebraic equations are accordingly representations of both these two modes of thinking, for a numerical or geometric relation can always be obtained from an equation. But the spatial (extensional) relations, despite their translatability into a line intuitable by sense or imagination, are not conceived merely as determinations of real space (extension as body); they are representations of space (extension) in the sense that the space with which the equations have to do is itself determined by the properties of the algebraic-numerical relations. The algebraic system, in other words, because it can determine positions solely by means of its internal properties, is a representation of space. But this represented space is just the one with which we have to do in the mathematical representation of optics. Cartesian figures, despite the identity of their appearance with Euclid's figures, are not the same. Euclid's figures are given, in the same sense that they are constructed, namely, by the mechanical method of ruler and compass. Descartes's figures, on the other hand, are constructed by referring them to an arithmetically constructed coordinate system: the space in which they are constructed is itself constructed. When Descartes speaks of the lines described by rays passing through a medium, we must realize that these lines are representations that are accessible only through mathematical thinking, or "pure understanding." *

But this imagined space has now become probative of real space because what formerly was regarded as real space, namely, distances that are immediately perceived, has been annulled by the theory of vision which reveals the systematic inaccuracy of these perceptions. The "real space" of immediate experience, for example, has been replaced conceptually by the telemetric triangle. It is a fitting outcome of the identification of body with space—that great monument to *la géométrisation à outrance*.† No wonder then that the world is a fable.

Men and Animals as Spiritual Automata

Animal automatism is subject to misunderstanding because of the inconsistencies among Descartes's accounts of it, and because of the ambiguities of the

---

* Descartes distinguishes between mathematical rays and material or real rays, which are not straight or indivisible; but the material rays are themselves imaginative constructs based on the assumption that the world is a plenum (AT II, 77). Boutroux wrote of Cartesian figures: "One must never forget that these lines are there only to represent magnitude in general. For imagination, they are geometrical figures, but for understanding they are pure quantities" (Boutroux, 1900, 31; also Klein, 1968, 203–06). See below, pp. 164–76.

† See Koyré's analysis of the geometrization of the world and the insuperable obstacles that it created for dynamics in Koyré, 1939, II, 49–53; III, 159–81.

terms "animal," "soul," and "reason" that arose owing to Descartes's innovations on the traditional meanings. In his own day and since, the doctrine was usually taken to mean that although animals possess the same organs of sensation and feeling as men, nevertheless, because they are machines, they are without soul or consciousness: they somehow have sensations but do not "think" them. This view, which Descartes espoused on several occasions, does not render the primary meaning of the doctrine, which is not a negative thesis about what animals lack. Rather, it is the positive theory that all motions observed in animals, and many of those in men, occur entirely by the "disposition of the parts" of the body.[36] Instead of disparaging animals, it is meant to express the proud confidence that mechanism suffices to explain all the behavior of animals without any diminution or reservation.

Animal automatism offends a prejudice that Descartes expounded on a number of occasions. To Henry More he wrote that we are accustomed to believe that there is in us "but a single principle of motion, viz., the soul, which . . . moves the body and thinks."[37] Owing to the similarities between animals and ourselves, we are inclined to attribute the same principle to them. The doctrine offends the belief that an incorporeal soul or will moves the body. But Descartes discovered that there are two principles of motion in men, one spiritual and the other mechanical. Investigating the matter more closely, he assured More, he at last recognized that all the motions of animals might originate from mechanical causes.

The destructive or critical edge of Descartes's automatism is directed at the Aristotelian soul doctrine, which incorporates the prejudice that Descartes overthrows. Aristotle distinguishes a nutritive, sensitive and motive, and rational soul, corresponding to the primary functions of plants, animals, and men. All these souls are incorporeal forms or activities of living bodies, and as such are inseparable from them; it follows that they are mortal, with the possible exception of the rational soul. The soul is understood to be the principle and cause of the material or physical processes of the body. This doctrine means that fundamentally there can be no physical explanation of these processes, since the causality exercised by soul is formal and final. Nevertheless, Aristotle is aware of the mechanical interpretation of animal motion. He uses the machine model himself to explain the lever action of bones and joints, and he even allows that the development of the embryo depends upon a mechanically produced series of motions. He believes, however, that the mechanical motions which exist in animals are initiated by sensation, imagination, and desire, i.e., the animal soul.[38] The animal is more like a well-ordered common-wealth than a machine.

Rather than denying that sensation and desire are causes of animal and human motion, Descartes asserts that these operations too are mechanical. The one statement that best depicts the grand sweep of the theory occurs at the end of the *Treatise on Man,* when Descartes summarizes the properties of his model of the human machine:

> I wish you to consider, finally, that all the functions which I attribute to this machine, such as digestion . . . nutrition . . . respiration, waking and sleep-ing; the reception of light, sounds, odors . . . ; the impression of ideas in the organ of the sensus communis and imagination; the retention . . . of these ideas in the memory; the interior movements of the appetites and passions; and finally the movements of all the external members . . . ; I desire, I say, that you consider that these functions occur naturally in this machine solely by the dispositions of its organs, not less than the movements of a clock or other automaton. . . . Thus it is not necessary to conceive that it has a nutritive soul, or sensitive soul, or *any other principle of motion* and life except its blood and spirits . . . which have no other nature than [that] found in inanimate bodies.[39]

These extremely large claims, or rather total claims, allow no exception or exemption from automatism. There is no other "principle of motion," meaning that reason or thought is not an exception, however often Descartes might assert this elsewhere. The paradox it poses is this: it seems that men and animals pursue and avoid things because of their perceptions and volitions, whereas Descartes's theory needs to affirm that the appearance of psychic causation is mere appearance, behind which lies a real mechanical cause.

MIND'S MACHINERY AND ITS CORPOREAL IDEAS

In order to render these conceptions clear, it is necessary to explain Descartes's model of the brain, which seems not to have been systematically investigated by any commentator. It should be said straight away that the model is a com-plete fable, and the analogies upon which it is based—the hydraulics of the fountains at Fontainebleau, and the pipe organ—are far-fetched and rather crude.[40] Furthermore, the brain anatomy it requires contradicts the facts as they were known at that time; the histology is sheer invention. While these deficiencies are important to the evaluation of Descartes's place in the history of anatomy and physiology, for the present purposes they are not significant. The model is merely a vehicle for the elaboration of ideas that far outstripped the empirical knowledge of the day.

The model revolves about two primary anatomical components, the pineal gland and the tissues of the cortex. Descartes imagines that the walls of the cortex can expand away from, or contract toward the pineal gland, which is situated in the center (see Figure 2). The extent of the expansion or contraction

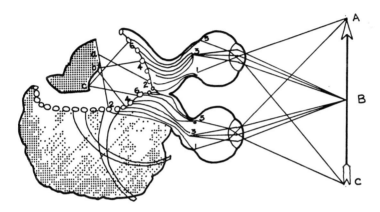

Figure 2. The walls of the cortex and the pineal gland. This drawing is an adaptation of figure 29 in AT XI, page unnumbered. Clerselier reports that the drawings for the *Traité de l'homme* were made by de la Forge and Gutschoven at his request (AT XI, xiii).

depends upon the quantity of animal spirits that enter the brain; the cavity is larger during waking than sleep, while in death the cortex closes the cavity altogether. The cortex is "nothing but a tissue" composed of nerve fibers, pores, and tubes, which interlace to form a net, as shown in Figure 3. The threads of the net are the nerve fibers, the interstices are the pores, and the tubes lead from the "knots" or intersections to the interior surface of the cortex, which faces the gland.[41] The tissue becomes denser toward the outer circumference of the cortex, where the nerve fibers become the "marrow" of the nerves that extend throughout the body. The tubes lead animal spirits into the network from the cavity of the cortex, where they may either distend the fibers so as to leave an impression—which is the basis of memory—or they may be carried off into the nerves to cause the motion of some member of the body.

The character of the spirits requires a brief explanation. There is in the heart

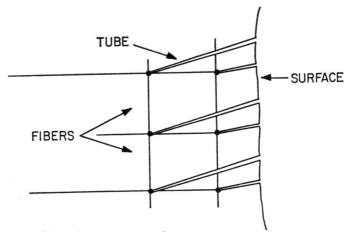

Figure 3. Section of brain tissue: nerve network

a "fire without light" which is the fundamental principle of life.* The heat from
it is the cause of the palpitation of the heart, and it also heats the blood. The
most agitated blood rises to the brain, where it is in effect a vapor, and so is
called the animal spirits.†

The pineal gland is attached to the floor of the cavity of the cortex by two
small arteries that constantly bring a fresh supply of spirits into the gland from
the heart. The rush of the spirits into the gland causes it to be floated, much
as a light ball will float on a vertical jet of water. This arrangement makes
it possible for the gland to incline from side to side, which is a factor that
plays a large role in the model. On the gland there are points, or orifices, from
which the spirits exit into the cavity, cross the intervening space to the cortex,
and enter the tubes that take them into the nerve network of the cortex tissue.[42]
The sense of the model depends upon the correspondence between the points
on the gland and the tube openings, for it is the mechanism by which the
topographical isomorphism of the organs of sense is reproduced in the brain.[43]

In the case of a visual sensation, the machine starts to work when an object
is presented to the eyes (as in Figure 2); the retinal image forms, i.e., a pattern

* *Passions* § 8; AT XI, 123, 202. The long discussion of the circulation of the blood that
occurs in the *Discourse* was significant because it showed that the *pneuma* (or vital principle) of
ancient physiology and medicine could be understood on mechanical principles. The materializa-
tion of pneuma has antecedents in Stoic and Epicurean theory, where it is already understood
to imply a material *hegemonikon* or sensus communis (see Pohlenz, 1950, 51; Bréhier, 1951,
48, 161, 165; Cicero, *De Nat. Deo.* II, 9). For the connection between these theories and the
Cartesian corporeal ideas, see below, p. 165, ns.

† For an account of Descartes's criticisms of Harvey's theory of the circulation of the blood,
see Gilson, 1930, 64–72 and DM, 406–07, and Passmore, 1958, 86–94.

of impacts is received upon the nerve endings of the retina; and these impacts cause the nerve fibers, which extend to the brain through the optic nerve, to open a corresponding set of tubes on the interior surface of the cortex (which in the figure is marked by the even numbers). Descartes likens the opening of the tubes by the impact of the nerve endings to the ringing of a bell by pulling a string. The open tubes, then, are isomorphic to the retinal impact pattern, which in turn is isomorphic to the object. The lines running from points *a, b, c* on the gland to the two sets of tubes 2, *4, 6* indicate the continuity of the isomorphism up to the pineal gland; and the diagram appears to indicate that the image is reinverted, although Descartes does not expressly discuss this interesting and important question of physiological optics.* In any case, once a tube is opened by a stimulus of a nerve ending in an organ, the animal spirits flow from the gland into the open pores.† For reasons not wholly clear, spirits flow only from those openings on the gland that correspond to the tubes which happen at that moment to be open. The lines of Figure 2 thus indicate the flow of the spirits from the gland to the tube, and it constitutes the sensus communis. The brain mechanics explain the facts of vision as they are expounded in the *Dioptric.*

From the model we see that the stimuli from the double organs of sight have been unified in the single topographical array of the gland and the streams of the spirits. Descartes attempts to explain the perception of distance and position by the various movements of the gland. As it inclines forward off the perpendicular, the points on the gland correspond to objects that are relatively closer to the eyes, whereas a backward movement causes the flow of the spirits to correspond to the tubes opened by the impacts of light coming from a more distant object.[44] The suggestion seems to be that the distances the gland moves, and its angles of inclination from the vertical axis, somehow make possible the computation of the telemetric triangle. But apart from the fact that the gland of necessity would move simultaneously in different directions if it were to preserve the impact pattern of the retina, Descartes lacks a mechanism to record the successive movements, since each of the motions is successive and discrete. Thus we reach the limit of the fabulous explanation of vision. The explanation of all other sensations follows the same pattern.

* The diagrams that accompanied Clerselier's posthumous first edition suggest the reinversion of the image; but they were prepared by Gutschoven and de la Forge at Clerselier's request. AT XI, xii–xiii.

† AT XI, 172, 181, 185. The model for this action is probably the pressure system of pipe organs. AT XI, 165.

Supposing that the action of the gland adequately assimilated the stimuli of the organs, the relationship between the sensation and the spirits is such that the distribution of the points emitting spirits from the gland determines a "figure . . . which is traced in the spirits on the surface of the gland." [45] The term "idea" denotes "all the impressions that the spirits are able to receive in leaving the gland," which is to say that "idea" applies to any representation, whether of sensation or imagination, that occurs in the sensus communis.* It is interchangeable with "thought." The famous dictum that the pineal gland is the seat of the soul simply means that the figures on the surface of the gland are the location of the soul's representations, which in traditional terminology are said to be in the sensus communis, although it is apparent that in Descartes's model we have not the notion of a psychic container in which sensations are housed. Two consequences of the model, of great importance to the Cartesian mind doctrine, are that all sensation is located in the brain and that the organs are mere conductors of stimuli. Not only is this unlike Aristotle, who has sensation occurring both in the sense organ and the sensus communis, but it is also the basis for Descartes's replacement of the distinction between the sensitive and rational soul by the principle that sensation is a cognition. Furthermore, the identification of the perceived image, sensible or imaginative, with the animal spirits (a brain process, in current parlance) is altogether contrary to what nearly every commentator understands the term "idea" to mean for Descartes, to say nothing of its bearing on the doctrine that the soul is an incorporeal substance.† It is not an isolated statement but, on the contrary, provides the explanation of those passages where Descartes speaks of "corporeal imagination" and "corporeal ideas." Moreover, it cannot be a causal theory, because it is indispensable to both the theory of automatism and the epistemological doctrine that an "infinitude of figures" suffices to express all sensible things.

The significance of the doctrine of corporeal ideas, to anticipate briefly the *Meditations,* may be seen in its bearing on the cardinal idealist proposition that there is immediate knowledge of thoughts or ideas only. The optical theory of vision implies this result; but the brain model makes it completely explicit. Whereas in the *Meditations* the idealist position is attained only by doubting

---

* AT XI, 176–77. This is the consistent use of "idea" in the *Treatise,* e.g., 177: 25, 178: 10, 181: 12, 183: 6. Also AT III, 19–20, 48–49, 264.

† Lenoble (1950, 164) attributes an occasionalist doctrine to Descartes on the basis of passages in which he speaks of the spirits occasioning ideas. He does not mention the present passage, nor others in which the spirits are said to cause ideas.

the existence of body, with the brain model Descartes exhibits a species of idealism that asserts the corporeality of ideas. The brain model shows the idealism to be inseparable from materialism, or the subjectivity of thought inseparable from its objectivity. It therefore suggests that thought and extension are coordinate principles. Further, the corporeality of ideas, which is a consequence of the exclusion of every other principle from the world but extension, provides a physical basis for the methodological assertion that it is impossible to imagine anything without cognizing extension, i.e., that it is necessary to cognize extension in all that is imagined. In the sequel this intersection of ontology and epistemology will assume great significance. Finally, note that the identification of the figures of the spirits with ideas cannot be made on the basis of premises available to physics; it requires in addition the subjective experience of the physicist. This injection of non-physical knowledge into physics has also occurred in the optics, when Descartes explains the perception of color, proving that science requires access to the res cogitans in order to explain the res extensa, Descartes's metaphysics is governed by the need to know the res extensa in order to determine res cogitans.

REFLEX MOTION

If all the motions of animals can be accounted for on the basis of mechanical principles alone, without invoking the soul or volition as a cause; and if this is also the case for the human machine, then Descartes's theory of animal automatism has somehow to account for a mechanism through which sensation can cause motion, with the restriction that this mechanism be based only on mechanical principles. Descartes does not give his mechanism a specific name, but because it is applied first to involuntary motions, and then extended to voluntary motions, and because it is entirely based upon a co-ordination of afferent and efferent impulses, there is some justification for calling it "reflex," although it is not identical with the modern usage of this term, as Canguilhem has pointed out in his study of the origins of that concept.*

The involuntary sensory-motor circuit may be expounded by using Descartes's

---

* Canguilhem argues that the concept of the reflex was first formulated by Thomas Willis in *De motu musculari* (1670). Liddell, 1960, makes no attempt to trace the concept beyond 18th century irritability theories. Canguilhem's criticism of the text usually cited by those who attribute a reflex concept to Descartes is correct (Canguilhem, 1955, 43), but his constructive argument against the Cartesian origin of the concept seems unconvincing. He says that the model upon which the concept was based is the motion of light reflected by a mirror, where the incident ray corresponds to the afferent nervous excitation, and the reflected ray corresponds to the efferent response (ibid., 41). This is precisely the Cartesian model, not that of Willis.

example of the withdrawal of a foot from a fire. The heat of the fire acts upon the sensory nerves in the foot. This excitation is communicated to the brain through the nerves that connect the foot and brain; the effect there is to open specific tubes of the cortical tissue. They are just those tubes which, when the animal spirits pour into them from the gland, lead them down to the muscles of the foot through nerve pathways; there they enter the muscles, and cause them to distend so that they retract the foot from the fire. The link between sensation and motion, then, depends on the double role played by the animal spirits: they are both receptors and effectors. The figure impressed upon the spirits, owing to the fact that they enter just the tubes opened and no other, is perceived as pain; then, rushing into the foot, the spirits cause the required motion. A new phase of motion is thereby prepared, for the movement of the foot sends new excitations to the brain, which may have the further consequence of other, especially voluntary, motion.

Volition may be followed by either a perceived or an unperceived motion. Voluntary motion, properly speaking, is of the perceived type, while unperceived motion includes such things as the movements of the animal spirits that follow upon attention and recollection, or the movement of the pupil of the eye as we consider different objects.[46] According to the formula of the *Passions,* the "whole action of the soul" consists in the pineal gland's moving in the way necessary to produce the result that the soul has "willed." [47] Although the *Treatise on Man* never mentions volition, it does explain all of these voluntary acts. Voluntary motion proper, that is, where we conceive a specific motion that we wish our members to execute, depends on the principle that "the idea of this movement of the members consists only of the manner in which the spirits leave the gland, so that its idea [i.e., the "figure" of the spirits] is the cause of the movement.[48]

The difference between reflex ("instinctive") and voluntary motions is founded physiologically on the difference between sensory-motor mechanisms that have been "instituted by nature," and which for the most part are unalterable, and such new mechanisms as may be instituted by association. Descartes is modern in that just as he takes the phenomenon of involuntary movements as the starting point for the theory of automatism, so he takes the phenomenon of rote learning as the starting point for the explanation of voluntary motion. His two examples are the adventitious associations produced in the course of language learning and in training animals. In the latter case, an acquired habit is made to displace a natural or instinctive connection between sensation and motion. For although a dog is naturally disposed to flee at the report of a gun and to pursue a partridge, this relationship can be reversed.[49] The mechanism of reversal requires that perception, which either by nature or custom has been accompanied by appetition, be impeded by associating it with a perception of the opposite quality. Physiologically this means that new physical connections must be established among the memory images impressed upon the cortical tissue, and these in turn with new passions, whose physiological correlate is specific differences of quality (e.g. more or less agitation) of the animal spirits.[50] The mechanical model for this circuit is incomplete because Descartes found no way to tie in causes of qualitative changes in the spirits with external perceptions and memory.* But this circumstance does not obscure his meaning. From the point of view of experience or "prejudice," we normally say that fear or courage was the reason for this or that act. The passions as perceived are analogous to every other perception in that their causal efficacy lies not in the logic of the perception sequence, say, fear and flight; rather, we experience fear because a certain motion occurs in the brain, and the "voluntary" action which follows upon it is caused by the connection between that physical motion and other motions in the brain. The mind is purely a "spectator."

VULGAR DUALISM

Those statements in the *Discourse* and elsewhere which affirm a radical difference between men and animals are now to be examined, for that view is inconsistent with the clear implication of the *Treatise on Man* that men and animals are spiritual, i.e. thinking automata who vary only in degree.

The argument for the difference between men and animals stated in *Discourse* must be understood in the context of Descartes's initial statement on the nature of reason. The *Discourse* opens with the assertion that reason is the most "equitably distributed" of all things because no man desires "more" than he possesses. The irony of this assertion, which numerous commentators have remarked, is underscored in the next sentence in which Descartes expressly speaks for himself, declaring that the common opinion is probably not in error and that it "testifies" (not "proves") that reason is equal in all men. Shortly thereafter he avows that he would "like to believe" that reason is equal in

---

* The quality of the spirits is determined partly by natural disposition or the predominant "humor" of the individual, and partly by agitation of the heart and the quality of the blood. Since the quality is already determined when the spirits exit the gland, there is no mechanism by which they may be altered in the cortex by sense stimuli. This feature of the model caused Canguilhem to deny that Descartes has a true concept of reflex (Canguilhem, 1955, 41).

all, for it is the attribute which distinguishes men from animals, and he appears to follow the common opinion of the philosophers that reason is the "form" of a species. In his proof of the differences between men and animals, however, Descartes does not appeal to a "formal" difference at all, no doubt because he has banished from his world the scholastic "forms or qualities." [51] Instead, he argues that the absence of speech signifies the total absence of reason in animals. More precisely, since animals can be taught and machines constructed to utter words, he must prove the mechanical nature of those responses by contrasting it with the speech of men, who are able to reply appropriately to whatever may be said to them. He argues from the "remarkable" fact that the most stupid men, not excepting idiots, can "arrange different words together" in order to "make known their thoughts," while the same cannot be said of any animal. [52] In the course of developing this argument, Descartes asserts that "very little reason" is required in order to be able to speak; that men are "unequal," some being more teachable than others; that animals are teachable; that an animal which was as teachable as a man would be his equal; that brutes conceivably have "less" or "more" reason than men.* The peculiarity of the argument is that Descartes seems unable to deny all reason to animals without admitting the inequality of reason among men, although the initial premise of the argument requires the assertion of the equality of reason on pain of admitting that animals too possess reason.† Moreover, the argument for the complete absence of reason in animals begs the question and appeals to a dubious "fact." It is hardly evident that idiots can "respond appropriately" to whatever may be said to them; and when we consider that reason is the "power of judgment," it seems that idiots differ more from the intelligent men than they do from some animals. The question begging arises from the very nature of the argument about speech.

Descartes does not identify the power of speech with the differentia of men; it is, rather, an observable datum from which he infers the presence or absence of thought, which is the true Cartesian differentia. He challenges but does not disprove the possibility that beasts think, even though they lack intraspecies speech. Combining the admission of the inequality of reason in men with the weak arguments for the absence of reason in animals, plus the earlier

---

* Observe that casual remarks elsewhere in DM undermine the asserted equality of reason. Descartes says that he is "less able than others to distinguish truth from falsity" (DM 15), that God has given "some light" to each (DM 27); and that animals are teachable is acknowledged in *Passions*, § 50 & AM VIII, 135.

† Descartes expressly admitted inequality when he wrote that "the understanding of some is not as good as that of others" (HR I, 217/AT IX-2, 22).

premise that a specific difference between men and animals depends upon the equality of reason in men, leads us to infer that men differ from animals by degree.* This interpretation is supported by a further observation. The automatism theory of the *Discourse* is expressly said to summarize the findings of *The World* of which the *Treatise on Man* is a part. In the *Discourse,* the difference between men and animals is equated with the difference between men and the subtlest possible machine; yet in the *Treatise* the automatism doctrine is developed explicitly for a human machine, for which no organs or powers are assumed that might not also be possessed by brutes, and this machine can even imitate "most perfectly" the actions of "a true man." [53] One must recognize, finally, that Descartes's contrast between a man and a machine is spurious insofar as it suggests a human artifact. If nature itself is a machine, there is no reason why man might not be a machine also.

These conclusions might have been averted had Descartes agreed that in fact not speech but thought differentiates men from animals, and Descartes denies that animals, hence machines, think. The specific terms of this denial are that animals lack consciousness of the sensations and passions that are acknowledged to be in them.[54] This is a rather implausible statement, as continuous opposition to it testifies, for it is difficult to conceive sensations that are unsensed. To Plempius, Descartes proposed that animal sensation might be like our own experience of them when the mind is preoccupied;[55] to More, he acknowledged that it is impossible to prove that animals are unconscious because it is impossible to "penetrate inside them." But he argues that since admitting that they are conscious would entail the unacceptable consequence that their souls are immortal (or, that ours are mortal) it should be rejected on that ground.[56] The significance of this controversy seems to have been overlooked. If Descartes must deny animals consciousness of sensations and passions on pain of admitting that they possess a "rational soul," then for Descartes, unlike Aristotle, to sense is already to think. This doctrine, announced in the *Discourse* by the formula "raison ou sens," grounded in the *Treatise* by the attribution of "ideas" and "thoughts" to sensus communis of the man-machine, becomes authoritative in the *Meditations* by the substitution of res cogitans of the traditional "rational animal."

---

* For Descartes's account of how automatism can be interpreted and accepted by those who insist upon their "prejudice" that animals possess sensibility, see HR II, 244–45/AT VII, 427. Observe that Descartes attributes sensibility to animals in MM II, 14 and several times in *Regulae* XII.

It is not irrelevant to observe that the author generally credited with first having stated the man-machine doctrine, La Mettrie, himself acknowledges having found his doctrine in Descartes's writings.* But La Mettrie's modern editor and expositor rejects this testimony. La Mettrie, he thinks, read his own ideas into Descartes; for he can explain how he extracted those ideas only by interpreting "Cartesianism somewhat anachronistically in the light of [the "duplicity" of] eighteenth century literary tactics." [57] The seventeenth century, one gathers, was innocent and unironical.

* Vartanian, 1960, 191–92, 149. For the history of automatism among the early Cartesians, see the excellent essay in Balz, 1951, 106–57.

4 Demonic Legerdemain

In a dream the ego beholds bright colored figures . . . although
it does not receive any radiant stimulus from outside. There is
no doubt, therefore, that those figures are created by the mind.
. . . vision, then, is like a dream built on the basis of information
received by means of external stimuli and the peripheral organ of
sight.

Ronchi, *Optics: The Science of Vision*

The physical world, as Democritos so tersely expressed it some
2500 years ago, consists of emptiness and of atoms. What is built
of our sense modalities is *another world,* our own perceptual
world.

Linksz, *The Physiology of the Eye*

The Objectives of the *Meditations*

Descartes announces that the *Meditations* set forth the reasons by which he
persuaded himself that he had attained "certain and evident knowledge of the
truth." [1] The reader who wishes to follow this path is admonished to attend
diligently to the "order and connection" of his reasons, which is a deductive
sequence like that "used by geometers." [2] To all appearances we are promised
an argument *more geometrico,* hence a self-contained and complete argument,
to the most important truths. In previous chapters evidence has been presented
that creates a presumption against these claims; but since it is drawn from
sources largely external to the *Meditations,* this claim must also be judged on
its own terms in the context of the work.

THE ORDER OF REASONS

The declared objective of the *Meditations* is to refute the atheists and skeptics
by proving the existence of God and the immortality of the soul, "and at the
same time" to lay the foundations of science by treating "the whole of first

philosophy." [3] Yet mitigation or retraction of the claims about the order, evidence, and objective of the work already began in the Synopsis. He does not in fact prove the immortality of the soul, because it depends on premises that can be secured only from "the whole of physics." * Furthermore, two comments on the proofs of the existence of God acknowledge obscurities and difficulties that might be found in them; full clarification and satisfaction are promised only in the *Replies to Objections.* Yet the *Replies* contain far more than clarifications; they present new material on many subjects, material that cannot be deduced from the *Meditations.* The same, although to a lesser degree, is true of the *Principles,* which purportedly contain almost the same things as the *Meditations* and which were composed simultaneously with them. [4] If these two writings contain new material presented in a new order, then the *Meditations* do not present a self-contained argument, and the order and connection of reasons undulates uncertainly through many pages of Descartes's own commentary. To admit this, however, is tantamount to abandoning the notion that the sequential order of the *Meditations* is determined by the requirements of a deductive argument.

Such a conclusion may not be hastily drawn. A number of recent interpreters have taken the claim to a strictly ordered demonstrative argument with utmost seriousness; of these, Martial Gueroult is the most thorough and uncompromising exponent. To him the *Meditations* are "a profound monument, solid and geometrical like the fortress at Vauban." [5] Let us then consider his analysis of the order of reasons.

Despite his emphasis on the *series rationum* as a deductive sequence, Gueroult does not analyze the series into discrete propositions, as Spinoza did in his interpretation of the *Principles more geometrico.* The order of reasons is not so much a series of theorems derived from first truths as a "method," the "analytic" method of argument. Following Descartes, he distinguishes it from the synthetic method, which proceeds by the order of the subject. [6] The initial member of the series according to the order of reasons is the Cogito as "first knowledge"; the initial member according to the order of subject is God as the first truth. [7] Such observations outline an argumentative strategy, but they do not constitute an explanation of how Descartes applies the method of analysis, nor what it is, nor do they even prove that the method is in use in the *Meditations.*†

---

* HR I, 140/AT VII, 13. The title of the second edition replaced the initial claim of having proved the immortality of the soul by the more modest claim of having proved that body and soul are distinct (AT VII, v–vi). Observe that the proof to which he refers (MM VI, 9) does not mention the word "substance."

† Vuillemin has noted that in Cartesian mathematics synthesis and analysis are reversible, whereas in metaphysics they are not. The reason is that whereas mathematics is concerned only with

Spinoza is the only commentator to have displayed Descartes's "rigorous proofs" in such a way that each premise and inference could be scrutinized. In point of fact, the order of reasons as expounded by Gueroult is inseparable from his interpretation, the rigor of which we are merely assured.

Since he is committed to the sufficiency of the order of reasons, Gueroult maintains that, despite the *Replies* and correspondence, the *Meditations* are essentially complete and self-sufficient.[8] Yet he cannot state the objective of the work without reference to Cartesian method and physics. By proving the objective validity of clear ideas, metaphysics permits the universalization of mathematical physics, which up to this time had enjoyed partial success. The doctrine of the creation of the eternal truths, i.e., the doctrine of God's infinity and incomprehensibility, resolves the problem of the foundation of truth and the problem of the limits of knowledge which had been posed in the *Regulae*.[9] In sum, the task of metaphysics is to "generalize absolutely" the method by showing that the subjective certitude upon which it rests corresponds to "universal objective reason"; and to show, by the theological doctrine, that the exigencies of universal reason correspond to the world.[10]

None of these objectives is ever stated in the *Meditations,* which indeed do not even mention the method. But it is not merely the interpretation of the objective of the work that Gueroult is compelled to import from outside. The distinction between subjective and objective reason is of his own making, as is his interpretation of the regress to the Cogito as a regress to the "condition of the possibility of all knowledge." [11] His interpretation of the Cogito, which he is constrained to import from the *Discourse* and *Principles,* depends on the axiom, "In order to think, it is necessary to be," which is likewise absent from the *Meditations*. The doctrine of the creation of the eternal truths, which gives sense and body to the infinity of God, is appropriated from the correspondence and *Replies*. These examples could easily be multiplied. They show that the most determined and thoroughgoing effort hitherto at an interpretation of the *Meditations* as a single, self-sustained argument must in fact invent that argument by interpolating into the text much material for whose use Descartes left no guide. These vicissitudes seem to prove that the *Meditations* contain no order of reasons in the required strict sense. Descartes's statements on the order

---

proportion, metaphysics requires existence proofs, hence the notion of causality, which is alien to mathematics (Vuillemin, 1961, 273–74, 283–84). The proofs of the *Meditations* are in fact distinguished by no method but that of familiar syllogistic. The artificiality of the mathematical method as applied to metaphysics is apparent from Descartes's synthetic treatment of his main proofs, for which he requires ten definitions, seven postulates, and ten axioms to prove four propositions.

of reasons thus do not provide a sufficient hermeneutic for interpreting that work.

THE *Meditations* AS JUSTIFICATION OF SCIENCE

It is clear that one's treatment of the argument of the *Meditations* will vary according to the way he evaluates Descartes's foundational objective. There is wide agreement that the argument is meant to justify science, method, or reason: it is a validation of reason; or it is moved by the Kantian question, *quid juris?* The textual warrant for this interpretation is that the doubt calls into question the methodological rule of evidence, which previously had no basis other than Descartes's resolution to give credence only to clear and distinct ideas. As a result of the doubt, he now finds it necessary to ground this rule on the twin principles of the Cogito and a proof of the existence of a veracious God. This view of the foundational objective requires evaluation from the perspective of the First Meditation.

The vagueness and almost studied silence of the initial statement on the founding of the sciences is one of many reasons why the meaning of the text is so elusive. For some years Descartes had detected many false beliefs among those opinions which as a youth he admitted as true; now he is aware that everything constructed on this foundation is doubtful. His remedy is to sweep away the old foundations by doubt, so that he may raise a "firm and permanent" structure in the sciences. We are not told what precisely Descartes had built on the foundations he had from youth. Therefore we cannot at once tell what its relation is to Cartesian science. Still, as the sequence progresses it transpires that the old foundation was "the senses," and toward the end there is a reference to the structure that had been raised upon them: "physics, astronomy, and medicine and all the other sciences which depend upon consideration of composite things, are doubtful, while arithmetic, geometry and such like . . . contain some certainty and indubitability." [12] Can these be Cartesian sciences? If so, one must impute to the meditating Descartes the view that Cartesian science is uncertain because it is based on sense prejudice, although before and after the *Meditations* his claim is always that Cartesian science is certain because its foundation is mathematics and not the senses. It is therefore hardly credible that Cartesian science requires reform along these lines. The only other readily available science is scholastic Aristotelianism, which Descartes certainly thought dubitable and whose foundations the

Meditations are expressly said to "destroy." * There is no doubt that the soul conception criticized in the Second Meditation is Aristotelian, for it is initially characterized as the rational animal concept. It appears, therefore that the explicit foundational objective represents Descartes's position at a time prior to possession of Cartesian science, as he indicated to Burman in describing the standpoint of the First Meditation: "The author considers himself as one who has just begun to philosophize." [13] Evidently the explicit foundational endeavor is based on the fiction that Cartesian science does not exist. The fiction explains why neither Cartesian science nor its previous founding are mentioned; and why the sense doubt is conducted on the basis of ordinary skeptical objections rather than on the sophisticated arguments that might have been brought to bear from the theory of vision. Assuming that the *Meditations* justify or vindicate reason, can the explicit foundational intention be to justify a science whose existence they do not acknowledge? If so, how can that be squared with the statements of purpose according to which the *Meditations discover* the principles—God and the soul—upon which science is based as a deduction from first causes? Obviously, a determination about whether the *Meditations* justify science cannot be made until the relation of the metaphysical foundation to the previous foundation is understood.

While metaphysics is said to discover the principles of physics, nothing in the argument of the *Meditations* bears it out. The identification of matter with extension is asserted in the First Meditation without discussion and is never questioned at any point.† The basis for the identification given in the *Meditations* is the same as that given elsewhere—it is intuitively evident.‡ The extension of the world is in no way deduced from a higher cause. Except for the passage which identifies God with nature, extension is related to God only mediately, through the divine warranty for the methodological rule of evidence. For Descartes does not derive the extensionality of the world from God, but asserts its extensionality on the basis of his clear ideas of mind and body. The theological principle enters the argument only to guarantee the reliability of

---

* Beck (1952, 235) momentarily recognizes that the description of the composite sciences refers to the sciences as "practiced in his own day." He abandons this reading because he thinks that the reference to simple natures indicates that Descartes must have his own physics in mind.

† The analysis of wax is not a proof that body is extension, at least not according to Descartes's express statement in HR II, 63/AT VII, 175; cf. AM VIII, 122.

‡ MM V, 3–6, 16; MM VI, 1, 10. Observe that MM V, which, according to its title, is devoted to a discussion of the "essence" of material things, in fact never discusses that "essence."

reason's ideas. It might be applied equally to any and all rational claims, as Descartes on occasion indeed does.[14]

This peculiar state of affairs must be compared with the abandonment of the fictive nonexistence of Cartesian science in the Sixth Meditation, when Descartes appropriates his scientific theory of sensation to settle the problem which appeals to divine veracity and introspective analysis had failed to settle, namely, the determination of what is real in sensation. This explicit entry of Cartesian science is of decisive importance to the present question. Together with the assertion that body is extension, that the human body is a machine, and references in the *Replies* to the *Dioptric,* it shows that the affected nonexistence of Cartesian science is accompanied by tacit admission of its existence. More important, the appeals to science show the nullity of the project to found science by metaphysical doubts of the senses, since the method of doubt and introspective analysis "succeeds" only by appeal to the very science that it allegedly discovers or founds. Consequently, the sole achievement of the explicit foundation is to provide the divine warranty for the methodological rule of evidence, which is needed only because of the hyperbolic doubt that Descartes styles as "ridiculous" and one that "no sane man" would contemplate.[15] It seems, therefore, that the explicit foundational endeavor has no other objective than to satisfy the learned by inventing a theological derivation of the world, that is, by an imaginary replacement of extension with God in the genuine foundations. The explicit apologetic intention to prove the existence of God is one with the explicit foundational intention designed to shelter physics from the "hatred" of the learned, i.e. Descartes's apology for his physics. This level of the *Meditations* will be called its rhetoric.* The term is dictated by three considerations: it reminds us of the work's apologetic objectives; it correctly characterizes the argumentative origin of this foundation from a "hyperbolic doubt," for hyperbole is proper to rhetoric and poetry rather than science; and it implies a contrast with the true argument and objective of the work, which will be called "acroamatic." †
Let us consider the acroamatic foundation.

THE *Meditations* AS RECAPITULATION OF METHOD

The rule of order developed earlier implies that the *Meditations* are devoted to a foundational problem based on the fact that Cartesian science exists—a

---

* The rhetoric of the *Meditations* corresponds roughly to the "lofty and obscure" reasonings that are condemned in the *Regulae* and the *Discourse.*

† Clerselier used this term to distinguish Descartes's scientific and philosophic writings from his popular works (AT V, 629).

foundational problem that is immediately connected with the unadulterated foundation of physics, the principle that matter is extension without qualities whatsoever. The only direct justification of this principle Descartes ever offers appeals to the theory of sensation to explain how the belief in the external existence of qualities arises, and the true nature of our perception of extension.

The *Regulae* affirm mind and extension as dual first principles of knowledge in the sense that they exhaust all that the mind is able to know. While Descartes possesses intuitions of both simple natures, he requires an argument that they are exhaustive. An outline of it appears in Rule XII, which purports to summarize "all that went before" by expounding the right use of the mind's instruments (sensation, imagination, understanding) for obtaining clear cognitions. He notes that his exposition assumes a theory of what the mind is, what body is, and how the two are related, but he foregoes the explanation since he wishes to write "nothing controversial." Instead he hypothesizes a theory of sensation, whose details we now know from the *Dioptric,* which leads to the epistemological result that "the infinitude of figures suffices to express all the differences in sensible things." [16] This thesis is then related, via the suppressed theory of sensation, to a statement on the relation of mind and body. The "cognitive power" is a "single agency" which may apply itself to the corporeal images of the sensus communis in order to sense or to imagine; or it may act alone, without images, in which case it is called "pure understanding." True science depends upon the right use of each instrument, although their right use can be explained only by reference to a theory of the real relation between mind and body.

This outlook is the dominating philosophical motif of the theory of vision and of automatism; consequently, the foundation of science comes to depend upon understanding the nature of the mind, with respect to its "distinctness" and "union" with the body, as the point of intersection of the epistemological or methodological problem of the mind's cognitive relation to the world, in the sense of its cognizability as extension only; and the ontological thesis that the world is nothing but extension. The argument of the *Meditations,* as will be shown, recapitulates this problem complex in light of method and physics, that is, in a complete and final way. The unique achievement of this recapitulation, in virtue of which it is "foundational," is its capacity to unify the ontological and epistemological orders. The argument which consummates the unification would show that the "nature" of the mind can be understood in terms of its "distinctness" from body, i.e., that it can be reduced to cognition of objects or consciousness. The argument thus answers the ontological question about what the mind is, epistemologically or methodologically, in terms of cognition. The way is then open to assert that all the mind's objects are nothing but body, to which it is immediately "united." The two simple natures are related by the necessity of mutual implication, both in the ordo essendi and the ordo cognoscendi: in the former, because mind is an "effect" of extension, an effect which is not an extended thing but cognitions; in the latter because all that the mind is able to know clearly is extension. Mind and body are therefore the coordinate first principle of science. This interlocking relationship and reciprocal determination is the true "guarantee" of the correspondence between the world (ordo essendi) and the clear ideas of reason (ordo cognoscendi).

THE B-LEVEL ARGUMENT OF THE *Meditations*

The rhetorical and acroamatic levels are related to one another by a masterpiece of prestidigitation, examples of which have just been pointed out. The rhetorical level, which usually consists of the most conspicuous textual features, when properly examined becomes an image of the acroamatic level where Cartesian science is operative. The image is an intellectual counterpart of a visual field-ground illusion, whose peculiarity is that a single figure exhibits two entirely different pictures, according to which elements the viewer organizes as field and ground. The extreme abbreviation of the argument of the *Meditations* is the property that enables it to suggest two different comprehensions of its meaning. The variety of portraits in the gallery of Descartes exegesis results from attempts to piece together a single homogeneous image from fragments of two heterogeneous wholes. The present interpretation is an analytical dioptric whose objective is to achieve clarity by refracting the two images, thereby focusing them as clearly distinct wholes.

Sense Doubt

THE STRUCTURE OF DOUBT

Descartes undertakes to found immutably certain science by doubting the senses. He announces this plan without argumentative support, although its presuppositions are numerous and unevident. It assumes that the senses are known to be the source of the uncertainty of his opinions, and that the uncertainty can be rectified by a wholesale attainder on sense evidence. It assumes that certainty is attainable by the method of doubt, and that the residue of certainty that is presumed to survive the skeptical onslaught will be suitable as the first principle of science. If the doubt were an analytic method of discovery, it would present the remarkable spectacle of an investigation that began with sweeping assumptions about the nature of science that nevertheless proved to be true. But however that may be, these assumptions comprise the dogmatic basis of the doubt which alone gives it purpose and direction. The confirmation of the assumptions by the result is not a coincidence. The identification of the greatest certainty with the first principle of science, which the doubt postulates, is clearly derived from the pre-*Meditations* methodological concept of science as one which homogenizes the ordo essendi and the ordo cognoscendi by neutralizing sense prejudice. The program of the doubt is therefore the first image of Cartesian science that we encounter in the *Meditations*. But whereas Cartesian physics demands a discriminating evaluation of sense evidence, Descartes's rhetorical purposes lead to the heedless hyperbolic doubt which overthrows their evidence entirely. The hyperbolic doubt is latent in the rule governing the advance of the doubt, which is that if one member of a collection is uncertain, the whole collection should be rejected as uncertain.[17] It is a formula for throwing out the baby with the bath, or, as Gassendi protested, substituting new prejudices for the old. The rule simulates the valid inference that a counterinstance of a universal proposition falsifies it. It infers from the falsity of the universal affirmative to the truth of its contrary, i.e., from "not all *a* is certain" to "no *a* is certain."

The meaning of the sense doubt is subject to a significant misunderstanding of Descartes's own making. He calls it a withdrawal of the mind from the senses, which he expressly connects with the traditional religious meaning of a "meditation" as a withdrawal to the soul "separated from the flesh." [18] This anti-sensualism easily leads to the view that the doubt is a gradual regress from the lower to higher faculties. This is a double error. The doubt is directed not against the senses per se, but against opinions based on sense evidence—it is directed against prejudice or a species of judgment. The doubt aims to suspend "assent." The notion of the doubt as a regression from sense to understanding also introduces the basic misunderstanding that Cartesian mind consists of higher and lower faculties; instead, it is "one and the same power" that senses, is angry, and cognizes purely. The doubt does not exhibit the correction of a lower faculty by a higher, but exhibits reason, the "power of judgment," in the process of self-correction. Each stage in the process will locate and overthrow a specific prejudice.

The method of this process is the skeptical *alternado* between contradictories, the object of which is suspension of judgment.[19] Schematically, credence *p* is attacked by doubt *q*; credence makes a rejoinder to the doubt, which succeeds by revising p to meet the initial objection; p' is in turn attacked by a revised version of q, q', and so on. The theses and antitheses are so chosen that they form a series which shows the defects of prejudice.

SENSE DECEPTION

Descartes starts the process with the naive and straightforward objection that sense evidence should be doubted because the senses "sometimes deceive us." The credence against which it is directed is unstated; presumably it is that the senses are entirely reliable. The most torpid version of this prejudice is a trust so unreflective that no distinction between sensation and object is made at all. The mind in its earliest days "perceived magnitudes . . . and the like, which were exhibited to it not as sensations but as things . . . although it did not yet observe this distinction." [20] The skeptical objection thus represents a higher degree of reflection than the initial credence; hence its instructive value. But, the hyperbolic rule operates to infer that sense evidence should be rejected entirely. The riposte overthrows the hyperbolic inference by drawing a distinction between trustworthy and untrustworthy sensations. Although we may err in regard to minute or distant objects, there are others that "we cannot reasonably doubt," for example, that "I am seated by the fire." Sense prejudice has now reached a stage of maturity; it contains within itself a reflective moment.

Descartes does not explain here either the reflection by which the distinction between veridical and unveridical sensations was drawn, nor does he state the new principle of credence. Although they are indispensable for understanding the doubt, Descartes has displaced them to the Sixth Meditation; this is further evidence that the *Meditations* do not follow the order of reasons of its own argument. Recounting there his old beliefs, he tells of having observed the apparent changes in objects as his position and distance from them changed. He has compared two views of a round tower, one close and one far away, and concluded that only one of these observations is veridical, although they are equally "appearances." He has gone much farther. He reconciles the incompatibility by assigning the non-veridical appearance the status of a sensation "in his thought," while the other is a sensation caused by "objects similar to [it]." [21] Prejudice has now entered a theoretical level; it has an explanation, the copy theory of sensation, to back its credence; hence, it is not "reasonable" to doubt all sense evidence. The student of the *Dioptric* will already discern the invisible hand of Cartesian science controlling the meditations of the naive Descartes.

MADNESS

The first credential rejoinder trails off into the second skeptical objection as an afterthought. Descartes might doubt his conviction that he is dressed and seated by his fire if he "compared [himself] with persons devoid of sense, whose cerebella are so disturbed and beclouded by the violent vapors of black bile, that they believe themselves kings although they are really quite poor." Here for the first time science, albeit archaic Galenic medicine, enters the lists as a reason for doubt. The reflection has made a leap in sophistication. Whoever admits that sense organs are necessary to sensation must admit that the reliability of the sensed idea as a copy of the object will depend on the soundness of the organ; what then if the organ of all the senses, the cerebellum, is defective? Descartes has expanded the considerable body of theory latent in the first credential rejoinder to compel prejudice to distinguish between the sense organs and the sensus communis, whose seat is the cerebellum or, in Cartesian science, the pineal gland.

The madness conundrum attacks the principle upon which the first credential rejoinder was based. Veridical sensations are true because they are copies; they are copies because they are adventitious and because "the ideas which I received through the senses were much more lively, more clear, and even, in their own way, more distinct than any of those I could frame in meditation." * The sensus communis is the seat of sensation and imagination, or meditation. If adventitiousness, clarity, and distinctness are the marks of veridical sensations understood as copies of objects, they do not suffice to distinguish veridical sensations from imaginary impressions upon the sensus communis whose cause is not an external object but an aberration of the brain. The madness doubt, by conjuring up the possibility of clear, distinct and adventitious representations which nevertheless are not copies of external objects, undermines prejudiced credence.

But this doubt is rejected because it is hyperbolic: "They are mad, and I should not be any less insane were I to follow examples so extravagant." It is significant that the madness doubt is answered by appeal to the very criterion of clarity and distinctness which it purports to overthrow. The madman does

---

* MM VI, 6. Descartes uses the term "meditation" to denote "works of imagination" (AT X, 202–03). Observe, however, that first principles can be known "without meditation," i.e., directly by intuition (HR I, 205/AT IX–2, 5). This tends to confirm my view that the feigning of the doubt, and the dreaming theological metaphysics that results therefrom, is part of the rhetoric of the work.

indeed experience phantasms as though they were real objects, i.e., clearly and distinctly, but Descartes, who is not mad, can only *imagine* that condition. He cannot imagine that he is a king with the same vividness that he senses that he is seated by his fire.

DREAMS

The rejection of the madness doubt is followed by another afterthought that introduces the dreaming doubt. While he cannot doubt his sanity, Descartes remembers that he has dreamed things during waking quite as improbable as the experience of the mad; and while dream images do not seem as distinct (F.V. "clear and distinct") as his waking perceptions, nevertheless, after carefully considering the matter, he concludes that he can find no "certain" mark to distinguish waking from dreams. This so astounds him that he almost persuades himself that he dreams.

The dreaming doubt is a prime instance of the vagueness in the argument of the *Meditations* which has occasioned lively discussion of its meaning. Descartes succumbs to the doubt after carefully considering the matter, but we are not told what his reflections were. It is not even clear precisely how this doubt affects the status of sense beliefs, since the status of dreams with respect to reality is not explained. However, a determination of these questions is quite important because Descartes next makes the "supposition" that he dreams, which remains in force throughout the *Meditations*: in some sense Descartes writes a dreaming metaphysics.* The problem becomes even more complicated in the immediate sequel, where, despite the dreaming supposition, Descartes offers a series of rejoinders to prove that he knows something "real and true." These rejoinders evidently parallel the strange statements elsewhere that if we sense anything "clearly and distinctly," either in waking or dreams, we may be assured of its truth.[22]

Having assumed that he dreams, Descartes admits that all his present perceptions may be false in the sense that the objects they represent may not exist. This suggests that the dreaming state is one of total illusion. If so, the doubt would cease to be reasonable, since, as various authors have pointed out, such a hypothesis can be dissipated by a reductio ad absurdum: "If the conclusion were true, the premises could not be set up." For if all purported knowledge of

---

* See note, p. 111. The manner in which Descartes ultimately dispels the dreaming doubt (MM VI, 24) recalls the procedure he used in the famous dream vision of November 10, 1619; for when an apparition appeared to him, he had "recourse to reasons taken from philosophy" (AT X, 182).

reality is merely a dream illusion, the conclusion leaves no possibility of distinguishing reality from illusion in the premise; hence the conclusion can give no meaning to illusion.* Descartes seems to have deceived himself by a simple sophism. Rightly observing upon waking that he had a dream as vivid as a waking experience, he now infers that all waking experience may be merely a vivid dream, from which, however, he cannot awaken. Whereas the identification of the vivid dream as a dream was possible only because he possessed a mark—waking up—he now would efface that mark altogether. One cannot therefore reasonably doubt that he always dreams.

But it is doubtful that Descartes takes dreams entirely in the conventional sense. Even vivid dreams lie in the region of semiconsciousness, a region that the Cartesian mind doctrine is notorious for having ignored. The dreaming doubt seems for him to be entirely a problem for the waking intellect.† In the concluding paragraph of the First Meditation he likens his old opinions to the imaginary liberty that a captive may enjoy in a dream, whereas the "laborious wakefulness" of the doubt disturbs the tranquillity of sleep; and there is a similar remark in the Second Meditation. Owing to these deficiencies in the explicit argument of the dreaming doubt, perhaps it should be interpreted as an image of a genuine argument at the acroamatic level.

The madness doubt challenged the prejudice that sensations, clearly and distinctly perceived, are true copies of external objects by suggesting a species of perceptions that are clear and distinct and yet correspond to no external object. The dreaming doubt raises the same objection but without appealing to an aberration of the brain. Allegedly veridical sensations have the same status as dreams, imagination, and every other phantasm in that they are the immediate objects of thought through which reality is known. How then can we determine what in these perceptions corresponds to the reality which is supposed to have caused the veridical sensation. What is that reality altogether? The dreaming supposition, at the acroamatic level, means that prejudice has reached the stage of edification at which it accepts the idealist thesis that we have im-

---

* This argument was presented by W. H. Walsh (1963, 91). In a note, L. J. Beck criticizes Walsh for failing to notice that Descartes does not say that there are "no certain marks" by which the dreaming state can be distinguished from waking (Beck, 1965, 76, n. 1). But Descartes does assert this at AT VII, 19: 20-21. Frankfurt says that the reductio argument against the dreaming doubt is not only appropriate to Descartes's purposes, but "uniquely suited to them" (Frankfurt, 1970, 51). If so, it is strange that Descartes does not invoke it.

† There is no evidence in the *Meditations* that Descartes has any interest in the experienced inability to distinguish waking from dreaming, nor in the theoretical considerations to which it points, namely, the unconscious. The complete neglect of unconsciousness is one of the notable features of the Cartesian mind doctrine (MM VI, 6).

mediate knowledge of thoughts only. This means that the fundamental prejudice has been uprooted, as Descartes explains retrospectively in the Third and
Sixth Meditations:

> But there was yet another thing that I affirmed, and which owing to the
> habit which I had found of believing it, *I thought I perceived* clearly, al-
> though in truth I did not perceive it at all, namely, that there were objects
> outside me from which these ideas proceeded, and to which they were en-
> tirely similar.[23]

The sense doubt, in the final analysis, is directed against one primary prejudice
—the belief that we have immediate knowledge of external objects, or that we
perceive their external existence. This is the only obscurity that afflicts them.
The doubt does not challenge clarity and distinctness as a rule of evidence, but
forces the admission that external existence is only apparently clearly perceived.
It is not possible to discover from the *Meditations* why the doubt that founds
the sciences must center upon just this doubt. From the perspective of the First
Meditation, no more can be said than that it happens to issue from Descartes's
recapitulation of ancient skepticism. But in the course of clarifying his theory of
sensation in the *Replies,* Descartes gave the proximate reason for this doubt by
referring to his optical discovery that perceptions of space are due to "judgments of the understanding." [24] The metaphysical doubt thus incorporates the
finding that all knowledge of position and distance, and therefore of visual
objects as such, is estimated from two-dimensional retinal data.

REJOINDER TO THE DREAMING DOUBT

The level of sophistication attained by the doubting Descartes becomes clear
from the credential rejoinders made to the dreaming doubt. A series of successively revised statements about what may be "real and true" in our ideas is
terminated when he arrives at the position of Cartesian science, or a facsimile
thereof.

The rejoinder revives the prejudice that images of things, even in dreams,
must in some way correspond to real things perceived by the senses and asserts
that imagination and phantasms generally have their origin in the senses. Descartes seeks a grip upon reality by reflecting on the limits of the factitious fantasy. He suggests first that however he may fantasy, such general things as eyes,
heads, and arms are not imaginary. But then upon consideration of the depic-
tions of painters, he revises his estimate. Eyes, heads and arms may be imaginary, but colors at any rate are not. He thinks that there are other things,

"more simple and universal," of which all our "images" of things are made (*effinguntur*). "To this genus belongs corporeal nature in general and its extension, the figure of extended things, their quantity or magnitude and number, as also the location in which they exist, the time of their duration, etc." [25] We are not told in what sense these simple things are universal to all images, nor in what sense all images are made from them. Color, and presumably all qualities, are also included among the simples, although they are not mentioned in the subsequent paragraph on mathematics and composite things. But it is at least clear that Descartes has performed an analysis of sensation in terms of simples and complexes (or composites) that undoubtedly suggests the principle of Cartesian science, extension, as the universal out of which all images are made. The simple things have the advantage of certainty or undubitability because the relations obtaining among them are independent of questions of existence. Thus, at this stage Descartes needs only his doctrine of corporeal ideas to confirm this prejudice that the universals correspond to something "real and true." Cartesian science is accordingly immanent to the rejoinder. From the point of view of the acroamatic foundation, the doubt is now prepared to pass directly to the Cogito. But it is postponed because Descartes discerns a new set of reasons for doubt that threaten the foundation he has embraced.

The Theological Doubt

The introduction of the theological doubt deflects the argument from its announced intention to doubt opinions based on the senses. The primary evidence for this devolution of the argument is that the theological doubt calls into question the truths of mathematics, which have just been declared to be independent of existence. Furthermore, the reason for doubt is no longer drawn from sense evidence, but is based on an "old opinion." The theological doubt corresponds to what the *Discourse* characterizes as opinions gathered from "teachers." *
There is, however, a continuity between the sense doubt and the theological doubt. In both cases clarity and distinctness as a rule of evidence are called into question; but whereas the sense doubt drives the criterion from prejudice to reason, the theological doubt questions the rule as such. Up to this point, the hyperbolic doubt admits of an interpretation in conformity with Cartesian science, but from this point forward, the doubt attacks foundations of Cartesian

---

* The *Search for Truth* especially emphasizes the need to escape the "authority of masters" (HR I, 305/AT X, 496). See also AT V, 146.

science by attacking the first rule of the method.* It is an argument which considers objections that might be made to his foundations from the point of view of revealed religion. His response is the final solution to the strife between reason and revelation.

THE OMNIPOTENT GOD

The theological doubt is broached when Descartes recalls his "old opinion" that he was created by an omnipotent God. Perhaps God has arranged things so that no reality corresponds to his images of heaven, earth, or extended body; and perhaps he is deceived when he does sums or any simpler operation. Therefore, Descartes says, "We shall also doubt the demonstrations of mathematics and of its principles" because, as he wrote in the *Principles,* "we have heard it said that God who has created us can do whatever he pleases." [26]

It is important to establish the identity of this God. Some authors blunt the cutting edge of this question by treating it merely as an hypothesis or as an abstract possibility; but Descartes presents it as an ingrained opinion that he has acquired from others. It corresponds to what the *Discourse* calls the opinions of teachers that he had heard from infancy. It would appear, therefore, that the God in question is the biblical God. The same conclusion is reached by observing that the God whose existence is to be proved to the atheists is specifically the God taught by the Catholic Church, as Descartes noted to the Sorbonne faculty. Above all, throughout the *Objections and Replies,* both Descartes and his critics accept this identification without discussion.[27]

In addition to this identification, another must be considered. In the passage presently under discussion Descartes does not style God a "deceiver," but suggests only that the meditating Descartes might be deceived by him. However, the gloss on this passage in the *Principles* establishes the identity of the biblical God with the *deus deceptor* first mentioned in the Third Meditation: "We should have reason to think that God is a deceiver if he has given us [a perverted reason]." [28] Again he says in the *Replies*: "Unless reason tends toward truth . . . , God, who has given it to us, merits being regarded a deceiver." [29] The biblical God thus enters the argument as an objection to the reliability and self-sufficiency of reason.†

---

* The doubt breaks a number of methodological rules, e.g., never to assume the false as true (*Regulae* IV); the prohibition against "admiration" for "sublime and profound philosophical explanations" (*Regulae* IX, X); the injunction to study only those simple things about which unanimity is possible (*Regulae* II).

† Various critics complained that the doubt seems to endanger faith (HR II, 93/AT VII, 215; HR II, 274–75/AT VII, 471). Descartes frequently concedes this point (AT VII, 7, 247, 346; AT

THE ATHEIST REJOINDER

But is the doubt reasonable that an omnipotent deceiver exists? The credential rejoinder implicitly raises this question by doubting the doubt: "There may indeed be those who prefer to deny the existence of a God so powerful, rather than believe that all other things are uncertain." These persons, elsewhere identified as atheists, would rescue themselves from the hyperbolic doubt by affirming that the origin of the world and of themselves is "fate or chance . . . or a continuous succession of antecedents." This succinct description is reminiscent of Cicero's description of Stoic physics:

> Reason compels us to admit that all things happen by fate. Now by fate I mean the same that the Greeks call *heimarmene,* i.e., an orderly succession of causes wherein cause is linked to cause and each cause itself produces an effect. This is a sempiternal truth that flows from all eternity.*

The description is a reasonable facsimile of the universal necessity that permeates the Cartesian world. It suggests also the Stoic fatalism that Cartesian ethics invokes to remedy the irresolution that stems from the belief that there is outside us some power that disposes itself toward us favorably or unfavorably. It would appear, then, that the Cartesian conception of nature is the substance of the rejoinder to the theological doubt, particularly when one considers the sequence of the argument from the dreaming doubt forward. The rejoinder to that doubt formulates the idea of Cartesian science; it is then challenged by the idea of the biblical God, which is in turn countered by the cosmological conception required by Cartesian science. At this point in the argument, then, Descartes poses the alternatives as affirming the existence of the biblical God, which entails the uncertainty of all knowledge, and affirming the self-sufficiency of reason, which entails the denial of unqualified divine omnipotence. The rejoinder accordingly develops the strife between faith and reason incipient in the *deus deceptor* by exhibiting a complete disjunction between the "old opinion" and the requirements of science.

Descartes does not attempt to draw his skeptical rejoinder to the atheists from a new premise about the existence of God, but undertakes to show that an

---

I, 558; AT V, 153, 560). His better known position, however, is that the doubt is purely "metaphysical" and has no bearing on questions of faith and morals. This artificial limitation upon the scope of the doubt has seemed arbitrary to many interpreters. Gilson, for example, dismisses Descartes's disclaimer as "only a feint" (Gilson, 1913b, 268). See also Röd, 1964, 60.

* Cicero, *De Divinatione* I, 55. Descartes held that it was permissible to doubt the existence of God for the purpose of increasing our knowledge of him (AT IV, 62).

equivalent doubt can be deduced from the atheist premise. He argues that since error is a sign of defect, the probability of the atheist's being so imperfect as to deceive himself always increases as the power of the author to whom he assigns his origin is diminished. This reasoning is very strange. Its result is that whether Descartes regards his author as omnipotent or less than omnipotent, he may be deceived in all things. L. J. Beck suggests that this reduction shows that there can be "no question of choosing between a theistic and an a-theistic solution" to the metaphysical problem raised by lack of knowledge of the origin of our being.* Yet closer inspection of the argument shows that it presupposes the theological doctrine, developed in the Third and Fifth Meditations, that God's perfection is implied by his omnipotence, and that both together constitute the reason for his veracity. Indeed, to explain why the atheist is subject to complete doubt, including doubt of mathematical truths, Descartes says that in the absence of knowledge of the true God, the atheist is subject to the deus deceptor doubt.[30] The atheist would reply, of course, that he does not believe in any God, and that his conception of nature, so far from being the occasion for a doubt of the existence of the world or the validity of mathematics, is precisely the conception that supports the immutability of both. The root of these difficulties is the unreasonableness of the theological doubt. But rather than enter now upon a discussion of that wide-ranging topic, let us accept the appearance of the argument that upon either premise about his author, Descartes has reason to doubt the reliability of reason.

THE MALIGN DEMON

At this point the doubt comes to a halt, having apparently reached its extreme limit. Descartes now discusses the need for adopting a method that will impress his doubts upon his mind and restrain his old habits of credence. The method he adopts is not the skeptical epoche, toward which the doubt seems to have been aiming, but the astounding procedure of "allowing [himself] to be deceived, and for a time pretending that all these opinions are entirely false and imaginary." For this purpose he introduces the celebrated malign demon: "I will then suppose, not that the supremely good God, the fountain of truth, but some malign demon, who is both supremely powerful and cunning, employs all his energies in deceiving me." [31]

It is for good cause that the demon has been the subject of much commentary and debate. Not only is he the axis of the doubt, at least at the rhetorical level

* Beck, 1965, 70. Kenny (1968, 34) also remarked the oddity of the argument against the atheists, but does not find it significant for the strategy of the doubt as a whole.

of the work, but he is also quite mysterious. The demon presumably epitomizes the deus deceptor and atheist doubts; but since they are different doubts, it is by no means clear how the demon relates to them. It has been argued that the demon doubt is distinct from the other two, or that one of several varieties of identification occur—the deus deceptor with the demon; the atheist doubt with the demon; the deus deceptor and atheist doubt with the demon.* Every commentator assumes, as is only natural, that the Second Meditation is conducted under the aegis of the demon, whatever his identity; and yet a genium is not mentioned there nor elsewhere in the *Meditations*. He is not glossed anywhere in the *Replies,* nor does he appear in any of the other three accounts of the doubt.† His one ephemeral appearance, however, has engraved his insubstantial figure on all studies of Cartesian metaphysics. It is neither possible nor necessary to discuss all alternatives. Instead we will show that a coherent interpretation can be obtained by identifying the demon with the deus deceptor. There are three main objections to such an identification: the natures of God and a demon are different; the quality of the demon and deus deceptor differs, both with respect to good or evil and power; and the origin and function of the deus deceptor differ from the demon.

The first objection is removed by the expressions Descartes uses to describe the deceiver in the Second Meditation. In the summary of the doubt just prior to the Cogito, he is said to be "some God, or whatever other name it may be called," which suggests that "genium" could be substituted without changing the conception. In the same context he is called "some deceiver, I know not what (*nescio quis*), supremely powerful and cunning." Later he is described as "some deceiver, most powerful and . . . malign." [32] The final reference speaks of the deceiver as the power who "created" Descartes. [33] The Third Meditation, whose reference is definitely to the omnipotent, deceiving God, preserves the expression *aliquis Deus* introduced in the Second Meditation. [34] This thorough conflation of the attributes and names of the deus deceptor and demon is sufficient reason to set the first objection aside.

The transformation of the omnipotent God, of whom Descartes has heard it

* Beck, Gouhier, and Alquié agree in holding the three doubts distinct; Kenny and Röd identify the deus deceptor with the demon; Kennington identifies the atheist and demon doubts, which agrees with Gueroult's view that the demon represents "the absolute form of atheism," although Gueroult further identifies the atheist and demon doubts with the deus deceptor. Kennington and Gueroult were anticipated by Hamelin, who wrote that the demon is the "personification de la violence que fait peut-être subir à l'esprit la nature peut-être irrationelle de l'universe" (Hamelin, 1921, 118).

† The deus deceptor, atheist, and demon doubts are all absent from the DM; the demon is omitted in the *Principles,* while the *Search for Truth* omits the atheist and demon doubts.

said that he is good, into an evil demon occurs through a series of dialectical steps. Throughout the doubt Descartes studiously avoids mentioning the theological tradition, but it makes one brief appearance in the objection that God's omnipotence is governed by his goodness. This consideration is rejected on the grounds that if it is evil to be deceived in all things, it is evil to be deceived in some, and of the latter we cannot doubt. Latent in this reasoning is the heterodox syllogism: an omnipotent God deceives me, and deception is evil, therefore God is the cause of evil. By calling his evil deceiver a "demon," Descartes makes this problem of providence visible without uttering the "criminal blasphemy" it contains.

This interpretation is recommended by the argument of the *Meditations.* Meditations III to VI pose the traditional problem of providence in terms of the need to reconcile divine omnipotence with the evil of error; since the later arguments refute doubts raised earlier, the argumentative plan requires that the possibility of an evil God has been considered. This strategy may account for the fact that none of the authors of *Objections* raised any questions about the difference between God and the demon. Furthermore, Descartes explains to the Sorbonne faculty that in order to refute the atheists in a final way, he must consider their strongest arguments.[35] This plan perhaps explains his otherwise strange silence about the traditional theological solutions to the problem of providence, for in the circumstances they beg the question: the atheists have examined the traditional proofs and remain unpersuaded.* Indeed, the transition from the deus deceptor, to atheist unbelief, to the evil demon, simply follows the Epicurean dilemma. If there is a God, either he would prevent evil, but cannot, in which case he is not omnipotent; or he can prevent evil, but will not, in which case he is evil. Descartes's embellishment of this tradition is the premise that it is evil or "sin" to err; its source, we learn from the Fourth Meditation, is the tacit identification of virtue with knowledge.

Other evidence that a demon is introduced as a deliberate fiction only to con-

---

*HR I, 134–35/AT VII, 3–4. Descartes's remarks to the Sorbonne faculty about persuading the atheists, cited here, must be compared with his preemptory reduction of the atheist position to skepticism in MM I, 10. His initial statement on the traditional proofs is that they are "like so many demonstrations" and that it is impossible to invent new ones. Yet Descartes disavows having recourse to them because a multitude of demonstrations implies that there is no single demonstration that is truly certain, and Descartes's new demonstration is more certain than mathematics. Thus it seems that the atheists were after all not entirely wrong to doubt the traditional proofs. Yet strangely, Descartes does not claim to be able to persuade the atheists. Rather, the Sorbonne faculty should use its authority to silence the atheists and rid them of their spirit of contradiction (HR I, 136/AT VII, 6). The "refutation" of the atheists therefore seems to be more a public show of a refutation whose purpose is to pile up a "mass of evidence" that will impress the ignorant.

ceal the blasphemy of the doubt is found in Descartes's defense, to the curators of the University of Leyden, against this accusation. To defend Descartes against the charge that he regards God as a deceiver, his protagonist in a public debate cited the passage where Descartes supposes not the "supremely good God, the fountain of truth, but some malign demon." To this the critic replied that the demon was nevertheless styled "supremely powerful" (*summe potens*), which is true of God only.[36] Speaking for himself to the curators, Descartes does not deny that summe potens qualifies the demon as omnipotent; instead he argues that by this reasoning anyone who speaks of demons or gentile gods should be charged with identifying them with the true God, since they all have some one of his attributes.* The supposition of an omnipotent deceiving demon is a supposition per impossibile, he adds, because deception is incompatible with divine perfection.[37] Descartes must withdraw the true God from the doubt, since as the source of truth he provides no occasion for doubt, and he is certainly not a deceiver; he is, in fact, the veracious God of the Third Meditation. The confusion arises for Descartes's critics because, unlike him, they identify the true God with the biblical God, which Descartes has indeed transformed into an evil, omnipotent deceiver, and therefore, into an "impossible" or "contradictory" concept.† The final stage of the doubt is not a reasonable doubt, but there is a reason for it.

THE COGITO AS REJOINDER TO THE THEOLOGICAL DOUBT

The obstacle to science articulated by the deus deceptor-demon doubt is an image of the traditional position of the Church on the relation between faith and reason. Theology holds that because of his fallen nature, man's powers do

---

* AT V, 8/AM VII, 299; also the remarks to Burman in AT V, 147, 150–51. Kennington's argument (1971, 411–46) that the choice of the expression "summe potens" rather than "omnipotens" implies the finite power of the demon is conducted without reference to these texts, although they exhaust, I believe, Descartes's commentary on the subject. It also makes no reference to the fact, upon which the Leyden dispute is based, that in the usage of the day these expressions had the same denotation. In view of the opposition that this phrase cost him, it is difficult to understand why, if Descartes wished the power of the demon to be conceived as finite, he did not say so.

† In commentary to Burman on the phrase summe potens as applied to the demon in MM I, 12, Descartes says that "here the author utters a contradiction, for *summa potentia* is inconsistent with malice" (AT V, 147; also 150–51). Neither the final stage of the doubt nor the arguments that follow in the later Meditations can be understood unless it is recognized that the doubt is, strictly speaking, contradictory or unreasonable. This fact is stressed in many passages in addition to the above: HR II, 41, 42, 245/AT VII, 144, 145–46, 428. Defending himself against Bourdin's demonstrations of the absurdity of the doubt, Descartes says that in MM I he pretended that he "was not attending to anything which I clearly perceived" (HR II, 266/AT VII, 460). If the doubt is literally interpreted, we must believe that Descartes thought that the sciences could be founded by first banishing from his mind all his clear and distinct ideas.

not suffice for his salvation; he requires the guidance of revealed truths. "In this life we do not see by vision but by faith." [38] St. Thomas gave this doctrine its canonical form. He argues that there are two orders of truth, those of reason and those of faith. Although Grace does not destroy but perfects nature, nevertheless it is of higher dignity and by right has authority over the other; for philosophy, as the work of reason, is fallible, while sacred doctrine, the word of God, is infallible. In the event of a clash between reason and faith, the presumption is against reason: "Whatsoever is encountered in the other sciences which is incompatible with the truth [of theology] should be completely condemned as false." [39] St. Thomas therefore puts philosophy in the high, but subordinate, station of "handmaiden" to theology. The autonomy of reason is thereby lost.

The key premise of St. Thomas's argument is the fallibility of reason, which is admitted by most of antiquity except in regard to logical truths. Descartes seems to have concluded that the autonomy of reason could be reestablished if an argument were discovered which showed the infallibility of reason—its immutable, unshakable certainty—after conceding all and more than theology might urge against reason. The concession is the hyperbolic doubt that God might have given him a perverted reason, so that he is deceived in all that he clearly and distinctively perceives. Exaggerated though it is, the doubt nevertheless reflects the unrest of reason subordinated to faith, as Descartes indicated with unsurpassed clarity on the occasion of Galileo's recantation: "I confess that if [the Copernican theory] is false, all the foundations of my philosophy are false also, for they most evidently demonstrate this [theory]." [40] The concession of hyperbolic fallibility is however double-edged. It changes the attitude of reason from that of a docile captive who enjoys the thought of freedom in its dreams, to that of a rebel, jealous to assert his rights.

This transformation is pictured by the absurd and tortured posture of the demon hypothesis. By a deliberate act of will, Descartes allows himself to be deceived by pretending that all his former opinions are false. On its face, this proposal seems to be flatly impossible: to be aware that one is pretending to believe the opposite of what he believes is to dispel the pretense. And yet this is the posture of reason when it "sacrifices reason on the altar of faith." It is an image of the common theological position, accepted by St. Augustine as well as Descartes, that it is by will rather than reason that we assent to revealed truth, since its truths cannot be comprehended by the understanding.[41] From this perspective, the light of reason that contradicts faith assumes the aspect of demonic deception, as we learn from St. Augustine:

Because Satan sometimes "transforms himself into an angel of light" in order to test those who need testing or to deceive those deserving deception, nothing but the great mercy of God can save man from mistaking bad demons for good angels, and false friends for true ones, and from suffering the full injury of this diabolic deception, all the more deadly because it is cunning beyond words.[42]

The fact of faith is the proof that the evidence of reason can be doubted. A doubt is possible only where the tug of evidence is present. It has become clear in the recent literature that Descartes affirms the impossibility of doubting clear and distinct ideas when they are immediately perceived, but there is a "retrospective" or "second-order" doubt directed against the perceiver as such, even as we might doubt the veracity of a source without disputing what that source affirms. For Descartes this doubt is confused and unreasonable, but a doubt nonetheless. The Cogito is the rejoinder to the theological doubt that rescues reason from the shadow region of irresolution.

The recent emphasis by almost all authorities on the "order of reasons" or argument of the *Meditations* has resulted in an unfortunate neglect of their pronounced dramatic elements, which are integral to the argument. Although it is known that the *Meditations* partially simulate the mode of Loyola's *Spiritual Exercises* and other writings of that genre, in which, among other things, temptations by demons appear, little attention is paid to this significant fact.* The last stage of the doubt and its refutation by the Cogito is certainly a moment of high drama, which deserves study in light of the religious antecedents to which the *Meditations* are known to refer.

By propounding his doubts, Descartes, the evil demon, so to speak, assumes the shape of a good angel:

You can doubt the truths of mathematics and the existence of the world, my friend. Do you deny it? Well come and look, I will show you that it is quite easy. You believe in God and all his miracles; and that the legions of Satan are spreading lies and deceit everywhere. You believe these things. Why then do you not admit that you are helpless against these infernal powers? What

---

* Fessard, 1956, 246–54; Beck, 1965, 28–38. There is more than a nominal connection between the *mauvais génie* who appears in the posthumous *Olympica* and the malign demon of the *Meditations*. Both appear in the context of dreams, both raise the problem of providence, both are counterposed to the "spirit of truth" or to certainty, and in both cases the apparitions seem to represent the religious alternative to philosophy. See Kennington, 1961, 199–203.

basis has your prideful confidence in things that seem evident to you, when all the while you believe that reason is weak and mendacious?

The siren song of the doubt seems intended to provoke reason to consciousness of its own nature. Such, at any rate, is its effect upon the persona that Descartes assumes, for the Cogito is enunciated as a cry of defiance: "Let who will deceive me, he can never cause me to be nothing while I think that I am . . . or that two and three make more or less than five, or any such thing in which I see a manifest contradiction." [43] The doubt brings reason to consciousness of its own nature; and in that moment, it recognizes that the theological doubt is not reasonable. This insight Descartes expresses by writing that "even if [God's veracity] could not be proved, we are *by nature* so disposed to give our assent to things we clearly perceive, that we cannot possibly doubt their truth." [44] Or again: "It is irrational to doubt that which we clearly apprehend on account of [divine omnipotence], which we do not clearly understand and ought not understand." [45]

These considerations may explain why nothing short of the resources of the Cogito can defeat the theological doubt. Various authors have shown that the demon may be reduced to a logical absurdity by an internal argument appealing only to the principle of contradiction. Descartes could look to the dialectical keenness of the whole scholastic tradition as a proof that such refutations would not answer his purpose; for indeed, the Augustinian Cogito, and the medieval logical analysis that developed from it, was just such a logical reductio ad absurdum of universal deception.* Logic will not suffice because Descartes must grapple with an attitude or belief held despite proofs and rational evidence. His tak is not to refute proposition, but to change an attitude. The Cogito can effect the change because it is a material truth about the *reasoner*. It is a necessary truth about a contingent existent: "I am, I exist, is necessarily true each time I pronounce it, or mentally conceive it." [46] The Cogito brings thought to consciousness of its nature, that is, to self-consciousness. In that moment the mind apprehends an objective limit upon deception, for the Cogito exhibits to thought a limit upon omnipotence circumscribed by thought itself, indeed, *my* thought. This truth, however, mediates the awareness of the nature of rea-

---

* *City of God*, XI, xxvi. Léon Blanchet has thoroughly scrutinized this tradition in his outstanding study, *Les antecédents historiques du "je pense, donc je suis."* His work, and that of Gilson based upon it (1930, 191–201), clearly show that Descartes stands in this tradition, despite his evident wish to disassociate himself from it. For a brief summary of Descartes's position, see DM, 295–98.

son to affirm the truth of what it clearly and distinctly perceives. That nature has the character of necessity; we "cannot prevent" ourselves from affirming all that we clearly perceive. It is a necessity that "not even Zeus can conquer." But the necessity may be obscured to the reasoner; his bon sens may be corrupted by a deep-seated self-doubt.* Necessity remains nonetheless; it "leads the willing and drags the unwilling."

In its attempt to give credence to two orders of truths, the mind is enfeebled by the irresolution that results from its being dragged by the necessity of its nature to affirm the evidence of reason as its own. It is reduced to bondage. By bringing reason to consciousness of its inner nature, and embracing that nature, fully aware of the blasphemy it contains, the Cogito emancipates reason from all restraints of piety: it empowers a self-consciously secular reason. The exact meaning of Cartesian metaphysical certainty is defined by this embrace or assent to the clear evidence of reason. The truths of mathematics and logic are no more evident and certain to Descartes than they were to other philosophers; his method adds nothing to their indubitability. Cartesian certainty is distinguished rather by the act of will, or "resolution," that affirms this evidence as a whole.† An unshakable and immutable will is the basis of the autonomy of reason. Just as it was by an act of will that assent to truths above reason was made, now, thanks to the consciousness that freedom of will is the "only thing that truly pertains to us," Descartes exercises the virtue of generosity to affirm that alone which is truly his own. The courage of resolute generosity drives away the fear that sundered the irresolute soul into two halves, one longing for another world outside our power, the other tugging it back to itself. By eliminating this strife, the generous soul acquires "security," the good conscience that springs from the will's self-consistency (homologia).[47] But because the autonomy of reason is won through a struggle, its virtue has the character of an embattled spiritedness, which was so clearly discerned by Gerhard Krüger: "Self-consciousness constitutes itself in defiance of all omnipotence. This is not 'Christian inwardness'; rather, here begins in philosophy as such the rebellion against Christianity that we call Enlightenment."[48]

---

* On the theological origin of this self-doubt, see Krüger, 1933, 225–34. The present analysis incorporates the principal results of Krüger's outstanding essay.

† The guarantee for the unshakability of this will is that it is determined by "nature" or "natural inclination." See MM IV, 10; V, 6, 12, 14. The *Passions* interpret love, hence self-love, in an Aristophanian manner as love of one's "other half." See *Passions,* §§ 90, 91, 107; and below, 191.

The Theology of the *Meditations*

Although according to the present interpretation, the Cogito establishes the self-sufficiency of reason from its own resources, Descartes nevertheless returns to the doubt posed by the deceiving God. He now declares that he has "no reason" to believe that God is a deceiver, nor any grounds for believing that there is a God at all. The doubt is therefore "very slight, and so to speak, metaphysical." [49] But presumably because he is writing a metaphysical treatise, he determines to look into the matter. The result is his proof of the existence of God, who is perfect, veracious, and the source of all truth. His omnipotence, moreover, is limited by the principle of contradiction.[50] The proof satisfies Descartes that his rule of evidence, that clear and distinct perceptions are true, is wholly reliable because "no contrary reason can be brought forward which could ever cause me to doubt [them]." [51]

This theological justification of the rule of evidence is part of Descartes's ad hominem argument to the learned. Since they require a theological foundation, he gives them one that complements the achievement of the Cogito. For the import of his doctrine of the veracious God is that, in the strife between reason and faith, God sides with reason, thus conferring divine sanction upon reason's clear and distinct perceptions, which must be true if God is not a deceiver. One could, if he wished, view the doctrine as the metaphysical basis of Descartes's remarkably candid empirical statement that "since we were men before we became Christians, it is beyond belief that any man should seriously embrace opinions which he thinks contrary to that right reason that constitutes a man, in order that he may cling to the faith through which he is a Christian." [52] This theology is followed by a theory of error according to which God has given Descartes the capacity to prevent himself from falling into "error and sin" ever, provided that the assent of his will is governed by the resolution never to judge the truth of matters that are not clearly perceived by the understanding.[53] But since we assent to the truths of revelation only by the will's acceding to what the understanding does not comprehend, his theory appears to abolish faith.

Such an interpretation, it may be objected, tacitly assumes that the theological doctrine of the *Meditations* is a detachable episode, whereas in fact the theology is a response to a problem that lies at the very roots of Cartesian metaphysics. The formulation given the problem by L. J. Beck would command the agreement of most recent commentators. Descartes's subjective point of departure places ideas between the mind and reality. On this supposition, the "subjective criterion of truth [that clear and distinct ideas are true] is not enough to secure that knowledge of the real which he requires." [54] The subjective or psychological conviction, expressed by Descartes's incapacity to doubt clear ideas, must be complemented by an objective or logical criterion (the veracity of God) that guarantees the correspondence between ideas and the order of the world. [55]

The attempt to convert subjective to objective certainty is admittedly afflicted by the difficulty known as the "Cartesian circle": clear and distinct ideas must be used to prove that clear and distinct ideas are true. There is some apprehension that Descartes might have pickled himself permanently in subjective idealism. Commentators have come to Descartes's assistance with a variety of solutions.

Supposing that one or more of them successfully frees Descartes from his circle, we are nevertheless afterward confronted with a theory of divine omnipotence which seems to demolish the possibility of proving the existence of a veracious God who guarantees anything whatever. "It must never be said of anything," Descartes wrote to Arnauld, 'that it is impossible to God. . . . I should not even dare to say that God cannot make a mountain without a valley or that one and two does not equal three. [56] If God can create contradictory states of affairs, and if his actual creation is not governed by goodness or truth, which themselves are determined by the fiat of the creating will, then any attempt to prove that God guarantees a correspondence between our ideas and the world must shatter upon the rock of God's "incomprehensibility." * No wonder Descartes omitted this doctrine from the *Meditations,* for it is impossible to reconcile with the whole rationale of the veracious God. It is vain to appeal to the immutability of the divine will to rescue the veracious God; for if the divine will is immutable, it is idle to say in the first place that God can create contradictions that we, owing to the nature of our conceptual powers, could never detect.†

---

* Surveying the texts in which Descartes acknowledges the incertitude and weakness of our knowledge of God, Alquié was led to suggest that the "Cartesian sense of Being is only sense of absence" (Alquié, 1950, 331–32). For the texts, see AT V, 133, 193.

† According to MM III, 27, there is no unrealized potentiality in God, since that would be a mark of imperfection; so that whatever he can do, he has done. But according to the DM, *World,* and *Principles,* there is no plurality of worlds; consequently, the veracious God has not the potency of the omnipotent God. If the latter exists, however, he must have actually created a plurality of worlds, none of which is tractable to reason. Gueroult attempts to reconcile omnipotence with veracity by saying that God did not create unintelligible states of affairs or other worlds because *"he did not want to make* [them]" (Gueroult, 1953, II, 35). This statement is

There is one significant difference between the deus deceptor and the omnipotent God of the unofficial theology; Descartes no longer implies that God
is malevolent or a deceiver. The reason, presumably, is that Descartes now
understands that whatever God does is good because he does it; that it betrays
ignorance of God's omnipotence to presume to judge his goodness or perfection.[57] Thus, the "hyperbolic certainty" resulting from the proof of a veracious
God, which is saddled with the problem of explaining the possibility of error,*
is followed by a theology of omnipotence that reduces Descartes to his original
subjective certainty. For although God may have created any state of affairs
whatever, nevertheless, Descartes avows that *he* can conceive them in only one
way, in accordance with the nature God has given him.[58] Therefore, it is irrational to doubt our clear and distinct ideas because of the divine omnipotence
that we neither comprehend nor should comprehend. Here indeed is the
reductio ad absurdum of the theological doubt. If it can be reasonably entertained, it is impossible to refute; but it cannot be reasonably entertained.

> [There are some perceptions] that are so perspicuous, and so simple, that we
> are not able to think of them without believing them to be true. . . . We are
> not able to doubt them, unless we think of them; but we cannot think of
> them without at the same time believing them to be true . . . hence, we can-
> not doubt them.[59]

Strictly speaking, Descartes cannot cast doubt on his clear ideas even by "feigning" that God is a deceiver. This representation is only an allegory of the confused mind torn between faith and reason. This Descartes stated with the
utmost clarity compatible with maintaining the effectiveness of his drama:

> What is it to us, though per chance someone [the doubting Descartes] feigns
> that those things of which we are firmly persuaded, appear false to
> God . . . ? What heed do we pay to that absolute falsity, when we by no

---

based on no text, and contradicts Descartes's assertions, admitted by Gueroult, that God's ends
are inscrutable. Moreover, according to Gueroult, God has created a contradiction in uniting
the mind with the body (ibid., 65). There may be a theology of an omnipotent God, but it
cannot be a rational theology.

* Descartes's hyperbolic certitude, to borrow Gueroult's apt phrase, is theologically no less
embarrassing than the hyperbolic doubt; for since it is contrary to the fact that we err, Descartes
is once more compelled to question divine veracity (MM IV, VI). His final word on the matter
is that "notwithstanding the supreme goodness of God, the nature of man, inasmuch as it is
composed of mind and body, cannot be otherwise than sometimes a source of deception" (MM VI,
23). Thus, a preposterous doubt of reason is followed by an unredeemable guarantee of it, the
upshot of which would seem to be that there is no alternative to reliance upon reason, however
fallible.

means believe that it exists or even suspect its existence? We have supposed a persuasion so firm that nothing can destroy it, and this persuasion is clearly the same as perfect certitude.[60]

The thought that subjective persuasion may be "absolutely false" is idle because it cannot be consummated as a reasonable doubt and because if it were, it could not be redeemed. It follows, therefore, that the refutation of this doubt by the veracious God, with its assurance of an absolute truth to guarantee subjective persuasion, is equally idle. The Cartesian circle thus appears to be the legerdemain by which things in no need of proof are made to depend on things not susceptible of proof.

Although the veracious God is inconsistent with the omnipotent creating God, their effect for Cartesian science is the same. The first appropriates God to the philosophers. But that gambit seems to have been too bold to maintain in an undiluted form; it was also necessary to acknowledge that the Church, and the God of the Church, might decree that things are otherwise than reason believes them to be. To compensate for this tension, Descartes seems to have been determined to push omnipotence to such an extreme that the divine edicts are removed entirely from the competence of rational scrutiny, so that they would wither away as irrelevant to science. The creating God is a candidate as the unknowable *hypokeimenon,* the *Ding an Sich.**

It ought not be concluded, however, that the theology of the *Meditations* is only a *deus ex machina* produced to win the applause of an audience. Some have maintained that Descartes cannot make the transition from the subjectivity of the Cogito to objective truth unless the Cogito itself is based upon a *prior* knowledge of God.[61] Descartes's assertion that God is the first truth upon whom all others depend must not be interpreted, these interpreters argue, as the canard that Descartes proposed, namely, merely a guarantee of clear ideas when they are not being considered.† Rather, his argument, that it is only from knowledge

---

* Gilson's early appraisal of the motive for the doctrine of the creation of the eternal truths has not been overturned by any subsequent study. He claimed that "it consists essentially in a justification of the new physics by the metaphysical conceptions that Descartes found in his milieu; it is an adaptation of the theology of the Oratory to the physics of efficient causes" (Gilson, 1913b, 73). Bréhier's well-known article on the subject confirmed this opinion, and lately Cronin, despite some criticisms of Gilson and Bréhier, largely agrees with them (Cronin, 1966, 73). Alquié declared that the theory states the "a priori conditions of technical science" (Alquié, 1950, 104; 94–97).

† There is no question but that this rather frivolous notion of the divine warranty has the greatest authority of the texts, e.g., MM V, 14–15; HR II, 38/AT VII, 140; HR II, 115/AT VII, 345; AT V, 178. But see the much stronger statement of the DM, HR I, 105/DM 38. Of the many expositions of this argument that have appeared in recent years, the one that best harmonizes

of God's infinity that he knows his own finite existence, must be taken seriously. The first certainty in the ordo cognoscendi must be grasped in light of the first truth in the ordo essendi, in such a way that "I exist, therefore God exists" becomes an evident proposition.[62] It is proposed that in effect the argumentation of the Second and Third Meditations is a discursive explication of a single intuition in which the finite thinker knows himself in and through the infinite God.*

The present interpretation can accommodate this view by equating the divine infinite substance with extension, and by replacing the hyperbolic doubt of the existence of the world by the authentic idealism of Cartesian optics, for which the existence of the world is a certainty.† By restoring the whole apparatus of atheist credence, i.e., Cartesian science, to its rightful place in the order of reasons, the true foundational doubt comes to light. As a result, the finite Cogito will be seen to be mediated by prior knowledge of the infinite substance, in the specific form of physiological optics and automatism. The problem about the relation between cognition and reality is no longer an attempt to prove the existence of objects outside of thought, but an attempt to show how corporeal ideas found and unite the ordo cognoscendi to the ordo essendi in the fundamental dualism of Cartesian philosophy.

----

with the texts while omitting nothing important is Kenny's interpretation. He argues that the doubt calls into question only the (general) rule of evidence, while particular clear and distinct propositions remain unaffected because they are indubitable; Descartes may therefore establish the validity of the rule by using his particular indubitable propositions to prove that God is not a deceiver (Kenny, 1970, 687–90). I fail to see how this analysis redeems the circle. Descartes cannot, on penalty of committing a circular argument, use the rule of evidence, established by the proof, to certify the proof; but if it remains uncertified, it depends only upon the subjective incapacity to doubt the propositions that were used in the proof; consequently, the general rule depends upon subjective certainty; nothing, therefore, has been proved. Given the wholesale doubt of reason, Descartes's argument has the same efficacy as a madman's proof that he is not mad. The most impeccable logical argument cannot overcome the devastating effects of the initial doubt.

* Gueroult, 1953, I, 245. Röd argues that the proof in effect restores the original "consciousness of reality" that receded under the onslaught of the doubt. It is not, strictly speaking, a proof but a "showing" of reality (Röd, 1961, 150–51).

† The textual authority for this reading is the statement of MM VI, 11 that "Per naturam enim generaliter spectatam nihil nunc aliud quam vel Deum ipsum; vel rerum creatarum coordinationem a Deo institutam intelligo" and the subsequent interchangeability of God and nature as the cause of sensations (MM VI, 15). The identification is even more explicit in DM, for an account of which see Caton, 1970, 239–41. It is sometimes suggested that these formulations merely follow scholastic usage derived from the precedent of St. Augustine. (For the scholastic version, see Gilson, 1913a, 198). There is hardly any doubt that the scholastic precedent enabled Descartes to speak this way without being challenged by such theologians as Arnauld, even as his Cogito was legitimated in advance by the Augustinian tradition. The important question is whether Descartes's use of this precedent is not as disastrous for Christian theology as his Cogito is for the traditional soul doctrine.

5   The Essence of Cartesian Subjectivity

The subjective phenomenon of consciousness—the sense of awareness that is more real to the individual than anything else—has
qualitative attributes that render it completely incapable of being
derived from or accounted for by any combination of physical
principles known today.

Wooldridge, *The Machinery of the Brain*

The Object and Plan of the Second Meditation

Descartes claims to have "expended as much care" in the composition of the
Second Meditation as he did on "anything I have ever written." The care shows
in its strong architectonic. The Meditation opens with a summary of the doubt,
followed by the argument which culminates in the certainty of his own existence. The remainder of the Meditation is an inquiry about what this "I" or
"something" is. The "what" question is repeated three times. On each occasion,
Descartes considers some aspect of his old opinions or prejudices about his
nature. Each inquiry terminates in a revision of the prejudice that provoked the
question, and a corresponding positive assertion about the mind. The first
"what" question (MM II, 4) leads to a review of the old belief that the soul is
a unity of faculties. MM II, 6 rejects all faculties except thinking, and enunciates
the first *sum res cogitans*. The "what" question arises anew because of the need
to explicate how mind or reason is related to what had previously been regarded
as the faculties of the soul, especially sensation and imagination, which leads
to the second assertion of sum res cogitans, where it is related to the "modes" of
thought. In MM II, 10 the "what" question reappears as a doubt that the mind
is better known than body. The subsequent analysis of the piece of wax explicates the relation between mind and its modes, and body and its modes.

The architectonic may be represented as in Figure 4. At each of the peaks, a
discovered truth about the mind is stated. The troughs represent doubts about
those truths that in every case arise from prejudice, or from an insufficiently

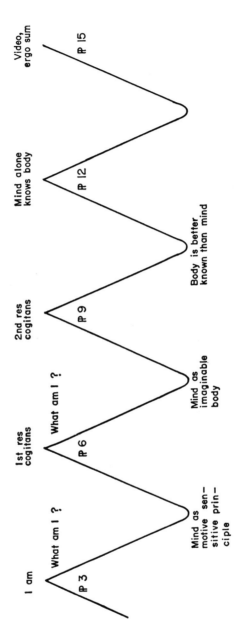

Figure 4. Plot of *Meditations* II

clear conception of the nature of the mind. The troughs, therefore, represent backsliding into the realm of prejudice, and each peak represents a response to the particular prejudice that precedes it. That each peak is a response to a particular doubt is of some importance to note; for the character of each doubt provides guidance for the correct interpretation of the truths asserted, some of which appear to be inconsistent, especially the first and second enunciations of sum res cogitans. At the same time, the limitation of Descartes's discursive exegesis must be noted. Since the mind is a simple nature, it is apprehended properly only by a "simple intuition." Consequently, each truth, properly understood, is identical with the remainder. The argument is therefore less a stepwise construction of a concept than the progressive defeat of prejudices that obscure a single intuition.

Interpretation of the Meditation would be appreciably easier if prejudice were the only obstacle to understanding. Unfortunately, since these prejudices are also by and large the traditional opinions that Descartes is anxious to conciliate, we are compelled to move once again, step by step, from the surface argument to its genuine sense. Indeed, in this respect the difficulties presented by the Second Meditation are greater than those encountered in the First. Not only must the entire argument be adjusted for the spurious doubt of the existence of body, and a spurious substance conception of res cogitans, but in the *Replies* and *Principles* Descartes makes crucial modifications of the apparent meaning of various arguments.

Ambiguities of the First Principle

The Cartesian first principle is the "simple and easy" knowledge which, according to the program of the *Regulae* that is executed in the *Principles,* initiates a deduction of all things that the mind can know with certainty. For this reason it is especially significant to understand that principle with complete clarity. Yet it is presented in a variety of ways that are by no means obviously equivalent. The most abbreviated statements of the first principle (in the *Discourse* and *Principles*) render it in the formula, "I think, therefore I am." This formulation appears nowhere in the *Meditations*; instead, "I am" is said to be necessarily true when uttered or conceived. The purport of this deviation, however, is rendered ambiguous by remarks in the *Replies* which treat the Cogito as virtually present in the Second Meditation.[1] The posthumous *Search* announces "I doubt, therefore I am" as first principle, although this formulation is said to be equivalent to the Cogito.[2]

Since Descartes never indicates that the diversity of formulations reflects a change of mind on his part, it is reasonable to assume that he thought of them as alternative formulations of one and the same thought. But the diversity of formulations and the multitude of expositions are testimony that the thought to be expressed probably cannot be expressed fully and unambiguously by any formula.*

Nearly all Descartes's commentary on his principle revolves about the meaning of its three terms and how they hold together. It divides into two types of exposition, one of which treats the Cogito as an intuition, the other as an inference. Although each contributes something essential to the explication of the principle, each is misleading in an important respect, as indeed nearly all commentators agree.

THE Cogito AS INTUITION

Descartes couples his stress on the Cogito as an intuition with warnings that the simplicity of the insight is obscured by the belief that it is syllogistically demonstrated, or by apprehensions that the terms "thought" and "existence" require definition prior to the enunciation of the principle or, again, by the belief that the Cogito requires a reflexive cognition to prove that thought is known.† The knowledge expressed in the Cogito is prereflective in the sense that it can never fail to be present to continuous internal experience.[3] The scholastics are particularly subject to such misunderstandings, as is especially clear from the *Search for Truth,* where Descartes's spokesman Eudoxus repudiates the objections of the scholastic Epistemon:

> I do not believe that anyone has ever existed who is so stupid as to need to learn what existence is before being able to conclude and affirm that he is; the same holds for thought and doubt. Indeed I add that . . . nothing persuades us of them except our own experience and this consciousness and internal testimony that each finds within himself when he examines things.[4]

---

* This point has been systematically argued by Wolfgang Röd, who asserts that "cogito, ergo sum" should be understood as an explication of the first principle rather than as its adequate expression (Röd, 1959–60, 190).

† HR I, 324/AT X, 524; HR II, 241/AT VII, 422; *Prin.* I, § 5. See Beck, 1965, 103–05. To Burman Descartes remarked that "to be conscious is to think and to reflect on one's thought at the same time" (AT V, 149). The view that Descartes must prove his simple ideas still appears in the secondary literature. Frankfurt, for example, rejects "cogito" as a premise for the argumentation of MM II, 3 on this ground (Frankfurt, 1970, 110).

In the later writings, the terms "perception" and "experience" have replaced the "intuition" of the *Regulae,* but the conception remains the same. The *Regulae* teach that first principles are known by intuition of simple natures, which are "seeds of wisdom" native to the mind, that is, which are not acquired by study and reflection. Moreover, the *Regulae* provide an important clue to understanding Descartes's perplexing inconsistency in affirming and denying that the Cogito, in part or whole, is an inference (*raisonnement*). Intuition and deduction differ in that no movement or succession of ideas enters into intuition, whereas deduction is just the illation of the necessary links (*vincula*) that obtain between ideas.[5] However, when deductions are simple and brief, so that the movement, at its conclusion, may be comprehended in a single perception, "we thereby suppose that it is presented to us by intuition." Consequently, one and the same activity may be regarded as both an intuition and an inference, depending upon which aspect is stressed. In terms of the *Regulae,* cogito, ergo sum expresses a simple proposition in which two simple elements are united by necessity.[6] Descartes's examples of such propositions bear directly upon the *Meditations.* "If Socrates says that he doubts everything, this necessarily follows: therefore this at least he knows—that he doubts."[7] Other examples are "I am, therefore God exists," and "I understand, therefore I have a mind distinct from body." The "therefore" expresses the necessary tie between two simple natures, my thought and my existence. The natures do not exist separately from one another, although they are distinguishable by thought. Thought and existence differ in that existence is among those simples which are common to mind and body. This commonness plays a crucial role in the argument to the first principle, since just the "existence" of body is doubted. Descartes finds that he can doubt that existence is inseparable from bodies or extended things, but not that it is inseparable from his thinking. This inseparability is the necessary relatedness expressed by "ergo." Leibniz correctly stated Descartes's thought when he wrote that "to say 'cogito, ergo sum' is not really to infer existence from thought, since to think and to be thinking [*penser et être pensant*] is the same thing."[8] They are the same in the sense that the whole proposition is grasped in a single intuition; yet there is a movement from one simple nature to the other which needs to be expressed. For this reason, Descartes often speaks of his concluding sum or of sum following from cogito, even though a formal inference is not in question.

Although the theory of intuition and deduction is indispensable for understanding the logic of the Cogito, by itself it is not adequate for several reasons.

One is that the argument to the Cogito in the *Meditations* and elsewhere seems to be an enthymeme or some type of formal inference.* A more serious problem is the inconsistency between the claim that the Cogito is prereflective and known to every man, and the fact that insight into the first principle can be obtained only at the termination of the doubt. According to the first view, thought and existence are known simply through what we continually experience; according to the second, it is only by means of the doubt that we obtain a clear concept of thought. The inconsistency is manifest in the contradictory claims that the first principles can be known "without meditation" and that "in metaphysics, nothing causes more difficulty than making the perception of its primary notions clear and distinct." [9] It is evident that the prereflective Cogito cannot be the Cartesian first principle, because the latter stands or falls with its power to certify itself as the first certainty, whereas the former has no necessary connection either with doubt or with first principles. Furthermore, the Cartesian Cogito leads to sum res cogitans, a proposition alien to bon sens, but entailed by the doubt. Indeed, the specific difference between the unphilosophic Cogito and the Cartesian Cogito becomes visible when Descartes represents its achievement as distinguishing mind from body, or, what comes to the same thing, as containing in itself sum res cogitans. This interpretation is presented in the *Principles,* where he says of cogito, ergo sum:

* Hamelin initiated what might be called the modern approach to the Cogito when he rejected the old view that it expresses an intuition or judgment, on the grounds that the old view took no account of the progressus marked by the "ergo" (Hamelin, 1921, 133). Basing his exposition upon Descartes's remarks to Burman on the relation between *sum* and the syllogistic major, "whatever thinks, exists," he claimed that the Cogito is an inference from thought to being, but only in the order of knowledge. The major is "implicitly" invoked, "but it is not a universal transcending me: the syllogism founds itself and justifies itself in the Cogito" (ibid., 134). Every significant interpretation after Hamelin sought above all to determine the true sense of the "ergo." Arnold Reymond denied Hamelin's contention that the progressus was a formal inference or that the major represented an ontological proposition. Appealing to Russell's interpretation of universals as material implications without existential import, he argued that the progressus was an *act* of thought which verified the major (Reymond, 1923, 548–53). Hamelin's self-grounding syllogism thus became a self-certifying act of thought. This was the state of the question when Heinrich Scholz renewed the inquiry in 1931. He replaced "cogito" by "dubito" and interpreted *dubito, ergo sum* as a material implication, and called it the "Grundsatz" of Cartesian metaphysics. It is the initial premise of a *modus ponens* argument to *sum,* which is the "Grundschluss" of Cartesian metaphysics. In this way Scholz hoped to have reconciled Hamelin and Reymond, since the inference does not violate Descartes's strictures against premises that transcend the region of the "I" (Scholz, 1961, 85–86, 93–94). In an outstanding culmination of fifty years' scholarship, Wolfgang Röd integrated these and other studies with a thorough-going attempt to treat the first principle as a presuppositionless beginning. His resolution of the inference vs. intuition problem depended upon distinguishing between a "Grundlegung" and "Grundlage," where the former, signified by the "ergo," is an act that generates the first certainty (Röd, 1959–60). This essay has unfortunately not been noticed by recent English-speaking interpreters.

This, then, is the best way to discover the *nature of the mind* and the distinction between it and the body [F.V. and that it is a substance entirely distinct from body]. For, in considering what we are who suppose that all things apart from ourselves [F.V. our thought] are false, we observe very clearly that there is [nothing] . . . that may be attributed to body that pertains to our nature, but only thought; and consequently this notion of thought precedes that of all corporeal things and is most certain; since we still doubt whether there are any other things in the world, while we already perceive that we think.[10]

A few paragraphs later Descartes distinguishes this insight from the prereflective Cogito when he observes that those who do not "philosophize in an orderly way," i.e., who have not followed the path of the doubt, do not understand by the "I" merely their minds, but also their bodies.[11] If the Cogito "distinguishes" the mind from the body and thereby determines the nature of the mind, the deficiencies of the Cogito as an explication are apparent, since the formula contains no reference to the excision of corporeal attributes from the concept "I think," which is achieved by the doubt.

Such considerations seem to show that Descartes misrepresents the case when he says that the Cogito may be established upon the prephilosophic notions of thought and existence. It is correct to say that they are the initial data; but they undergo revision in the course of the doubt, as we have shown in the previous chapter. The transition from the doubt to the first certainty represents the moment of the genesis, or constitution, of the new notion of "thinking," consequently, of "I," etc., which the Second Meditation explicates. The very terminology "simple nature" is misleading as applied to Cartesian mind because it connotes something given and discoverable, as one might find a shell by the seashore. Instead, Cartesian mind comes into being, as it were, by and with the assertion of the first certainty.

THE Cogito AS INFERENCE

The *Discourse* states that the truth of the Cogito is based on the principle that "to think it is necessary to be." Similarly, the *Principles* enumerate this "axiom" as one of the conceptions presupposed by the Cogito. These admissions are part of the fuel for the debate whether cogito, ergo sum is an enthymeme whose suppressed major is some form of the axiom just mentioned.*

* In addition to "in order to think, it is necessary to be," Descartes mentions the following prior principles: "Whatever thinks, exists," "no predicates pertain to nothing," and "he who

This problem has been discussed at length in the recent literature, which in the main rejects the syllogistic interpretation and, indeed, any formal interpretation of the "ergo." * A consideration that supports this reading, but which to my knowledge has not been noticed, is that Descartes himself is solely responsible for the debate. Although it is usually said that the syllogistic interpretation was first advanced by the authors of *Objections* II, that is an error. Instead, Descartes injects it gratuitously in reply to an objection that had not been made to an assertion (the Cogito) that does not occur in the *Meditations*. He rejects the syllogistic interpretation because the true relationship between the major ("whatever thinks must exist") and the conclusion is the opposite of what a deduction would require. The truth of the major is derived from the particular proposition, cogito, ergo sum. In fact, he claims that all general truths are derived from particulars.[12] He does not mention that he had proposed the major in the *Discourse*. He proposed it again in the *Principles* without acknowledging its repudiation in the *Replies*. It looks as though, having begun the debate, Descartes was reluctant to let it die. The problem is to determine which side Descartes favored.

It seems plausible that Descartes stirred up the debate as a foil. The Cogito argument was a well established part of the scholastic tradition when Descartes took it over. Arnauld thought it obvious that Descartes had appropriated "the doctrine laid down by St. Augustine . . . as the foundation of his whole philosophy." [13] While Descartes refused to acknowledge his antecedent, he did

---

thinks is not able not to exist while he thinks" (AT V, 147; *Prin.* I, §§ 7, 11, 49). Gueroult attempts to reconcile Descartes's strictures against a syllogistic interpretation with his admission that he presupposes "in order to think, etc." by distinguishing that "axiom" from the proposition Descartes cites as the major—"whatever thinks, exists." He claims, without textual authority, that the latter does not assert existence, while the former does (Gueroult, 1953, II, 310). Yet there are four, not two, prior principles, and Descartes derives the so-called "axiom" from the principle of contradiction and "no predicates pertain to nothing" (*Prin.* I, §§ 7, 11). Moreover, Descartes treats "whatever thinks, exists" as equivalent to "in order to think, etc." For, in the well-known remark to Burman on the syllogistic interpretation, he identifies the major "whatever thinks, exists" with the axiom which the *Principles* acknowledge precedes the Cogito, and that axiom is "in order to think, etc." (AT V, 147). Finally, Gueroult is faced with the difficulty that "in order to think, etc." is not mentioned in the *Meditations*; he claims that it is present, but expressed in the first person (ibid., I, 51, n. 2). But according to Descartes, the whole difference between the axiom or major and the Cogito is the first person reference of the one and the generality of the other (HR II, 38/AT VII, 141; HR II, 126/AT IX–2, 205).

* One of the best recent defenses of the syllogistic interpretation is Marc-Wogau's thorough study, which is made in full awareness of the evidence for the intuitive interpretation. He argues that sum is concluded from "if I think, I must be" (which is known intuitively), and "I think." He justifies his interpretation by appeal to the *Regulae*, where $(2 + 2 = 4) = (3 + 1 = 4)$ is said to be known intuitively and deductively by reference to the axiom "two numbers equal to a third are equal to each other" (Marc-Wogau, 1954, 146, 148). The syllogistic interpretation has been defended more recently by Kenny, 1968, 51–55).

admit that the authority of Augustine was useful to "shut the mouths of those small minds who have cast suspicion on this principle."[14] Apparently Descartes thought that his scholastic audience would be inclined to a syllogistic interpretation of his principle, and accordingly catered to this inclination in order to give himself the opportunity to contrast it with his own thinking.[15] It is therefore tempting to dismiss the whole episode as an academic exercise.

Unfortunately, the matter is not so easily disposed. Examination of the argument to the first principle in the *Meditations* shows that a new major premise lurks in the background. The relevant part of that argument, which consists really of rhetorical questions, is this:

> I myself, am I not at least something [*ego aliquid sum*]? But I have already denied that I had senses and body. Yet I hesitate, for what follows from that? Am I so bound to the body and senses that I cannot exist without them? . . .] Then without doubt I exist also if he deceives me, and let him deceive me as much as he will, he can never cause me to be nothing so long as I think I am something [*quamdiu me aliquid esse cogitabo*]."[16]

The conspicuous presence of the "I" as a "something" (aliquid) makes it appear that Descartes does not claim direct knowledge, an intuition, of the "I" that thinks, but instead infers it as the subject of attributes (doubt, thoughts) that are directly known. Consequently, "I think" is a hypothesis combined with a fact, while "I exist" is exclusively an inferred result. Nor may this aliquid be dismissed as an episode on the way to a conclusion known intuitively, since immediately thereafter Descartes takes up the aliquid as the starting point for the progression to sum res cogitans. This reading seems to be confirmed in the *Principles,* which accurately state the "axiom" or major premise to which the argument implicitly appeals:

> But in order to understand how the knowledge of our mind which we possess not only precedes that which we have of our body, but is also more evident, it must be observed that it is very manifest by the natural light . . . that no qualities or properties pertain to nothing; and that where some are perceived, there must necessarily be some thing or substance on which they depend.[17]

The major, "whatever thinks, exists," and its variations, is a special case of this prior principle drawn from scholastic metaphysics. The "quality or property," of which Descartes is certain, is doubt or, generally, thinking. Thanks to the axiom, he infers that there must be some res or substantia upon which that property depends; therefore, the "something" (aliquid) must exist. Accordingly, it seems that Beck is correct in saying that the "necessity derived from the fact [that I think and therefore exist] . . . is an ontological necessity."[18]

There are a number of important consequences of this interpretation. The "I" whose existence is the first certainty is already determined as a substance. But since this substance is inferred, the immediate certainty of existence peculiar to the prereflective Cogito is displaced by a mediated (inferred) metaphysical certainty (since it presupposes a metaphysical principle). It follows that the "facticity" of the prereflective Cogito is replaced by a metaphysical proposition. Furthermore, it would appear that the position of the Cogito as the first principle is irrevocably lost. Not only does it seem to presuppose a large part of the Aristotelian substance metaphysics, but this metaphysics is never subjected to examination in the course of the *Meditations*. What is more to the point, if existence is established by recourse to the metaphysical principle, Descartes could conclude from corporeal attributes (extension) to the existence of body with the same certainty that he concludes to his own existence; and knowledge of the existence of mind and body would have the same status. Not only would that in itself destroy the privileged position of his own existence in the *Meditations,* but it would also destroy the precedence of thinking as the "attribute" from which he infers his existence, since any attribute would do equally well. Without the precedence of thinking, however, Descartes cannot advance to sum res cogitans.

The subversiveness of the persistent syllogistic interpretation to the clear thrust of the Cogito suggests a return to our original suggestion that it is a foil. The foil is not narrowly confined; rather, Descartes initiates the dispute, one surmises, because he knows that the foil is planted deeply in the argument of the *Meditations*. The foil is the aliquid, whose determination Descartes seeks on three occasions in the Second Meditation. The aliquid question is the form assumed by the substance question in the Second Meditation. By rejecting the syllogistic interpretation of the Cogito—and that is the only formal interpretation Descartes ever suggested—the foil is implictly rejected in its entirety, i.e., the idea of a formal deduction of the first certainty and any traditional substance interpretation of the "I" that thinks are rejected. The true meaning of the thinking "thing" must be latent in the correct interpretation of the Cogito.

The Self-Grounding of Certainty in the Cogito

Descartes concludes the argument of the doubt with the assertion that "'I am, I exist' is necessarily true whenever I pronounce it or mentally conceive it." Having rejected formal interpretations of the first principle, we disregard any attempt to construe this statement as a proposition about a proposition and instead look for the relation between two certainties rather than between two propositions. The assertion may be recast as: Whenever I conceive or think* my existence, it is necessarily true that I exist. The formulation expands and renders more exact the lapidary cogito, ergo sum. What is at stake in the conclusion is not the proof of sum; sum has already been asserted in the course of the argument ("There is no doubt, then, that I am, if he deceives me"). Instead, at issue is the necessity that ties together Descartes's existence with his thinking it. Specifically, his certainty of his existence is sufficient condition for affirming in truth that he exists. As he remarks in MM III, 2, he is assured of the truth of this statement not by the axiom invoked in the *Discourse,* but by clear and distinct perception. The first principle, therefore, exemplifies the first methodological rule that clear and distinct ideas are true, which the doubt had challenged. It also vindicates the methodological claim that there are simple natures that can be known *per se nota.*

The necessary coincidence of certainty with truth in the first principle must be understood by contrast with the situation in the doubt. Descartes is uncertain of the existence of corporeal things; he perceives, as he thinks, images of them, but the existence of the objects imagined eludes him. However, in the case of his own existence no such gap between thought and reality is possible: the being of the object thought is guaranteed by the thinking of it.† The necessity of the first principle is not of the character of an eternal or logical truth. Logical truths are independent of their being thought, whereas the Cartesian principle is not; further, logical truths are not about contingent existents, whereas Descartes's thinking and existence are contingent. This is so even if the sense of the principle is interpreted to mean: "All occasions of my thinking are necessarily occasions on which I exist." Certainly Descartes's expression lends itself to such an interpretation, which is but a step away from the axiom "Whatever thinks, exists." That the principle should edge over in this direction

---

* Frankfurt has refined distinctions so far as to deny that "concipitur" used in this passage means "cogitatur," and he makes his interpretation turn upon this point (Frankfurt, 1970, 101–02). In commentary to Bourdin on this passage, however, Descartes says: "Sed *mente concipitur* nihil hic aliud significat, quam *cogitatur*" (HR II, 281/AT VII, 480). Frankfurt's refinement upon Descartes leads to the unusual statement that "there are times when a person can realize that he is [not] . . . thinking that he exists, and at such times *sum* cannot be derived from [*cogito*] . . . [but] a person can never be aware that he is neither uttering *sum* nor conceiving it in his mind" (ibid., 111–12).

† This point is brought out with particular clarity in the *Search for Truth*: "But my doubt and my certainty did not relate to the same object; my doubt regarded things only which existed outside me, my certainty concerned me and my doubt" (HR I, 325/AT X, 525).

is not surprising in view of the claim that the axiom is derived from the Cogito. But the particular truth from which the derivation begins should be: "By thinking my existence (now), I clearly perceive that I necessarily exist." *

The necessary compresence of Descartes's thought of his existence with his existence must be understood in the perspective of the doubt. Corporeal things lack that compresence; they are dubitable. The existence which Descartes thinks, therefore, must be of a special kind: it must be "incorporeal," i.e., it must be thought existence. Descartes therefore knows the truth of his first principle— the necessary co-incidence of his existence with his thinking—only by distinguishing the mind from the body. That distinction is consummated by the thought that places the existence of bodies in doubt; and that very doubt discloses the certainty expressed in the first principle: "I know very well that what I am, inasmuch as I doubt, is in no wise what I call my body . . . otherwise, doubting of my body, I should at the same time doubt of myself, which I cannot do." † The necessary tie between thinking and existence is therefore not a relation that constitutes one of the properties of a simple nature understood as an "object" given prior to the doubt, nor is it the case that the tie is available in the pre-philosophic experience of one's own existence. Instead, the tie is produced by the final stage of the doubt; more precisely, the doubt terminates itself by the production of the tie. For Descartes's recognition of the indubitability of his existence (as distinguished from the dubitability of bodies) produces the certainty of his presence to his thinking; the certainty is "unshakable" because that presence is generated by that very act of thought. The tie is necessary because thinking (or doubting) his existence necessarily makes that existence available to thought. "I think," and "I exist thinking," are the same thing, as Leibniz held; but their sameness is necessary exclusively in virtue of thinking the first principle.‡

* Both Gueroult and Frankfurt in effect merge the Cogito with the axiom (Gueroult, 1953, I, 51; Frankfurt, 1970, 106).

† HR I, 319/AT X, 518. Similarly, in the Preface to the *Principles* Descartes writes: "Thus in considering that he who would doubt all things cannot yet doubt that he exists while he doubts, and that what reasons so, in being unable to doubt of itself and yet doubting all else, is not what we call our body but what we call our soul or thoughts, I have taken the being or existence of this thought as the first principle." (HR I, 208/AT IX-2, 9–10).

‡ This analysis is completed below, pp. 148–50, where it is integrated with sum res cogitans. The interpretation offered here agrees in essentials with Röd's result: "In jenem Akte, in dem ich mich meiner selbst vergewissere, *erzeuge* ich eine Beziehung zwischen den Gewissheiten, das ich denke und ich bin. . . . Auf diese Beziehung weist das 'ergo' hin. . . . Weil [sie] erst im Vollzug der Grundgewissheit *entsteht*, ist sie nicht früher als diese selbst" (Röd, 1959–60, 191). Similarly, Heidegger, 1962, 80–81. Hintikka's influential interpretation of the Cogito as a performance resembles Röd's interpretation, owing perhaps to a common parentage in Reymond's "existential self-verification" view of the Cogito. He virtually echoes Röd when he writes that

It is essential to this analysis that it recognizes no distinction between Descartes's certainty of his existence when he thinks his existence, and his certainty when he thinks any cogitatio. The indifference is indicated by the generality of "cogito." As Descartes said repeatedly in many different contexts, including MM II, 15, not only dubito, but also video, ambulo, or any cogitatio whatever suffices for establishing the necessary connection, so long as they are taken exclusively as cogitationes, although dubito takes precedence because the concept of "thought" is constituted by the doubt. The reason for the interchangeability of "I think my existence" and "I think (any thought)" is that the existence he thinks is not separable from his cogitationes, which indeed is why he can move on to assert sum res cogitans. Therefore, simply in "I think," Descartes knows his existence in the required sense. As Descartes stated to Hobbes and Gassendi, the Cogito is not reflexive in the sense that it requires a thought which is certain of an earlier thought, since that would produce an infinite regress; instead, the entire reflection is immediately given in "I think" (any thought). That indeed is the condition upon which Cartesian self-consciousness can be empirical consciousness. The same consideration decides the question whether ego is an inferred aliquid or intuitively known. What must be said is that although it is not an aliquid, it is known relative to cogitationes exclusively. The ego can in no way be imagined, although it is immediately known. The search for the aliquid is a concession to the opinion that whatever cannot be distinctly imagined cannot be distinctly perceived. The defeat of this prejudice is the decisive moment in the construction of Descartes's untraditional substance concept. These statements will be expounded thoroughly as we advance through Descartes's own exposition of his principle. Similarly, the adjustments that must be made in the foregoing exposition of the Cogito to compensate for the rhetorical doubt of the existence of body will become clear in the sequel.

The First Sum Res Cogitans

In accordance with the exegetical plan of the Second Meditation, Descartes represents himself as concluding to his existence without having attained dis-

---

sum is indubitable *"because* or *in so far as* it is actively thought of. In Descartes's argument the relation of *cogito* to *sum* is not that of a premise to a conclusion. Their relation is rather comparable with that of a *process* to its *product"* (Hintikka, 1962, 16). His characterization of this process as a performatory utterance seems, however, to produce an inconsistency in his account. A performatory utterance is a publicly observable event independent of introspection (ibid., 13–14, 19), so that Descartes's attempt to deny his own existence fails for the same reason that the attempt to deny one's own existence to another fails. Yet he calls the Cogito an "insight" and claims that it requires a "verb of intellection" like cogitare rather than an observable activity such as ambulo (ibid., 31).

tinct knowledge of what he is. In the argument of the doubt, he notes that he doubts the existence of the "senses and the body," but he is not sure "what follows from that" and he now reverts to this question. After reviewing his old beliefs, he reiterates the doubt and concludes that he is a thinking thing. The absence of any new argument in addition to the doubt is one indication that the sum previously concluded was already sum res cogitans, as Spinoza asserted.[19] The transition from the old beliefs to sum res cogitans is intelligible only on the condition that the rhetorical argument for that conclusion is replaced by the theory of animal automatism.

THE REJECTION OF "RATIONAL ANIMAL"

Descartes formerly believed himself to be "a man." His attempt to say what he meant by that falls neatly into two parts. In the first, he indicates the significance of the question by considering the standard scholastic answer: "Shall I say that I am a rational animal?" Both predicates are rejected because they lead to many other questions that carry the inquiry far beyond the available evidence—Descartes's own "nature." In the *Search for Truth*, Eudoxus explains that the Aristotelian definition brings inquiry to a halt only upon the assumption that we already know what is rational and animal; but in the absence of such knowledge, the definition invites inquiry all the way to the summa genera, dragging us into a "metaphysical maze" from which there is no exit.[20] Descartes therefore shuns this method of inquiry, and holds to what he can know directly by self-inspection.

But the Aristotelian definition is not disposed so easily, for the second attempt to say what a man is reproduces the Aristotelian soul conception modified in one or two important respects. He understood the human body to be, he says, all that can be observed in a "corpse." * The "nature of body," about which he had "no doubt," he thought was anything defined by a figure which occupied place and which could be perceived by all the senses. Body is Aristotle's soma. Aristotelian that he was, the prejudiced Descartes did not believe that body had the power of self-movement, nor of sense and understanding. To explain these attributes, he had recourse to the soul, in virtue of whose "actions" or powers Descartes considered that he was nourished, walked, sensed things, and thought.[21] These "actions" are evidently the nutritive, sensitive, and rational faculties of the soul: the animate principle that moves the corpse-body. There

---

* The characterization of the bodily as that which pertains to a corpse is discussed as a vulgar error in *Passions*, §§ 5–6. It is of a piece with the prejudice that the soul animates the body.

are, however, two important deviations from Aristotle that plant the seed of Cartesian physics. He thinks that the human body is a machine, and he refrains from calling the composite a "form" or "substance."

Although Descartes presents no critique of this conception, it contains one statement that is later made thematic, and which, when thought through, leads directly to Descartes's critique of Aristotle. Having observed the "actions" of the soul, the prejudiced Descartes did not much consider what the soul is; but when he did consider it, he "imagined that it was something extremely rare and subtle like a wind, a flame, or an ether, which was infused throughout my grosser parts." [22] This shows that by raising the what question, Descartes meant to inquire about the constitution of the soul in virtue of which it is able to cause the "actions" of nutrition, locomotion, etc. He necessarily frames his answer in terms of what can be "imagined," because he seeks to know how the soul acts on the body. Aristotle must refuse an answer posed in these terms. The soul as "form" of the body is nothing corporeal and therefore its causal efficacy cannot be "imagined." The "what" of the soul is just the activities observed in animate beings; these acts are the form that shapes the material and efficient causes, i.e., soma, so that the body assumes the arrangement that enables it to perform the functions that constitute its "what." Descartes thinks that to answer in this way is to introduce occult causes and therefore to abandon the possibility of assigning observable causes to biological processes.

Such reflections are naturally suggested by the text when the *Meditations* are examined in light of the *Discourse* and the *Dioptric,* and they lead directly to a problem about the objective of the *Meditations.* If the *Meditations* are intended as a justification of Cartesian science, why does Descartes state here a soul doctrine that is anterior to Cartesian science? How is it that the theory of automatism, at which Descartes merely hints, is not explicitly stated as the theory with which his mind doctrine must come to grips? This outstanding omission is intelligible only within the explicit perspective of the *Meditations* to found science ab initio, i.e., upon the fiction that Cartesian science does not exist.

Let us now consider that argument that overthrows these old beliefs. Since Descartes considered himself a composite of soul and body, he examines each in turn. The form of his question is whether they "pertain" to himself, i.e., he seeks an attribute of the aliquid. Corporeal attributes are dismissed out of hand. Nutrition and locomotion, as faculties of the soul, are rejected because they presuppose the existence of the body, which is doubtful. The same is true of sensation. As for thinking, Descartes declares: "Here I find it. Thought (cogitatio) alone cannot be separated from me [F.V. I find here that thought is an attribute which pertains to me]." [23]

The only argument present in this reasoning is just the doubt of the existence of body, as Arnauld, Gassendi, and other critics observed.[24] Moreover, Descartes retained this reasoning in every other presentation of the conclusion "sum res cogitans." It is especially clear in the *Search for Truth,* where Polyander rejects nutrition, locomotion, and sensation as pertaining to himself because "I know very well that what I am, inasmuch as I doubt, is in no wise what I call my body . . . otherwise, doubting of my body, I should at the same time doubt of myself, and this I cannot do." [25] But since the doubt merely reiterates the argument of the Cogito, the "I" whose existence is disclosed is evidently res cogitans. Only the exigencies of explication cause Descartes to represent them as distinct. Thus, in the *Principles,* the Cogito is explicitly identified with res cogitans as being one and the same conclusion.[26] It must be emphasized, therefore, that Descartes definitely commits the paralogism of inferring res cogitans from the dubiety of body.

Granted that Descartes believes himself to be a thinking thing, it is not clear just what "thinking" embraces. Since he arrives at this determination by slicing away the nether layers of the Aristotelian soul, it appears, as Gassendi pointed out, that he identifies himself with Aristotle's "separated reason" whose Cartesian counterpart is *intellectus purus.*[27] The interpretation appears to be confirmed by Descartes's reply to Gassendi, in which he explained that "the principle by which we are nourished is wholly distinct from that by means of which we think . . . [I consider, therefore, that] the mind (*mens*) is not part of the soul, but the whole of the soul which thinks." [28]

This interpretation raises the problem of the relation between the first and second res cogitans. The second enunciation defines res cogitans by enumeration of its "modes," among which are understanding and sensation. How is it that sensation and imagination are excluded from the first res cogitans, while in the second, understanding or pure intellect (assuming for the moment that they are the same) is only a mode? Gueroult argues that the inconsistency may be resolved by distinguishing two senses of quid, namely, what is the essence of the substance (res) and, what are the accidents of the substance. When Descartes says "res cogitans, id est, mens, sive animus, sive intellectus, sive ratio," he means that pure intellect is the essence of thinking substance; more precisely, thinking and pure intellection are one and the same thing. It may nevertheless be construed as a mode because the "manifestation of pure intellect is an accident, although not pure intellect itself, as distinguished from all the other modes, which are contingent in relation to the substance." [29] Gueroult cites no text to support his reading, which is troubled by two difficulties: it requires that when res cogitans is identified with intellectus, etc., the latter terms explicate the former, whereas the reverse is clearly the case, since the true meaning of the latter was formerly unknown; secondly, there is nothing in the text at MM II, 9 to indicate that intelligens is listed qua its accidental manifestation. The primary objection, however, is that Descartes never speaks of pure intellect as anything but a mode. This is quite clear in the *Regulae,* where pure intellect is one of four "applications" of the "cognitive power." In the *Principles,* thinking is divided into two general modes, "perception, or the operation of the intellect," and volition; pure intellect is listed as one of three modes of perception.[30] Therefore rather than constituting the essence of thinking, pure intellect is only a mode.

ANIMAL AUTOMATISM POSITED

The proper interpretation of the first res cogitans comes to light both by close attention to the prejudice it replaces, and to Descartes's commentary in the *Replies* upon this segment. The crux of the transition is that on the basis of his prejudices, Descartes cannot understand how the power of self-motion and the power of sentience or thought (sentiendi, vel cogitandi) can pertain to body; yet he arrives at res cogitans by attributing all the powers of the soul, except thinking, to body. It is difficult to apprehend how he can achieve this result merely by doubt, as is especially clear in the case of sensation. For if thinking is the residue of doubt, to separate sensation from thinking requires that he doubt that he senses. Descartes indeed rejected sensation because "one cannot sense without body, and besides, I have thought I perceived many things during sleep that I recognized in my waking moments as not having been experienced at all." Sensations have the same status as imagination. But that merely renews the question: how does Descartes distinguish thinking from imagination merely by doubt? Imagination is not mentioned in the passage at all. Nevertheless, it is certain that Descartes cannot distinguish imagination from thinking by means of doubt, for he is able to doubt the existence of body only by construing sensations as imaginings.[31]

Pressed by Gassendi for clarifications, Descartes modifies the literal statement of the *Meditations* while claiming to reproduce what he had "expressly said": he referred nutrition to body alone, while motion and sensibility he referred "for the most part" (maxima ex parte) to the body, "and ascribed nothing of them to the soul, except insofar as it is a thought." [32] The modification evidently shifts the meaning of the first res cogitans toward an identity with the second. That the shift represents Descartes's genuine view becomes apparent from examining the *Principles,* where the identity of the Cogito and res cogitans is asserted: those who do not philosophize in an orderly way fail to observe that the doubting ego is res cogitans because they do not realize that:

> By themselves (*per se ipsos*) they ought only to mean their minds (*mente,* F.V. *pensée*), but because they believed that it was their bodies which they saw with their eyes, touched with their hands, and to which they wrongly attributed the power of sensation, they did not distinctly comprehend the nature of the mind.[33]

We have now come full circle. From one point of view, sensation is exclusively a power of the mind; from another, of the body.

When Descartes wishes to rescue his theory from such inconsistencies, he abandons all pretense of deriving res cogitans solely from the doubt, and he appeals forthrightly to the *Dioptric*: sensation is corporeal insofar as it is a "cerebral motion," but it is a cogitatio insofar as that motion produces the perception of a quality.[34] The interpretation of the doubt as an allegory of Cartesian science is thus vindicated by the details of the Second Meditation and Descartes's commentary thereon. The transition from the old beliefs to res cogitans is not effected by the doubt, but by covert interposition of automatism. The true meaning of the first res cogitans can be understood only by recognizing that Descartes knows what to attribute to mind because of his prior knowledge of what to attribute to the powers of the human body.

Clearly, the specific revision of old beliefs that occurs in this passage is the rejection of the "faculty" conception of the soul. The soul has no power to cause nutrition, locomotion, sensation, or thinking. All these powers, indeed, all powers, must be attributed exclusively to the body. "It may be easily proved," Descartes wrote in the *Principles,* "that our mind is of such a nature that the motions which are in the body are alone sufficient to cause it to have all sorts of thoughts, which do not give us any image of the motions that cause them." [35] Nothing may be attributed to the mind but the bare perception of the effects of these motions.

This outcome constitutes a partial answer to the question about the aliquid. It is correct to imagine the soul as some wind or subtle fire, i.e., animal spirits, for the spirits are indeed the cause of all the activities traditionally attributed to the soul. Only it is an error, which Descartes rectifies in MM II, 7 to identify these unknown motions "with the self that I know."

Passing over this question for the moment, let us integrate the result attained thus far with the statement on the "temporal" character of the thinking thing.

Descartes writes:

> I am, I exist, that is certain. But how often? Just when I think; for it might possibly be the case that if I ceased entirely to think, I should likewise cease altogether to exist. I do not now admit anything which is not necessarily true; I am, therefore, strictly speaking, a thinking thing.[36]

If Descartes's existence is thinking, and if, as the necessary truth of the Cogito showed, that existence is always known because it is thought, then it is never the case that he is certain of his existence when he does not exist, nor, conversely, that he ever exists but does not know it. When Descartes ceases to think, he ceases to exist.[37] This thesis expresses the great paradox of res cogitans. Prejudice is convinced that "I" do not cease to exist when asleep or otherwise unconscious. But for Descartes, the belief in the continuity of the self is a function of the prejudiced conflation of mind and body. Again it was Gassendi who, recognizing this latent consequence, pressed Descartes with questions.[38] Presumably to avoid embracing the implications of this view for his rhetorical substance doctrine, Descartes turns Gassendi's objections into a new channel, but in such a way as to acknowledge in passing that to cease to think is to cease to exist: "But why should [the mind] not always think, when it is a thinking substance? Why is it strange that we do not remember the thoughts we had in the womb or in a stupor? * Although the principle is acknowledged, the explanation renews the error of prejudice. The authentic sense of res cogitans is that my existence is wholly contained in my thinking; it does not lie outside myself, inaccessible to thought. The prejudice that I continue to exist through sleep, even though I do not think, depends upon conflating mind with body by way of the belief that the body is "part" of the self: if my body endures through sleep, then I do as well. Descartes's allegation that we continue to think during sleep, or in the womb, is of the character of a hypothesis, whose truth cannot be known; or rather it is a transparent absurdity, since it is impossible to think and not know that one thinks. Descartes in fact does not believe this absurdity, for he writes that "sleep . . . every day takes from us . . . the power of sentience, which is afterwards restored upon waking." † As the *Discourse* expressly

---

* HR II, 210/AT VII, 356. To Burman Descartes said that the "soul can never be without thoughts" (AT V, 150).

† *Prin.* IV, § 196. Sentience is identified with thinking in MM II, 5: *sentiendi, vel cogitandi.* This important equivalence is almost universally neglected.

notes, sleep and waking are functions of the body-machine. The *Meditations* underscore the contingency of thinking by the argument that the ego, as a dependent and imperfect thing, has no power to sustain its existence, and therefore depends every moment on the power of God. Res cogitans comes and goes as the activity of the brain waxes and wanes.* But it is permanently present to itself.

In summary, the appearance of the Second Meditation is that Descartes argues to sum res cogitans on the premise of the doubtful existence of body. As a result of this dreaming argument, res cogitans is interpreted in the framework of prejudice, for when Descartes affirms that he knows only thoughts, he implicitly invokes the common belief that thoughts are mental or spiritual things, as distinguished from material external objects. It therefore appears, as the criticisms of the *Objections* amply testify, that the aliquid has surreptitiously been determined as a spiritual substance.

The inverted reasoning of the dreaming world is, however, an image of the inverted reasoning of Cartesian science. The function of the dualist physical theories in the argument is to mediate the acroamatic meaning of res cogitans. The mind is not a soul, i.e., a unity of faculties, because the powers of sensation, imagination, locomotion, etc., are functions of the body which is their cause. At the same time, the prejudiced belief in the incorporeality of thoughts is latently destroyed. For this reason, res cogitans must be and is at this point determined irrespective of whether cogitationes are spiritual or corporeal; the aliquid question remains open until the Sixth Meditation. The thinking thing is determined by the respective "modes" of thought that it thinks. The ontological question of what the mind is has thus been resolved into a methodological answer, which construes the being of mind in terms of its respective cognitive relations toward the world (its modes of thought). At the same time, the modes of thought are grasped from the point of view of their genesis as modifications of the body. Accordingly, they are constituted both subjectively, as the modalities through which the world is known, and objectively, by the material causes which thoughts either make known or conceal, and hence, ontologically with respect to their relation to the body. Therefore, the ordo cognoscendi and the ordo essendi intersect. How they are pieced together by the theory of corporeal ideas and the theory of pure intellect will be discussed below.

---

* Beck notes (1965, 110), apropos this point, that at this juncture in the *Meditations*, "we cannot justifiably go even as far as Hume's 'congeries of perception.' "

The Second Sum Res Cogitans

In the attempt to find an imaginable concept of res cogitans, Descartes renews the question of what is the sum res cogitans, and concludes that, rather than constituting a mode through which the mind can be conceived, imagination is one of several powers, or modes, by which the mind thinks. This assertion is consolidated by Descartes's analogy of body with wax, in which he distinguishes what can be known of body by imagination and sense, from what is knowable only to understanding. Thus, in the remainder of the Second Meditation, Descartes undertakes to clarify the nature of the thinking thing by an analysis of its modes of thinking.

The argument of the preceding segments anticipated several important aspects of the advance to the second res cogitans. After admitting that he does not know that he is not a "wind" or other subtle corporeal substance, Descartes goes on to commit once more the paralogism of inferring from doubt of the existence of body that it is an incorporeal thinking thing. The positive result is the specification of thinking in relation to modes, which corrects the misleading first res cogitans. For our interpretation, this doctrine is the keystone of the Cartesian theory of mind.

MODES OF THOUGHT

The second res cogitans is defined by enumeration of modes of thought. The list is incomplete and unaccompanied here by a statement of principle. Later, thoughts are divided into two classes, understanding and volition, according to their functions in judgment. Understanding includes "ideas," which are "as it were, images of things" as well as sensation, imagination and pure understanding. Volitions, which include emotions, appetites and judgments, "add" something from the mind to the idea we have of a thing. The added thing (aliquid amplius) may be a judgment (affirmation or negation), an "instinct," prejudice, or emotion.[39]

These classifications are aquired in that pure understanding is a mode of one of the two "principal modes," and "perception or understanding" is in turn a mode of "thinking" which is also "understanding" or "reason." It is pertinent to inquire what the unity of the "principal modes" is, and how it becomes diversified.

Evidently the unity of the modes is the unity of res cogitans, which in turn is the "essence of thinking substance." It is correct, but not very helpful, to say that the unity is consciousness; for the question arises immediately how consciousness differs from *perceptio*. The equivocations upon understanding and thinking arise because Descartes is operating with two notions of perception, both of which are essential to his purpose, and each of which defines a twofold meaning for each of the modes.

In one sense, perception is a modification of a substance.[40] This meaning is a transformation of the traditional notion of perceptions as the "affects" or "passions" of the soul. The character of the transformation is reflected in the fact that res cogitans is determined independently of knowledge of the substance that undergoes these "affects" or modifications. It is so determined because that substance is the body, or more exactly, the brain. The other meaning of perception is the proper sense for res cogitans, namely a mode of thinking. Sensation and imagination are modes of thinking body, just as universals, for example, are a mode in which we use "a single idea to think the individuals that have a similitude among themselves."[41] These two meanings, which Descartes does clearly distinguish, are nevertheless conflated in almost all his writing, among other reasons because he must maintain a parallelism between conceptual and physical modes, which are unified in the *ideas corporeas*.* However, the unitary meaning of thinking (thoughts or modes) that ties the respective modes together is obtained with the constitution of res cogitans through the doubt. It is just the self-consciousness of "I think," that is, the idealism that I have immediate knowledge of thoughts only. This constitutes a conception of thinking because it shatters the spurious objectivity of prejudice which unwittingly projects its sensations onto the world, or which mistakes its own subjectivity for the order of things. The unity of res cogitans is consciousness of the subjectivity of the knower; it *is* the subjectivity of the knower. Its stance is that being is being for me; knowledge is the perspectivity of *my* thinking.

Problems about the identity of the "I" which thinks arise when the two meanings of thinking—as perception and conception—are conflated. The "I" in the first sense is not a substance underlying modifications but immediate awareness or consciousness, the whole of which is perspicuous in any given perception. Any other subject will turn into either the brain or Hume's "bundle of impressions," or the empirical ego of British empiricism, which for the most part conceives the subject as the recipient of impressions.† Insofar as British

---

* Below, pp. 165ff., 180.
† Ernst Mach nicely illustrated the Cartesian empirical ego interpreted as immediate intuition. Intrigued by C. F. Krause's apothegm, "Problem: To carry out the self-inspection of the ego. Solution: It is carried out immediately," he wrote: "In order to illustrate in a humorous manner

empiricism retains Cartesian idealism, it approaches the Cartesian empirical consciousness which is the immediacy of relatedness to "perceptions" qua modes of cognition of objects.

What initially differentiates the modes is the qualitative differences that factually and adventitiously obtain among them; what differentiates them as cognitions is Descartes's appraisal of their respective value as "instruments" for cognizing the world; thus they become modes for cognizing things. The analysis of wax makes an assay of sensation, imagination and understanding. Later in the *Meditations,* other modes are examined as well.

THE WAX

The analysis of wax is provoked by the carping sensualist in Descartes who still believes that objects perceived by senses and imagination are better known than the unimaginable thinking thing. Imagination has previously been defined as the "contemplation of the figure or image of a corporeal thing." The strategy of the argument is to defeat the objection to the unimaginability of res cogitans by showing that not even body can be adequately conceived by imagination, but by understanding alone, with the paradoxical result that both mind and body are known only "supersensibly."

Using wax as an example of a common object that we believe we clearly comprehend, Descartes illustrates his point that extension is the one attribute that endures through all its changes by noting that the sense qualities, size and figures suffice to enable him to recognize distinctly the "body" that the wax is, even as he subjects it to alterations.* He therefore concludes that the abiding sameness—the essence of the wax—could not have been perceived by the senses, since all qualities are now altered.

The conclusion is questionable. Why might not the sameness of the wax before and after the changes be inferred from a continuous perception of a

-----

this philosophical 'much ado about nothing,' and at the same time to show how the self-inspection of the ego could be really carried out, I embarked on the above drawing." The drawing he produced is a view of his room from the left eye (Mach, 1959, 19).

* See especially MM III, 19. The reasons governing the choice of the example are complex. Augustine had used it in *On the Immortality of the Soul* to illustrate an argument that the mind is unchangeable. Descartes, however, sees a parallelism between the modifications of wax and of thoughts: "I see no difference between the piece of wax and the diverse figures it receives . . . its ideas are put in the soul partly by impressions which are in the brain, and partly by dispositions that have proceeded from the soul itself. . . . Similarly, the wax receives its figures partly from other bodies which impress it, partly from figures or other qualities already in it . . . and partly also from its own movement" AT IV, 112–13. This aspect of the modes doctrine is discussed below, pp. 178–80.

spatially distinct lump as its shape changed? Would he have judged it the "same" object if instead of holding it to the fire, he had burned it? Burning the wax would play to Descartes's hand, because he now shifts the analysis from sensation to imagination. He apprehends as the sameness of the wax a "body which previously appeared to me as perceptible (*conspicuum*) under these [sensible] modes, and now under others." He "imagines" a body to be a flexible and movable thing, that is, one capable of assuming different figures. But if it assumes a variety of figures, then the wax will be comprehended only if all its possible figures—an infinite number—are comprehended.* But imagination cannot comprehend the infinite.† Therefore, it is only with the mind that he perceives or intuits the wax (*solis mentis inspectione*).

Gassendi, among others, thought Descartes's analysis was a sophism transparent enough to "ensure a schoolboy a beating from his master," for it seemed to him that Descartes was claiming to have an intuition of the substance of the wax independently of its "vestments," the sensible accidents.[42] Descartes agrees that the objection is well-taken: "If we desired to strip a substance of those attributes by which we apprehend it, we should utterly destroy our knowledge of it," for the more attributes we know, the better we know a substance.[43] His object was not to prove that substance can be known in the absence of its attributes, but that extension alone is the essence of the wax.[44] This defense does not remedy the difficulty, because there are inconsistencies in Descartes's account of what clear and distinct knowledge of extension consists of. The account in the Second Meditation, which is corroborated by two further restatements, denies that figure belongs to the essence that he knows.[45] But in MM III, 19, recounting the results of the analysis of the wax, he claims to have clearly and distinctly perceived in the wax figure, place, and change of position, although not sense qualities. Here the problem is joined. Descartes surely cannot know *this* wax without taking cognizance of the "sensible vestments" by which he could perceive the particulars of its figure, place, etc.; without them, the wax that he knows by the mind could not be the "same" that he senses and imagines but seems to be nothing more than pure space, that is, abstract undif-

---

* In commentary on the wax example, Descartes denied that figure belongs to the essence of wax. AT VIII, 123.

† In *The World*, it is a point of some importance that "imagination seems able to extend to the infinite," for that is the condition upon which the world can be "feigned" in "our fantasy" (AT XII, 32, 33). Of course, neither imagination nor pure intellect comprehends, i.e., encompasses, the infinite. Descartes's remarks on the infinite are complicated by his wish to distinguish the positive infinity of God from the privative infinite of mathematics and the "indefiniteness" of the world. Koyré's discussion of this question shows, I think, that in fact Descartes had only one conception of the infinite, and that is the mathematical conception (Koyré, 1957, 110–24).

ferentiated extension. Can this be known by an "inspection" of the mind? Does the mind "comprehend" its infinite possibilities more than imagination? These questions must be answered by reference to the Cartesian notion of cognition by pure intellect.

In the second half of MM II, 12, Descartes appears to veer sharply away from the pure intellect interpretation. Now he determines that, contrary to his former belief, he never did perceive the wax by the senses or imagination. He corrects his previous assertion that the sensibly perceived wax is the same as that perceived by the mind: he only "judges that it is the same, from its having the same color and figure." By noticing that he only judges them to be the same, Descartes becomes aware that he never knew the wax except by the mind. The error is analogous to believing that the figures passing in the street are men, while in truth, under the coats and hats, they are automata. Coats and hats are to their bearers as sensible properties of the wax are to extension. To say that it is the same wax is to attribute sensible properties to the extended thing, whereas, Descartes wrote More, the objective of his analysis is to show that sensible properties do not belong to the wax itself.[46] By asserting that our "sense knowledge" is in fact not "the sight and touch affected by means of organs, but solely the *thought* of seeing and touching," [47] Descartes corrects the vulgar view that perception of the wax outside me, in all its panoply of qualities, is a sense perception, and says that it is a perception of "understanding alone . . . as I have proved, in my *Dioptric*." * Once again, an analysis that purportedly embodies only logical reasoning upon the data of consciousness in fact depends upon covert appeal to a scientific theory. The assertion that we know the wax by understanding alone turns out to be equivalent to the assertion that we have immediate knowledge of thoughts only, or that all the modes of thoughts are cognized exclusively by understanding. Similarly, it is not imagination that beholds a figure or shape, but mind in the mode of imagination. Sum res cogitans.

The Achievement of the Second Meditation

Recognizing the ambiguity of the terms "sense" and "understanding" as they occur in the passage, the interpretation of "faculties" as "modes" can be understood. Earlier we stressed that the idealism arising from Cartesian optics stands prejudice on its head, for Descartes reverses the ordinary belief that sensations represent to us what is real, while imagination is a fictive reproduction of sen-

* HR II, 252/AT VII, 245. Note the identical reference to animals in this passage and in MM II, 14.

sation. This is the thought guiding the analysis of wax. To say that sensation is a mode of thought is literally to deny its appearance as an immediate given, by interpreting it in terms of the theory of the genesis of sensation, and so to cognize sensation, i.e., to transpose its immediacy into a concept. Sensing therefore becomes a manner or mode, of thinking objects. For an explanation of the details of that cognition, Descartes's analysis of wax must be viewed in context. It will be recalled that in the analysis of imagination in MM I, 6, which is staged on the assumption that waking and dreaming (i.e., sensation and imagination) are indistinguishable, Descartes undertook to determine what was "real and true" in all these ideas by seeking the universal things of which they are composed. This notion is resumed in MM II, 12, which states that clear perception of the wax is attained when one knows "the elements . . . of which it is composed." MM I, 7 specified these elements as modes of extension; in MM II, 7, imagination is said to be the "mode" of thought under which extension is perceived, and imagination is in turn identified with the sensus communis as MM II, 14. The sensus communis is the "central organ" which perceives all sensations and imaginations. The figures, motions and other attributes of extension that come to the sensus communis through the senses are available there for consideration in abstraction from the sense qualities. To cognize sensation in this way is to cognize it under the aspect of imagination. It is therefore the imagined object only that represents what is "real and true" in sensation. This is so even though color and every other qualitative difference signifies real differences, because those qualitative differences are understood to be real only insofar as they can be transposed into the schema of imagination; for example, as the spin of particles causes differences in color. The real world is not that of sense, but the world as cognized in the mode of imagination, with the indispensable aid of pure intellect. It is not surprising therefore that Descartes later proves the existence of the world from imagination. Descartes so often speaks of sensation and imagination in the language of prejudice—as faculties and as merely immediate perceptions—that he makes it unusually difficult to extricate the non-trivial sense in which they are cognitions. Sensations are not cognitions for just anyone; they are cognitions only for one who *thinks* the world. We have denied that this thinking has the character of a logical analysis of the data of consciousness although it has something in common with that procedure. Descartes *becomes* a thinker by interposing between himself and prejudice a theory or concept of the world that provides an intellectual optics by which he conceives reality, or knows it "with the mind" rather than the senses. That world conception, as we have argued, has certain implications for what Descartes is, which is the job of the *Meditations* to draw out. It strips him of every attribute but the one he cannot without absurdity deny. The thinking thing knows himself as thinker because he knows himself through the mediation of his world concept. He literally and strictly becomes a thinking thing only by thinking himself in this way: as a thinker he is a self-production. It is in this spirit that after the analysis of wax Descartes returns to the fundamental objective of the Second Meditation which is that the perception of any object is sufficient to give him knowledge of the mind. Ambulo, or video, are sufficient premises for concluding sum res cogitans.

> If one takes due precaution, he will find that all propositions from which we are also able to conclude to our existence are of the same character, namely, that with them the existence of the body . . . is not proved at all, but only the soul. . . . And although it may be doubted whether it is the same nature that thinks or occupies space, yet nevertheless . . . the soul is known only as intellectual.[48]

Translating out of the language of the spurious doubt, Descartes means that he is certain of himself because he has conceived every last scintilla of the world as extension and nothing else, and therefore he is a thinking thing, notwithstanding the possibility that animal spirits or some other subtle matter might be doing the thinking. For mind is nothing but the respective "modes" of thought, or the cognitive relations in which I stand toward the world.

We have argued that the foundational achievement of the *Meditations* is to show thinking and extension as the coordinate first principle of science, by the device of unifying the ontological and epistemological orders at their point of intersection. The unification does not and cannot occur by an intuition, but only by an argument intended to prove the necessary cohesion of thinking and extension. The essential design of that argument is now before us. Descartes arrives at his notion of mind by the mediation of the ontology of the world as extension and the automatism theory that follows in its wake; in turn his notion of mind mediates his ontology of the world as extension. If we think the world as extension, then mind must be conceived as a thinking thing; and conversely, if we think the world clearly, it must be as extension. The crucial place of corporeal ideas in defining the reciprocal necessity of thinking and extension for one another has not yet been expounded and to that extent the force of Descartes's argument is not yet whole. Nevertheless we are able to discern how this circle—the true Cartesian circle—envelops a whole that founds science. Descartes intuitively knows his first principles, the simple natures, thought and extension. They determine ontologically what there is, because the truth of clear and distinct perception is unproblematic. The Cartesian foundational problem is not to defend the immutability of these principles against a doubt that could never be defeated if it were successfully raised, but rather the need to secure access to a world wholly divested of quality—it is the methodological problem of outwitting prejudice that conceals the world. To this end Descartes undertakes to assay what the mind is able to know, which includes, but is not exhausted by, an assay of how the instruments of thought may be used to effect the access. From his fundamental physical principle Descartes derives a theory of sensation which marks out the character and limits of the data upon which those instruments can be set to work. The theory of sensation—a physical theory with full ontological commitment—is therefore necessary to complete the methodological endeavor. But conversely, the physical theory cannot be generated without reference to the extra-physical sensations as they are perceived, and other instrumentalities of the mind. This mutual mediation of physics and method, of ontology and epistemology is present in *Regulae* XII. The recapitulation of method, that is, metaphysics, is a discursive unpacking of a single insight that implicates simultaneously method and physics. The serial order of the parts of philosophy do not ultimately represent the internal cohesiveness of the system, or its idea.

6 The True Man

The Cartesian Image of Man—and accordingly the Image of Nature—ends in confusion.

A. G. A. Balz

The Plan of Meditation VI

The basic theme of the Sixth Meditation is the union of mind and body, that is, their union and their distinctness.* Although it has no sharp architectonic, nevertheless it divides naturally into two main parts, with part one extending from paragraph one through ten, part two from paragraph twelve through twenty-four.

Part one begins with a proof of the existence of the body from imagination (MM VI, 1–3) which leads to the first and only explicit distinction between imagination and pure understanding to be found in the *Meditations,* and relates modes of thought, especially imagination, to the body. Descartes then proposes that the existence of body can be established by considering sensation (MM VI, 4), which leads to the first discussion in the *Meditations* of the foundations of old beliefs or prejudices (MM VI, 5–7). Concluding that the old beliefs are insufficient evidence for the existence of body, Descartes recapitulates the argument of the First and Second Meditations (MM VI, 5–9), which issues in the proof of the real distinction between mind and body (MM VI, 9), followed by the second proof of the existence of imagined body (MM VI, 10), which is based on an obscure appeal to sensibility. Part one as a whole, then, is an attempt to find the unity of mind and body.

Part two is generated by the need to clarify the relation between sensation and imagination in regard to the existence of body. The competing evidence of sense and imagination causes Descartes to reflect further on divine veracity:

* Descartes wrote Princess Elizabeth that he had said "almost nothing" about mind-body unity in MM VI (AT III, 664–65; also HR II, 132/AT VII, 213). In view of its proof of the "substantial union" of mind and body, this is something of an exaggeration, but perhaps Descartes was thinking of the status of the question relative to the *Passions.*

perhaps after all, he says, his nature is such that he is deceived always. To resolve this problem, two new concepts of nature are introduced: nature as God, or the "order and disposition of things" God instituted; and "my nature" as the "complexus of all the things God has given me." On this basis, Descartes gradually brings to light the scientific concept of nature that hitherto has been suppressed. In addition, in the first half of part two Descartes considers, not the ocular evidence for the external existence of objects, but the tactile evidence of pain as evidence for the existence of my body, thus giving the argument a decisive turn because it raises the question whether res cogitans must be modified in view of the mind's attachment to the body, i.e., whether pain and the passions generally are thoughts.

In the second half of part two, after showing that judgments based on tactile sensations are as liable to error as visual sensations, Descartes has to reconcile the manifest errors of "my nature" with the premise that it consists of the "complexus of things" God has given me. This he does by a new statement of the unity of mind (MM VI, 19) and the theory of automatism, by which he is able to explain the errors of "my nature" and thereby solve the problem of the existence of body. Thus, the final solution to the metaphysical problem of the veracity of the senses is the scientific theory of the genesis of sensations and not metaphysical propositions about divine veracity.

The *Meditations* conclude with a necessary but not a sufficient explanation of mind-body unity. The problems posed by the mind's attachment to body in the experience of appetition and passion require further treatment, which is presented in the *Passions*, where the ostensible "true man" turns out to be an automaton.

The First Proof of the Existence of Body

The "proof" of the existence of body from imagination is rapidly and obscurely enunciated, and then followed by clarifications, a procedure that is often followed in the *Meditations*. The context of the proof is the discussion, in the Fifth Meditation, of the similarities and differences between the concept of God and mathematical concepts. In accordance with the statement that mathematics does not consider the existence of its objects, in the Fifth Meditation Descartes undertakes to show that the concept of God is distinguished by the fact that in it the notions of essence and existence are inseparable. The Sixth Meditation opens with the statement that material objects may exist "insofar as they are considered as objects of pure mathematics," because they are clearly and distinctly perceived. We know already from the Fifth Meditation that this perception is by imagination: "I am able distinctly to imagine the quantity which philosophers commonly call continuous, the extension in length, breadth, or depth, that is in this quantity, or rather in the object to which it is attributed." [1] In the Fifth Meditation, Descartes remained uncertain whether such objects have existence outside his thought. Now this uncertainty is renounced. Mathematicals may exist because they are clearly perceived, and:

> further, the faculty of imagination which I possess, and of which experience tells me I make use when I apply myself to the consideration of material things, is capable of persuading me of their existence; for when I attentively consider what imagination is, I find that it is nothing but a certain application of the faculty of knowledge to the body which is immediately present to it, and which therefore exists (*applicatio facultatis cognoscitivae ad corpus ipsi intime praesens ac proinde existens*).[2]

It would seem from this argument that the existence of body may be known from its essence, just as the essence of the mind can be known from its existence. It would appear that there is not one, but three beings in which essence cannot be separated from existence. Be that as it may, the argument advances toward a more exact grasp of the sense in which mathematicals do and do not exist outside thought. MM VI, 2 introduces the distinction between imagination and pure understanding or pure intellect, which explains the manner of their existence in thought, whereas the subsequent paragraph explains obscurely how, from the imagination of body, its existence may be known.

The argument from the imagination of body to its existence is of special interest because it shows how Descartes combines the appearance of asserting that mind is a separated intellect, to which sensation and imagination do not necessarily belong (MM VI, 6 & 12) with the modes doctrines of MM II, 9. Imagination, as distinguished from understanding, is said not to belong to the "essence of my mind." This statement conceives imagination as a faculty, because it is said to be a "power . . . in me." In MM VI, 1 & 2, however, imagination is conceived not as a power but as a mode of thought, for imagining is the "application" of the "faculty of knowledge," i.e., the mind, to an immediately present body. The faculty conception of imagination is implicitly overthrown in MM VI, 3, when Descartes explains why that faculty is not part of himself. If the mind were so joined to some body that it could consider or contemplate that body when it pleased, that would explain what imagination is; understanding, on the other hand, would occur when the mind "turned away" from this body to contemplate some ideas that it has from itself. Although this explanation is still enigmatic, it nevertheless becomes clear that understanding or pure understanding is not the essence of mind while imagination is merely an accident, but both are equally modes of applying one and the same power of knowledge, i.e., mind or understanding. The explanation of why imagination does not belong to the essence of mind suffices also to explain why pure understanding does not belong to the essence of mind, for the explanation abolishes the conception of powers of the mind altogether.

Nevertheless, the "body" to which the mind turns when it imagines is still a mystery. Imagination tends to be conceived in the prejudiced sense as inner and psychic, as distinguished from body which is outer and physical. But the faculty conception must be abandoned since the mind has no inner and outer for the same reason that it is not a unity of faculties. Mind is only the respective modes of thought. One of the most important clues for interpreting imagination is the identification of it with the sensus communis (MM II, 14). Another clue is given in the *Replies* when Descartes distinguishes between ideas and corporeal images: "And thus it is not only images depicted in the imagination that I call ideas; nay, to such images I here decidedly refuse the title of ideas, insofar as they are pictures in the corporeal imagination, i.e., in some part of the brain." [3] This implies that the "body" to which the cognitive power turns when it imagines is the image at the pineal gland. The theory of pure intellect and its relation to imagination turns on this identification.

The distinction between imagination and pure intellect (MM VI, 2) manifestly invites comparison with the statements that emerge from Descartes's analysis of wax. In the earlier discussion, Descartes denied knowledge of body to imagination, attributing it rather to an "inspection by the mind," but in MM VI, 2 it is said that imagining is the "intuition" of an image. The intuition of body is what distinguishes thinking in the mode of imagination from thinking in the mode of pure understanding, which conceives body without an intuited image; Descartes can conceive a chiliagon although he cannot imagine its thousand sides. What is true of figure is true of number, which to intuition or imagination is "nothing but the thing counted."

The theory of pure intellect is in effect a theory of abstraction, although Descartes developed it only so far as was necessary to meet the requirements of mathematical abstraction. Although fragments of the theory are scattered throughout his writings, and something of a scholasticized version is presented in the *Principles,* albeit with its connection to mathematics entirely severed, the only systematic statement is in the *Regulae.*

A Theory of Abstraction

As we approach the *Regulae,* it will be convenient to restate our findings, up to now, regarding the relation between method and the investigation of the powers of the mind. The objective of the method is to establish certainty in the sciences by instituting a mathesis universalis. Mathematics is a small peninsula of truth whose dominion is to be extended to a dark continent through methodological workmanship. The continent is the region of immediate sense experience, or prejudice; for the world as it appears to us is like a dream illusion. If the sense world is radically false, it cannot serve as the principle of experience—as the path of access to the world as it truly is. A knowing, scientific access to the world must be constituted in accordance with the requirements of certainty, i.e., mathematics. Unlike other sciences, mathematics can be disengaged entirely from the world, prejudiced or real; it need not consider "existence." The principle of experience for the discovery and verification of its truths are the intuitive and discursive powers of the mind working alone, or in abstraction from the world. To project a mathematical comprehension of the world is accordingly to project the replacement of sense experience by mathematical knowledge or mathematical reason as the principle of experience. For Descartes, the principal methodological problem is the institution of empirical consciousness, mathematically conceived, as the principle of experience. That is, the institution of universal mathematics requires the transposition of the immediately experienced world into the homogeneous frame of mathematical concepts, hence the mediation of sense experience by mathematics. It requires the inversion of the sensed world.

In general, the solution of the principal methodological problem takes the form of an investigation of the powers of the mind as the "instruments" of knowledge; *Regulae* XII in particular sets forth the whole plan of the solution, as Descartes expressly notes. But why should the solution take this path?

"I think" is the fulcrum of certain science because it provides the immovable point for the dissolution of the world as immediately experienced. It loosens the moorings of that world by destroying the prejudiced belief in its reality; and it does so by conceiving the world as being *for me.* The lever is the scientific explanation of the genesis of perception, for this account of the difference between sensation and thing yields a positive concept of the immediately given world as *mediated:* it enables me to think the apparently real world of immediate experience as only an idea or thought, through which I have access to the real world. In order for the mind to have access to the real world through the apparent, it is necessary that there be at least one element common to them, and that element is extension. The prejudiced world is like a narrow and rocky strait that connects the harbor of knowledge that the mind has from itself with the ocean of the real world. The vessel which negotiates this dangerous passage is imagination. And *Regulae* XII is the chart.

IMAGINATION AND PURE INTELLECT

Descartes begins his exposition by noting that it presupposes an explanation of what "the human mind is, what body, and how it is informed by mind." But he has omitted this explanation because he desires to write "nothing controversial." [4] Nevertheless, he includes some of the most important fragments of this explanation, which are interspersed through the Rule. The explanation is nothing but the scientific account of the genesis of perceptions.

Two or three crucial premises control the reflection as a whole. The first is that sensations are real modifications of the sensorium, as wax is really modified by the seal. The corollary is that the sensus communis and imagination are "genuine parts of the body, of sufficient size to allow [their] different parts to assume various figures." [5] The second premise is that the "infinitude of figures suffices to express all the differences in sensible things." The word *experimendis* ("express"), which means "to force, squeeze, constrain," continues the seal-wax analogy; the word choice indicates that the diagrams by which Descartes illustrates this conception are models of possible nerve excitation patterns in the sense organ. This interpretation is further confirmed by the remark that when "the external sense is moved by some object, the figure which is impressed on it is carried off to . . . the sensus communis instantaneously." Evidently Descartes has in mind the brain model which was considered in Chapter 3. Finally, the sensus communis may be stimulated by motions that originate in the organ of external sense, or that originate from the "stored impressions" or "traces" on the brain. To mark this difference, he distinguishes imagination and memory from the sensus communis. Notice that this is not a distinction of faculties in the traditional sense of powers of the mind. The sensus communis and imagination are merely two different ways in which *the brain* may supply impressions to the mind. The gland is the seat of both imagination and the sensus communis.*

---

* The *Regulae* stress the difference between the sensus communis and imagination, whereas the *Meditations* identify them. The psychology of the *Regulae* is more directly under the influence of scholastic usage than the later writings. According to scholastic psychology, the sensus communis

The upshot of this explanation is a completely mechanical, corporeal conception of the powers traditionally attributed to the soul, as is indicated by the several conspicuous references to the fact that all these operations can be performed by animals.[6] It also means that whenever the mind senses, imagines, or remembers, it perceives an actual body. Metaphysically, this doctrine is the unique Cartesian solution to the problem of idealism: we may know material objects from ideas, because ideas are themselves corporeal.* Methodologically, it signifies that the real world is the imagined (extension and its modes) world, for sense qualities are not "real." However, the real body actually perceived (the sensus communis) is only a representation of the reality which it is the business of science to know; and that in the representation which it

---

and imagination were two of four "internal senses," the other being the estimative faculty and memory. The principal difference between the sensus communis and imagination is that the former primarily apprehends present external things while imagination apprehends those things in their absence, and also divides and composes images and makes judgments (Gilson, 1913a, 165–66). The suppression of the sensus communis occurs when its office is primarily to perceive external objects, since one must either admit that those objects are perceived twice—once by the special senses and once by the sensus communis—or eliminate either the sensus communis or the special senses. According to Descartes's mature theory, the special senses are eliminated inasmuch as he denies that there is perception in the organs of the special senses; all sensation occurs at the "seat" of the soul, the pineal gland, i.e., in the sensus communis. But because his optical studies, combined with Stoic influences, have convinced him of the importance of the role of judgment even in sensation, the sensus communis, in its scholastic concept as receiving impressions, tends to be assimilated to imagination as a judging capacity. Consequently, Descartes tends to contrast "the senses," i.e., the external senses, with imagination; and in such contrasts the sensus communis is left idle, even though the later writings retain the term. The grounds for these terminological shifts are quite visible in the Replies to the Sixth Objections, HR II, 251–52/AT VII, 437–38. Another and related reason for the terminological instability is that the wax model of the sensus communis is entirely inadequate for the experienced phenomenon of simultaneous sensation from two or more senses, as well as for Descartes's model of the sensus communis as the *dynamics* of the motions of the spirits.

* As noted in Chapter 3, the theory of corporeal ideas is an inescapable consequence of the localization of the "faculties" of the soul. It is therefore not surprising to find in antiquity antecedents of the Cartesian corporeal idea theory, especially among the Stoics. Zeno held that the soul was a corporeal pneuma, and that sensations were impressions in the hegemonikon (the Aristotelian sensus communis). "But about this," Sex. Emp. writes, "they at once began to quarrel; for whereas Cleanthes understood it as involving depression and protrusion, just as does the impression made in wax by signet rings, Chrysippus regarded such a thing as absurd" (*Adv. Math.* VII, 228; also *Adv. Log.* I, 380). His reason was that the soul considers contraries together (e.g., a square and a triangle), although they cannot exist simultaneously in the same substance. The basis of the dispute is the question whether the soul is material. Cicero attributes to Zeno the materialist view, based on the reasoning that whatever acts or is acted upon is material (*Academica,* II, 39; also II, 18, 77). It is noteworthy that the need to account for the preservation of impressions drives even Aristotle to a literal interpretation of the seal-wax metaphor or a material interpretation of the image, although these views surface only in his discussion of memory (*De Mem.* 450 a30–b11; 453 a22–30; *De Som.* 461 b21–25). Conimbricinses, whose text was in use at La Flèche, speaks in the same vein when he discusses the localization of faculties (Gilson, 1913a, 266–67). See Beck, 1952, 28–29, and below, n. 180.

represents is the topographical isomorphism between image and the corporeal idea and its cause.

The conception of thinking which emerges from this explanation is an authentic statement of the sense of MM II, 9:

> It is one and the same agency which, when applying itself . . . to the sensus communis is said to see, touch, etc.; if applying itself to imagination . . . is said to remember; if it turn to imagination in order to create fresh impressions, it is said to imagine or conceive; finally, if it act alone it is said to understand . . . and is called "pure intellect." . . . It is properly called *ingenium* when it either forms new ideas in imagination, or attends to those already formed.[7]

The single agency that applies itself in diverse ways is consciousness, or the power of perception. The whole focus of the *Regulae,* as announced in the title, is the mode of consciousness in which it engenders, brings forth, or creates "ideas in imagination." The *Regulae* would direct this creative power by rules that put it in service of pure intellect (pure understanding). Ingenium* occupies a middle position between sensation and understanding, as well as between conception and reality. It is the medium through which the mind abstracts certain things from sensation, for example, the common sensibles, and also invents ikons or intuitable representations for its conceptions. As such, it represents the one point in the universe where body may be "formed" by mind.

The main interest of the distinction between pure understanding and imagination clusters about the difference between intuition, in either imagination or the sensus communis, and conception. In *Regulae* XIV, this distinction is made the basis for a theory of abstraction that is intended to clarify the origin and status of mathematical "entities" in their relation to the world. Specifically, the object is to expound the relation between the science of magnitude in general, which abstracts from both number and figure, and the imaginative representation of number and figure. The curious property of the discussion is that because Descartes begins with the abstract concepts as given, the thrust of his argument is not to show how abstract concepts are acquired from intuition, but conversely, to show how abstract concepts are instantiated by intuition.

Because pure understanding holds its concepts apart from imagination, it

---

* Although the Latin translation of DM renders *esprit* as *ingenium*, the only thing in common between the *Regulae* and DM use of the terms is the vague ordinary meaning "intelligence." DM indeed adheres strictly to the common meaning, for it explicates *esprit* as quickness of thought, distinctness of imagination and amplitude of memory. The ingenium of the *Regulae*, by contrast, is the operation of forming and receiving images.

generates a whole series of propositions about mathematical entities: "extension or figure is not body"; "number is not the thing counted"; "a line is the limit of a surface," etc.[8] These propositions are true of the figure, number, etc. considered by pure understanding. Yet these concepts cannot be directly represented by the imagination, for they have no direct instantiation either in imagination or sensation. The incommensurability of the conceived, as contrasted with the imagined or sensed mathematical, provides fertile ground for confusions and contradictions about their true nature. The geometer asserts that lines have no breadth, and surfaces no depth; "yet he subsequently wishes to generate the one out of the other, not noticing that a line, the movement of which is conceived to create a surface, is really a body; or that . . . the line which has no breadth is merely a mode of body." [9] In the scholastic terminology of the *Principles,* concepts of pure understanding are only "distinctions of reason." These entities are not "really" distinct from the objects of intuition to which they refer, yet they are conceptually distinct and for computational purposes are independent of them; thus, the arithmetician may ignore altogether that numbers are not objects distinct from the thing counted.[10] But if one forgets the instantiation of these concepts, they will be hypostatized into noetic entities that are "really" distinct from their instantiation, and one will attribute "mysterious properties" to them.[11] Accordingly, Descartes writes:

> We announce that by extension we do not here mean anything distinct and separate from the extended object itself; and we make it a rule not to recognize those philosophical entities which cannot be presented to imagination. For even though someone could persuade himself, for example, that supposing every extended object in the universe were annihilated, that would not prevent extension alone from existing, this conception would not involve the use of any corporeal idea, but would be based on a false judgment of the understanding working alone. He will admit this himself, if he reflect attentively on this very image of extension when . . . he tries to construct it in his imagination. For he will notice that, as he perceives it, it is not divested of a reference to every object, but that his imagination is quite different from his judgment about it. Consequently, . . . those abstract entities are never given to our imagination as separate from the objects in which they inhere.[12]

This conception is the basis for the identification of extension as body with the object of mathematics. Descartes notes that the identification is not the office of the mathematician, who considers extension merely as length, breadth, and depth, or as an imaginable picture, without "considering whether it is real body or merely space." [13] The mathematician has already made abstraction not only from the sensed particular, but also from the common sensibles as they are given in the sensed particular, or "subject," in the terminology of the *Regulae*. Descartes's idea is that the common sensibles in any given body or subject, which are really present in it, are the subject matter of mathematics and instantiations to which abstracted concepts refer. These concepts are dimensions, that is, "modes or aspects according to which a subject is considered to be measurable." [14] Thus, number is a dimension of extension, which itself has the two dimensions of order and measure, i.e., ordinality and cardinality.[15] Also weight and velocity are dimensions of a body, and in general, any aspect of a subject that can be measured is a dimension. Mathematical entities are only "modes of thought" by which pure understanding forms a being of reason by abstraction from subjects.

Backward and forward historical references may help to bring out the philosophic import of this theory. Its prototype is Aristotle's theory of the origin of mathematical concepts, which Klein has shown was assimilated to the mathematical tradition through Diophantus and Pappus.* Moreover, its function in both writers is similar. Descartes is in accord with Aristotle's critique of the Platonic conception of the independent noetic existence of mathematical entities; he agrees that they are derived by abstraction from actual bodies. To be sure, this interpretation contradicts those passages in which Descartes seems to affiliate himself with the doctrine of innate ideas.†　But apart from the plain sense of the *Regulae*, there are other passages that are incompatible with the notion of innate ideas. The *Replies* state that "our mind

---

* The argument is indirect. It is that the number concept of later Greek mathematicians assimilates Aristotle's critique of the Platonic *chorismos* thesis (Klein, 1968, 112–13).

† Apart from letters, the most important source is the *Meditations*. I do not believe that the term appears in the *Regulae*; it is alien to the Cartesian physiology of perception. Descartes reduces the doctrine of innate ideas to a triviality when he writes that all ideas, even of the sense qualities and the passions, are innate because they bear no resemblance to the cortical motions that cause them (HR I, 443/AT VIII–2, 358–59). He achieves the same effect when he likens the innateness of ideas to the propensity of certain families to contract gout! (ibid.; also HR II, 73/AT VII, 188.) Such statements seem designed to show in a humorous way the collision of the doctrine of innate ideas with physiology. Kemp Smith, among others, acknowledges that the innate ideas are a later development of Cartesian theory of knowledge, which is advanced specifically to deal with theological questions (Smith, 1952, 240–41). It may be added that in his polemic against Voëtius, Descartes, referring to the *Meno*, states the view that the doctrine of innate ideas implies the Platonic doctrine of reminiscence, which is surely not part of Cartesian epistemology (AT VIII–2, 166–67; also MM V, 4).

is so constituted by nature that general propositions are formed out of knowledge of particulars."[16] The same view is taken in the thematic statement on universals in the *Principles,* where an extensive treatment is given to the derivation of numbers from simple sense experiences.* These and other passages seem to indicate that the traditional notion of innate ideas, which Descartes apparently adopts, must be understood in the sense of the "seeds of wisdom" impressed on the mind "by nature," such as the idea of extension, which is impressed upon the mind by every sense experience.[17] For the empiricist Descartes, the Platonic number concept, according to which numbers are ostensibly noetic entities prior to particular minds and to particulars of the world, is a hypostatization of a being of reason: that is, Descartes considers noetic entities to be the creations of finite human minds, not objects with an ontologically independent existence.

Yet from the Cartesian point of view, if Aristotle correctly recognized the particular as the real—and he wavers on this question—he chose the wrong particulars. Descartes manages to combine, against Aristotle, the Platonic rejection of the sensed world in favor of a noetic world, with Aristotle's demand, against Plato, that the real be the concrete particular. The Cartesian extreme "Platonic" dissolution of the sensed world is complemented by an equally unyielding requirement that the real be available and accessible to intuition. Owing to this double movement, Cartesian epistemology is at once rationalist and empiricist, and indeed establishes this distinction as definitive. Empirical consciousness—"I think"—is the principle of experience. But empirical consciousness, by the appropriation of mathematics, constitutes itself as the framework of mathematical conceptuality. The axis of this reconstitution, to repeat, is the new Cartesian conception of imagination, which identifies the common sensibles as the real. The common sensibles are available in sensation, which the mathematical consciousness *conceives* as imagination. The common sensibles can also be abstracted from this source, reproduced in concepts, and studied by imagination and understanding. The relation between reason and sensibility is determined by the three modes in which the common sensibles or extension can be known—in sensation, imagination, and by pure understanding. Owing to the fact that imagination is a "real body," everything

---

* *Prin.* I, § 59; II, § 8. These passages direcly contradict the claim of the MM that mathematical entities are innate (MM III, 11; see AT III, 303), even the MM are by no means unambiguous in their assertion of innate ideas. In MM III, 21, Descartes explains how he derives various mathematical ideas; and the entire causal argument for the existence of God is that the idea of God is implanted or caused by God himself, which is to say that it is acquired from "outside."

imaginable is a possible existent, and conversely, nothing is imaginable that is not corporeal. Since pure understanding merely considers the "modes" of extension in abstraction from imagination, the mind remains tied to possible existence even when it has "turned away from body." Here we understand how Descartes determines "methodologically" what the "mind is able to know," i.e., the scope of its powers. The mind cannot think anything clearly and distinctly but extension; for sensation, imagination, and pure understanding are only three modes of cognizing extension; this is so because the sensus communis is itself a body. For this reason the Cartesian investigation of the limits of knowledge does not take the form of a transcendental deduction.

The corporeality of imagination and ideas is the nexus between the possible and the actual. As already discussed, uninterpreted sensibility cannot be the real, because, apart from the problem of quality, it gives no knowledge of imperceptible times and insensible magnitudes. Imagination and understanding working in tandem set the limits of the possible. For every concept of understanding, say, equations for lines, there is a corresponding imaginative representation, which the ingenium can imprint, from "inside," on the sensus communis. This is a "factitious" idea. Sensibility translates the factitious-possible into an adventitious-actual by providing external impressions that imprint upon the sensus communis a "figure" corresponding to the imaginative representation. The sensible figure will always fall short of the concept because gross observation cannot perceive, e.g., straight lines, rigid bodies, etc. But it is not always necessary because experimentation is able to make up the deficiency. Descartes, indeed, assigns to experiment just the role of discriminating between possible and actual existence.[18] Sensation is merely a mode of thinking which does not by itself determine the real. Reality is known only by the right employment of all the mind's instruments. That employment lies in the habitus of science that constitutes empirical consciousness mathematically conceived. The "impressions" of this consciousness are what is real: empirical consciousness is the principle of experienced reality.

This theory contains substantial anticipations of Kantian doctrine. Descartes has in effect stated the doctrine that understanding without intuition is empty, while intuition without understanding is blind. For having rejected the existence of noetic entities as "really distinct" from body, and having asserted their dependence upon the mind, Descartes in effect requires an intuitive instantiation for every concept. The representing-picturing function of imagination is analogous to the "schematism" of understanding, although for Kant it is time while for Descartes it is space. Finally, the Cartesian *ingenium* answers to productive imagination both in function and in stress. If the source of knowledge is the senses—if the mind does not passively receive ideas but must work them up from sensibility—then the "synthetic" or creative function of the mind becomes a matter of first importance. If we consider that the known real is always a mathematical structure "worked up" by the mind in the way just described, we begin to approach the view that the mind knows only so much of the world as it has put into it. But this view passes beyond Cartesian thinking into the terrain of transcendental philosophy.

The theory of abstraction seems indeed designed to prevent idealisms of various types, from the Platonic hypostatization of *entia rationis* to the Cartesian variety found in the *Meditations*. The doubt is undertaken in cognizance of the fact that sense objects are certainly perceived: "Even now [in the midst of doubt] I do not deny that these ideas of [earth, sky, stars and all other objects which I apprehend by means of the senses] are presented to my mind." [19] Even so, he conceives that body does not exist. This concept is identical with the idea Descartes criticized in the passage of the *Regulae,* quoted above. Should someone think that extension might exist even though all extended objects or substances in the universe were annihilated, this would be a "false judgment of the understanding working alone." This is the situation in the doubt, for Descartes does not deny that he possesses the idea of extension; he thinks only that he can possess this idea even though all real extended bodies are annihilated. The same criticism is found again in the *Principles* when Descartes states that those who distinguish extension (as an idea) from substance or from quantity "either mean nothing by the word 'substance,' or they merely form in their minds a confused idea of incorporeal substance." [20] The existence of body is guaranteed because it is impossible to separate its "essence" from its existence; corporeal nature, it may be said, is a necessary being. Consequently, Descartes is able to assert the existence of body on the basis of his *imagined* representation of extension, for this representation depends for its existence on corporeal imagination, which is a "real body" of definite dimensions; or rather, the imaginative representation of body *is* a body.

PURE INTELLECT AS SYMBOLIC THINKING

In order to expound the doctrine of pure intellect as a latent theory of symbolism, and to bring out some of its ambiguities, it is well to consider first the disagreement between Liard and Boutroux regarding the identity of the universal mathematics.

Liard holds with nearly all commentators that the objective of universal mathematics is a general science of proportions, i.e., a science that demonstrates theorems of arithmetical and geometrical proportions.[21] He opposes the view that Descartes's specific mathematical achievement is a new geometry because, despite the title of the *Geometry,* it is the algebraic aspect rather than the geometrical aspect of the work that is significant. Among other arguments in support of his position, Liard cites the letter to Mersenne in which Descartes distinguishes his achievement from that of his predecessor in algebra, Viète.

> If one compares what I have written on the number of roots of equations—on p. 372, where I begin to give the rules of my algebra—with what Viète wrote at the end of his book *De emendatione equationum,* he will see that I have determined generally all equations, whereas he has only given some particular examples . . . so that I have begun where he left off.[22]

This statement, Liard thinks, shows that Descartes's purpose in the *Geometry* is the reduction of all problems to finding the number of roots of equations. Liard writes: "This was the essential object of this universal mathematics, where relations and proportions are treated independently of any application to a specific material." [23] Descartes's aim was not an expansion or improvement of geometry, although this was a consequence of his endeavor, but an enlargement of algebra, which he sought to clarify by wedding it to geometrical intuition.[24] Analytic geometry is "only the consequence and so to speak the side effect of the constitution of a science more general." [25]

Although Boutroux contests Liard's conclusions by attacking his interpretation of the evidence, his more important thesis is that Descartes never attained his goal of a universal mathematics because it is in principle unattainable, since he contemplates a pure science of magnitude which uses only pure understanding.[26] Through such a science, the mind would be:

> in a state of passive contemplation [that was] always actual. Completed as soon as it began, it would not unravel, as we do, a long chain of theorems, for pure understanding embraces, at once and all together, all the truths that men discover one after another. From the point of view of understanding, for which time has no reality, it is not true that one proposition precedes

another which is given to reason: all are equally primitive and evident by themselves.[27]

From this point of view, the method is a make-shift device, the need for which signifies the imperfection of human understanding, which cannot dispense with sense and imagination.[28]

Boutroux's sketch of what is, in effect, a divine mind is an ideal that looms in the background of the *Regulae*. It helps to recognize that Descartes's formulations about the pure understanding working alone, without the help of imagination and sense, cannot be literally construed. Boutroux correctly remarks that "it is quite evident that, were the understanding able to resolve an equation by itself alone, it would have no need of symbols, but it cannot."[29] Descartes's description of pure understanding is confusing because in fact it never works alone. What he means by the "banishment" of imagination and the senses is abstraction from figures and numbers.[30] The abstraction is effected by using "brief notes," i.e., algebraic notation, which is an aid supplied by imagination and sensation. His account of this operation may be summarized as follows. When understanding deals with subjects in which there is nothing corporeal, imagination and sense can be of no use and therefore ought to be "divested of every distinct impression."[31] If understanding wishes to consider something that can be referred to body, it should form the idea of the thing as distinctly as possible, to the extent of making a sensible representation, e.g., geometric constructions. If it is desired to deduce something from a number of objects, e.g., the fourth term of a proportion, the "objects themselves [e.g., number signs] ought [not] be present to the external senses, but rather certain brief notes [i.e., letter signs]."[32] The observance of this rule is the right employment of the aids of understanding, imagination and sensation.

Understanding working alone and with aids is equivocal because there are two meanings of imagination (and sensation): it means the picture or ikon of something corporeal, and notation or symbolism. Notation, though visible and imaginable, is like pure intellect in that it stands in no direct relation to the world. This property of "symbol-manipulating" imagination is obscured by the stress on imagination as the corporeal mental counterpart to the extension of the world. But the utility of symbols to understanding is that although they are sensible-imaginable, i.e., themselves extended, they are not ikons of anything extended. As such, they are perfectly suited to "embody" concepts of pure understanding; they are so to speak "empirical data" that have no relation to the world.*

Although Liard, Boutroux and others have stressed the importance of Descartes's notational reforms to the success of his reform of algebra, it seems that the rule on notation (*Regulae* XVI) has not been adequately studied. The *Discourse* criticized the algebra of the day for the multiplicity of its rules that embarrass the mind and fatigue imagination.[33] The same objection is raised in *Regulae* XVI, but in such a way as to identify Viète's "rules of homogeneity" as the target of criticism.

To appreciate the directives of *Regulae* XVI, we must recognize the menial perspective of the *Regulae* as a whole. Their purpose is to show, step by step, how to achieve clarity of conception about each thing that comes before the mind. Consequently, Descartes is interested throughout in subjective and seemingly trivial nuts and bolts of thinking, such as the length of attention span, the development of mental habits, what order to follow, how to use imagination, and in general, its "capacity." The discussion of notation is entirely in this mode. Notation is called into being to serve the humble office of an aid to memory, which itself is only an aid to understanding. To expound his idea, Descartes relates the function and utility of mathematical notation to writing. This art has been invented as a support for memory. By providing a notation for thoughts that may be used to preserve them, writing frees the mind to turn its attention to other things. Speaking of his own notation for equations, Descartes remarks:

> By this device not only shall we economize our words, but, what is the chief thing, display the terms of the problem in such a pure and naked way that, although it omits nothing, there will be nothing superfluous to be discovered in it, nor anything to occupy the mind (*ingenium*) to no purpose by requiring it to apprehend a number of things at the same time.[34]

It is noteworthy that the terms "pure and naked" are so frequently used in connection with pure understanding, and that they are synonyms for "clear and distinct." The statement is virtually a recipe for perspicuous notation. Implicit in it is the demand that every element in the notation signify an element in the problem to be considered, and nothing more; and that every element of the problem be signified in the notation. The directive on notation

* According to Klein, this operation is the core of the "symbol-generating abstraction," which he believes to be the basis of the modern (algebraic) number conception (Klein, 1968, 174–75, 208).

fulfills the requirement of *Regulae* V, which is said to be the "sum of all human endeavor." The utility of notion lies not only in its directing our attention to those things and only those things that should occupy the mind, but also, as Russell pointed out, in what it enables us not to think about.

There is no doubt that Descartes understands his notational directive specifically in the context of the problem of analytic geometry, for the first part of the Rule reads: "When we come across matters that do not require our present attention, it is better to designate them by brief notes than by figures, even though the [figures] may be necessary to the conclusion." [35] Although this statement conceives the utility of notation too narrowly, in this context it throws a light on what Descartes means by abstracting from both numbers and figures, which is the point raised directly after the remark on notation just quoted. For the statement about abstracting from figures is followed immediately by an implicit critique of Viète's "rule of homogeneity":

> Note further that by the number of relations attaching to a quantity I mean a sequence of ratios in continued proportion, such as the algebra now received attempts to express by sundry dimensions and figures. It calls the first of these the radix, the second the square, the third the cube, the fourth the biquadratic, and so on. I confess that for a long time I myself was imposed upon by these names. For, after the straight line and the square, there was nothing which seemed to be capable of being placed more clearly before my imagination than the cube and the other figures of the same type; . . . but at last, after testing the matter well, I discovered that I had never found out anything by their means which I could not have recognized more easily and distinctly without employing their aid. I saw that this whole nomenclature must be abandoned, if our conceptions are not to become confused; for that very magnitude which goes by the name of the cube or the biquadratic, is nevertheless never to be presented to the imagination otherwise than as a line or surface, in accordance with the previous rule. We must therefore be very clear about the fact that the radix, the square, the cube, etc. are merely magnitudes in continuous proportion, which always imply the previous assumption of that arbitrarily chosen unit of which we spoke above.[36]

No other passage of the *Regulae* indicates more certainly the genesis of Cartesian geometry. The terms "quadratic" and "cubic" are the vestige of Viète's association of equations of successively higher degrees with figures of successively greater dimensions. Thus, the sum of two right lines is another right; their product, a rectangle. The product of a rectangle and a right, a solid. But the system comes to an abrupt end here, because, space having only three dimensions, there is no representation for equations beyond the cubic.* Descartes abandons this system altogether, replacing it by a system in which equations of any degree can be represented by lines only. This is above all what Descartes means by "abstracting from figure": linear coordinates suffice to express all difference between figures. This, in turn, is the key to the Cartesian notion of a general science of magnitudes. Viète's "rule of homogeneity" states that only homogeneous magnitudes may be compared, and those magnitudes are homogeneous that result from addition and subtraction, whereas multiplication and division yield heterogeneous magnitudes.[37] In the Cartesian system this distinction disappears. The law of signs (the fundamental theorem of the "algebraic" section of the *Geometry*), shows how any magnitudes may be compared, which is just the goal of a "general science" of proportions. Considered in its historical context, then, abstraction from figure means abstraction from the kinds of figure to which Viète had tied his equations. By showing how all equations could be represented by using only plane figures, Descartes gave a procedure for graphically representing equations that previously had no imaginative or sensible counterpart.

Although the lines Descartes uses to represent equations are for the imagination identical with any other line, to the understanding they are by no means the same. Cartesian lines result from the method of determining an infinite number of points in position. But this conception is entirely arithmetical and depends upon no imaginative representation of lines but upon computational rules intrinsic to algebra. The resulting line is thus a *schema of an equation,* i.e., of a conception accessible only to "pure understanding." As such, Cartesian figures are representations of space or body, although their "corporeality" is guaranteed by the doctrine of corporeal imagination. Jacob Klein has expressed this result forcefully in his argument that Descartes was the first to conceive geometry as a "symbolic science." [38] Cartesian space is symbolic because its figures are generated and conceived by computational methods that are independent of "existence" or the world. The post-Cartesian problem with respect to the ontological foundations of science is latent in this achievement.

---

* Viète, 1968, 325–26, 334–38. Brunschvicg observes that Descartes's generalized notion of dimension is the basis for his replacement of this correlation of figure and degree of an equation with the concept that relates degrees of an equation to a given unity (Brunschvicg, 1912, 110). On the same subject, see Liard, 1882, 57–58.

The Second Proof of the Existence of Body

Let us return to the Sixth Meditation. The proofs of the existence of body (paragraphs 1–3, 10) are separated by a proof of the "real distinction" between mind and body, which must be briefly considered.

THE REAL DISTINCTION BETWEEN MIND AND BODY

The achievement of the proof and its place in the "order of reasons" are subject to contradictory appraisals. One set of pronouncements says that the proof assumes the distinction between mind and body that was drawn in the Second Meditation, and by addition of new premises about the nature of body and the veracity of God that are gathered in later Meditations, proves that there is a "real distinction" between mind and body.[39] A real distinction, as distinguished from a modal distinction or a distinction of reason, is the epistemological correlate of a distinction between substances and a weaker claim than a substantial distinction, because it refers only to the necessity of conception rather than to the status of things.* It is one of the curious properties of the proof that the terms "substance" and "real distinction" are not mentioned; it concludes only that I am "truly distinct from my body," *insofar as* I am a thinking thing, and can exist without it. These reservations are explained in the Synopsis, where Descartes says that he would require a complete physics to prove the immortality of the soul, which would establish the premise that the modifications of the thinking thing do not imply its dependency on modifications of the human body.†

The nerve of the proof is the manner in which the transition is made from the distinct ideas of mind and body, which were established in the Second Meditation, and the conclusion to the "true" distinctness of mind and body. Descartes frequently stressed that in the Second Meditation he lacked the resources to conclude from his distinction that mind and body are different substances, or "really distinct." This point became a subject of dispute partly because in the *Discourse* Descartes had concluded, from the fact that he perceived himself to be only a thinking thing, that he in essence consisted ex-

---

*HR I, 141/AT VII, 13; *Prin.* I, §§ 60, 63. The transition from conception to things is based on the premise that the mind could not conceive itself to be completely different from body if that were not really the case. See especially HR II, 22/AT VII, 120.

†HR I, 141/AT VII, 14. For a strong denial that the "essence" of the mind does not include its modes, see HR II, 64/AT VII, 176.

clusively in thinking.[40] The trouble with this proof, as all critics urged and as Descartes admitted, is its assumption in the premises that thoughts or thinking are not corporeal.[41] However, the present argument does not differ in the slightest, as Arnauld and others complained, from the argument that is admittedly defective:

> And therefore, just because I know certainly that I exist, and that meanwhile I do not remark another thing that necessarily pertains to my nature or essence or nature, except that I am a thinking thing, I rightly conclude that my essence consists in my being a thinking thing.

The identity of the arguments in the Second and Sixth Meditations is brought out by the duplication of the "order of reasons" from MM I to MM II, 6 by the order from MM VI, 6 to 9, for in both cases Descartes argues, on the basis of the doubtful existence of body, that he is only a thinking thing.*

If one set of commentaries reduces the purportedly stronger proof of the Sixth Meditation to the admittedly inadequate proof of the Second Meditation, there is another set that claims for the latter the same strength that is purportedly found in the former; for Descartes definitely and repeatedly claims to know the mind as a substance in the Second Meditation on the basis of his doubt of the existence of body.† It seems, therefore, that the "proof" has no other purpose than to give men "the hope of another life after death" and to "establish religion." [42] From the point of view of the acroamatic argument, Descartes's position is indeed that he knows his essence to be thinking solely in virtue of his thinking it, as we have emphasized. But this claim is independent of the question whether thoughts might be modifications of subtle bodies such as the animal spirits: Descartes would nevertheless remain a thinking thing. Indeed, Descartes claims to have proved with unsurpassed efficacy that the mind, which is not a form, is substantially united to the body.‡

---

* Many passages assert and deny that doubt of the existence of body suffices to prove the substantial incorporeality of res cogitans, e.g., HR I, 101/DM 33; HR I, 440/AT VIII–2, 354 (where it is asserted that the mind can be known to be incorporeal even if we have no concept of body); HR II, 208/AT VII, 132; *Prin.* I, §§ 7–8; HR I, 208/AT IX–2, 10.

† Defending the distinction drawn in MM II, Descartes asserts that nothing more is needed to establish the real distinction than a clear and distinct conception of mind and body (HR II, 22–23, 32, 98, 102/AT VII, 121, 132, 221, 226, 227).

‡ See especially the revealing comment to Gassendi (HR II, 133/AT IX–1, 215, HR II, 102/AT VII, 227). Gueroult claims that the substantial union of mind and body is contradictory to reason and can only occur in the order of things because the omnipotent God sets aside, in this case, the eternal truths (Gueroult, 1953, II, 65). Of course, if Descartes accepts one miracle, there is no reason why he should not accept them all.

CORPOREAL IDEAS AS THE UNITY OF MIND AND BODY

To proceed now with the proofs of the existence of body, in paragraph 3, Descartes concludes with probability to the existence of body simply on the basis of the distinct idea known to imagination. In paragraph 10 he concludes with certainty to the existence of body. We shall argue, however, that the second proof appeals to no data not present in the first.

The proof is rather exotic. Descartes argues that sensation and imagination are modes of himself on the grounds that they cannot exist except in an "intelligent substance," since in their "formal concept" some cognition is implied. (The argument implies that animals are "intelligent substances.") He also knows "in me" (F.V.) such "faculties" as motion, change of figure, etc. These ideas of corporeal things must be attributed to corporeal substance, since no intellection is comprised in their concept. This statement deserves careful scrutiny. If the doubt of the existence of body is serious, the statement is gratuitous; and in any case cognized body is an idea, which forthwith throws it into the category of sensation and imagination, from which he wishes to distinguish it. The remark deserves comparison with MM III, 19 and 20, where the ambiguity is repeated in the claims that he might have the idea of corporeal nature wholly from himself, although corporeal nature is not "formally" (i.e., really) in himself because he is only a thinking thing. In any case, he argues that the "passive faculty" of receiving ideas of sensible things would be useless unless there were an "active faculty" in himself or some other thing that produced those ideas. Despite his argument to the contrary in the Third Meditation, he decides that the "active faculty" cannot exist in himself, because it does not presuppose thought; consequently it resides in God or extension. But since he has a "very strong inclination to believe" that the ideas are caused by corporeal substance, they must be so produced, else were God a deceiver. However, Descartes concludes only to the existence of causes for his ideas of body, and so the proof advances no further than the argument of paragraphs 1-3. The genuine problem for a metaphysical proof of the existence of external objects is how, in view of his very strong inclination to believe in the external existence of qualities, Descartes separates them out from extension.

The game is given away in the subsequent discussion, when Descartes no longer makes any pretense of deriving his results from an introspective reflection, but says that in order to separate extension from qualities, one must give an account of how the "active" and "passive" faculties are related to one another, i.e., of the manner in which the mind is united to the body. For this purpose, Descartes simply appropriates the theory of automatism.[43] The active faculty is the animal spirits. The faculties of perception or modes of thought are but so many ways in which the sensus communis may be affected by the spirits. Commensurate with the physiology of sensation, Descartes reiterates the conception of res cogitans as modes of thought.

> When I consider the mind, i.e., myself inasmuch as I am only a thinking thing, I cannot distinguish in myself any parts . . . For the faculties of willing, sensing, conceiving etc. cannot be properly speaking said to be its parts, for it is one and the same mind that wills, senses, and conceives.[44]

The mind has no parts because it has no faculties, all of which are powers of the body. Mind can be one and the same in all its "acts" because Descartes conceives them uniformly as cognition of corporeal ideas. Descartes is a thinking thing "insofar as" these cognitions occur; he is united with the body insofar as what he cognizes is nothing but body. This is the authoritative Cartesian solution of the relation of both the union and distinctness of mind and body. Physically speaking, the modes of thought are only modifications of the brain.

These modifications are the unknown "something" or substance about which Descartes has inquired. They are unknown in the sense that the immediate causes of perceptions qua animal spirits are not perceived; Descartes, however, identifies them with the spirits by reflection. That is the "substantial union" or identity of mind and body. Their difference is constituted by the fact that these modifications are cognized. In the previous chapter, the multiple meanings of a "mode of cognition" were analyzed, and in the preceding segments have explained how the modes are deployed for objective cognition of objects. Here we need but add that the identification of the modes qua perceptions with extension culminates the doctrine of modes by specifying a single mode or concept for cognizing both mind and body at once.* The culmination has, of course, been implicit and sometimes explicit in much of the foregoing analysis. It is the apex of Cartesian objectivity and it is the definitive unification of the

---

* Descartes implied the corporeal substantiality of thoughts in his parallel between the mind and wax and the mind and flame (AT IV, 113–14, AT V, 221). There are statements in which Descartes asserts that a spiritual stuff intervenes between the cortical images and the mind, but Smith (1952, 141–60) and Beck (1952, 122–25) have argued that this is merely an ad hoc hypothesis. Smith correctly observes that the corporeal idea theory frees Descartes from many common objections about the interaction of mind and body. One must doubt, however, whether there is any interaction at all, since the mind is not a substance to be "impressed" by the body or which can act upon the body. The correspondence with Elizabeth, in which Descartes appears to commit himself to the inexplicability of the interaction, must be evaluated in light of Descartes's evident reluctance to discuss the subject with her. See AT III, 692–93; AT V, 289.

ordo cognoscendi and the ordo essendi toward which the foundational endeavor was directed. At the apex of objectivity the subject is least conspicuous; he tends to disappear into the object. For that reason the union of mind and body may deteriorate into materialism. On the other hand, the objectivity of the object is a mode of my cognition; hence, the difference between mind and body may deteriorate into absolute idealism. These two monisms are the unavoidable permanent house guests of Cartesian dualism.

Mind-Body Unity

In the interest of a clear statement of the acroamatic concept of mind-body unity, we have abstracted from its context, where Descartes presents another, quite distinct notion of mind-body unity that seems to modify res cogitans. It is the prejudiced notion of that unity.

The problem is posed and discussed in a new terminology introduced expressly for this purpose. "Nature" now means God or the world order instituted by God. "My nature" is initially said to be the "complexus of all the things God has given me"; but the scope of the term is subsequently reduced to include only those things Descartes possesses insofar as he is "composed" of mind and body. The "teachings of nature" are certain "spontaneous inclinations" to beliefs that arise owing to the mind's union with the body. They are distinguished from habits of credence, i.e., prejudices, that "seem" to be teachings of nature, but are not.[45] Both together—the teachings of nature and prejudice—are beliefs that arise when mind does not judge of things alone, but "in conjunction" with the body. The principal object of the discussion is to determine to what extent the judgments that emanate from "my nature" may be trusted. But since "my nature" has previously been identified with thought, the assay of prejudice turns out to be the task of assessing just what "my nature" is. It appears that in the course of the discussion, res cogitans undergoes a revision. If hitherto Descartes has identified his nature with thought, he has nevertheless frequently introduced the qualifying expression, "insofar as I am a thinking thing." Now, however, he speaks of "my body, or rather the total me, insofar as I am composed of mind and body"; similarly, the "nature of man" designates the composite of mind and body.* Although we seem to have arrived at the "true man" promised in the *Discourse,* the appearance is nevertheless misleading. If res cogitans is revised, surely it is not because of the mind's union with the body. We have shown, on the contrary, that res cogitans is constituted by the ac-

---

* MM VI, 22–24. "My nature" is said to be res cogitans in MM II, 9.

roamatic concept of that union. In the *Treatise on Man,* the man-machine is the most perfect possible simulation of the "true man." At stake in the argument is not a reconciliation of a disembodied mind with the fact of its union, as is often said, but a reconciliation of two apparently incompatible notions of that union. Descartes is settling accounts with the prejudices he set aside at the beginning of the doubt. The sense of the argument is lost if this structure is not recognized. Descartes does not merely accept the teachings of nature; he criticizes them by reference to the automatism theory upon which res cogitans is based. Our interpretation will attempt to show that the purport of the argument is to revise prejudice to make it fit within the concept of res cogitans rather than the reverse. On the other hand, since res cogitans was obtained by explicit rejection of prejudice, we should not be surprised if the loose ends and incommensurables of the Cartesian mind doctrine put in an appearance.

THE "TEACHINGS OF NATURE"

The issue between reason and prejudice is joined when Descartes reflects upon what nature teaches about his relation to his body, of whose existence he is persuaded by pain and appetition. Owing to these sensations, he is led to believe that he is not related to this body as a pilot is to his ship, but that he is "intermingled" with it so as to form a single whole. If that were not so, if he were *only* a thinking thing, when his body is hurt he would contemplate the wound as a pilot contemplates damage to his vessel, "by the understanding only." In general, all appetites, pleasures and pains are not merely perceived but felt, and these feelings lead to certain inexpungible beliefs and actions.

Descartes deals with the teachings of nature by the double procedure of referring them to automatism and restating them in terms of res cogitans. The feeling of pain in the foot or hunger in the stomach does not prove that the soul extends throughout the body. After considering certain errors that contradict this belief, such as the feeling of pain in a phantom limb, Descartes argues that we perceive pain only from the motions of the brain, which give us the sensation of pain in the foot, although what is actually there is not a sensation but merely a local motion of nerves.[46] Consequently, pleasure, pain, and appetition are only thoughts, albeit "confused modes of thought that are produced by the union and *apparent* intermingling of mind and body." [47] This expedient preserves the unity of res cogitans for, as Descartes asserts in the context, it is one and the same mind that understands, wills, and senses. The problem is to understand "confused thoughts" within the dimension of res cogitans.

Thoughts are confused because they conflate teleological judgments with judgments of fact. Pleasure and pain, appetition, and similar sensations are the signs by which nature "truly teaches" the condition of the body with respect to its harm and benefit. "My nature" on the whole rightly "judges" that pain is to be avoided, and so on. But by inobservance and habit, these modes of thought, which taken by themselves are clear and distinct, are rendered confused and obscure when they are taken as sufficient evidence for inferring anything about the external existence of objects and their nature.[48] For we may have clear and distinct knowledge of all sensations so long as "we consider them simply as sensations or thoughts," i.e., so long as we "take care to include in the judgments we form of them that only which we know to be precisely contained in our perception."[49]

It seems that the terms of the problem are the same as the terms of the doubt, but with this difference—whereas belief in the existence of objects corresponding to ideas was suspended by reference to ocular evidence, now tactile sensations, feelings in the strict sense, occupy the foreground. If res cogitans incorporates an ocular-optical bias, then prejudice presents a difficulty because feeling has been ignored. Since pain is felt in the body, prejudice does not err by assigning it a corresponding similar objective cause: the error is the incorrect assessment of its location; that is, we do not judge that the pain is in the foot, we *sense* it there.* It appears that prejudice in general, but especially concerning feelings, is the objection to res cogitans. But why is it an objection? Does not the automatism theory after all assign sensations their correct location and settle the question about their causes?

The doubt is consummated by suspending judgment, considering ideas or perceptions merely as immediate data of consciousness. The theory latent in the doubt becomes explicit when Descartes distinguishes the two principal modes, understanding and volition, assigning to volition, in the mixed submodes of instincts, appetites, and passions, the role of judging of external existence. It is thanks to the doubt and the suspension of "confused thoughts" that Descartes arrived at the concept of res cogitans. But we cannot always suspend "judgment," since the requirements of life dictate prejudiced belief. It seems that Descartes ceases to be res cogitans, as Hume ceases to be a skeptic, when he leaves his chamber. Specifically, what is at stake here is whether "confused thoughts" or sensibility in general are modes of thought, as Descartes has previously claimed. If they are not, then presumably I am not exclusively a thinking thing, for they admittedly belong to "my nature."

---

* MM VI, 21, 23. In *Principles* I, 67, Descartes denies that pain is sensed in the foot.

The prejudice that external objects are immediately perceived would threaten res cogitans if its constituting thesis, that I have immediate knowledge of thoughts only, were understood to mean that the external existence of things is not *perceived* whereas the deliverances of sensibility are *perceived* as thoughts. This interpretation is incompatible with our argument that what constitutes a mode of thought is not its being an immediate perception or a datum of consciousness, but a manner in which the mind's "instruments" are conceived relative to their respective functions in knowledge, and that the constituting thesis of res cogitans is the *conception* of the subjectivity of the knower, which is mediated by the scientific theory of the genesis of sensations. We acknowledged, however, that the opposed interpretation that thoughts are perceived qua thoughts, is also present in Descartes's expositions of his principle, primarily but not exclusively in the form of attributing "judgment" of external existence to volition and its modes. This inconsistency must now be discussed.

Although there are Skeptic and Stoic antecedents for Descartes's strange doctrine of judgment, its support in Cartesian science is the theory that distance, position, in short, external existence is not perceived but inferred "by a simple act of imagination" and that in general, perceiving with the senses seems to be an acquired capacity. However, basic learning must be a mechanical and unconscious process, since our subjective experience is that we perceive objects external to ourselves and different from ourselves. When Descartes denies that we perceive external existence, he denies the subjective experience by appeal to the theory of the genesis of sensations, which locates all sensation in the brain. He thereby sets in the place of the immediate data of consciousness a discursive-reflective theory, i.e., he substitutes a concept for a perception, and then treats this concept from the point of view of experience as though it were a perception. Nevertheless, he does not carry through consistently the implications of the scientific theory, according to which external existence is not immediately perceived and all perceptions are put together from fragmentary data whose subjective quality is never experienced. If Descartes had carried through his critique of prejudice, the wholeness of "ideas" would have been replaced by a theory according to which the mind constitutes sensibility through unifying functions of a kind similar to those elaborated by Kant. In this way the argument that even sensibility is a mode of thought would have been vindicated. As it is, the theory of ideas functions as a last stronghold of immediacy against the potential threat of the doubt to dissolve all reliance upon intuition; thus, although according to physiological optics, figure itself is inferred, metaphysically Descartes appropriates it in its appearance as "ideas."

Other considerations to the contrary notwithstanding, the treatment of thoughts as perceptions is an indissoluble aspect of the Cartesian mind doctrine. It creates a schizophrenia within the thinking thing of which Descartes seems to be but half aware. Descartes asserts that thoughts are perceptions partly in order retain the immediacy of intuition without which his rule of evidence would collapse, forcing him into a forthright discursive grounding of truth claims. On the other hand, res cogitans is in fact discursively mediated; it is, we claim, a conceptual result. The reinstitution of the immediacy of perception leaves him no way to acknowledge the mediation and, indeed, forces res cogitans back to the position of prephilosophic empirical consciousness, but in the awkward posture that denies some of its most undeniable immediate perceptions. Consequently, Descartes finds himself pressed to explain the unity of res cogitans: it cannot be the mediated concept, for that is incompatible with understanding as perception; nor can it be prephilosophic empirical consciousness which believes itself to perceive objects, not thoughts. Thus, Descartes is reduced to proposing that a thought is anything of which we are immediately conscious, or whatever we experience "in ourselves," as if that were a solution rather than the symptom of his problem.[50] Briefly, that problem is an attempt to institute empirical consciousness at the level of reflection.

THE DIREMPTION OF RES COGITANS

Related to these difficulties is another problem which the Sixth Meditation treats more directly, but still allusively. We saw that Descartes immediately transforms the objection to the pilot-ship model of mind-body unity into a question of "confused thoughts." The point is, however, that not merely thoughts are at stake. Perceptions are followed by "impulsions" to act. The "motor" aspect of prejudice is discussed in terms of whether the errors of "my nature" that sometimes occur, such as the dropsical person taking water, can be reconciled with a veracious God. The analysis leads him to contrast the teleology of perceptions of harm and benefit with the mechanical explanation of appetition. According to the latter, it is purely adventitious that pain in the foot produces in the brain the sensation of a pain in that location; the motions of the animal spirits might have produced sensation of its location anywhere; indeed, it might have produced "sensation of anything else whatever," although that arrangement would not have "contributed so well to the conservation of the body."[51] But such teleological explanations have been declared "extrinsic" to nature. The body obeys the same laws of nature in sickness and health, even as the broken clock and working clock do. That the sensation of pain is fol-

lowed by the retraction of the foot from the fire cannot be explained by appeal
to its end. To do so would introduce the soul as a cause of motion, since we
should be compelled to say that the *perception* of pain was the cause of the
motion. From a mechanical point of view, it is conceivable that a burn to the
foot might cause a pleasant sensation, which would nevertheless be followed
by its retraction from the fire; for perception plays no role in the sensory-motor
circuit of automata—perception is a gratuitous by-product. Harm and benefit
are purely subjective experiences, no different from color qualities or sounds.
Still, this experience "persuades" Descartes that there is a body which is his
own; it defines "having" and "possessing" something that is his. Furthermore,
the experience causes him to think of himself as an actor or doer, as exercising,
in the Cartesian terminology, "volition." From a mechanical point of view, his
doing is no less illusory than other experiences. Res cogitans is based on the assumption that the body is the only agent; it incorporates the assumption by
reducing mind to respective cognitive relations or modes of thought. Can action
be conceived as a mode of thought? Nominally, yes; for volition is one of the
two principal modes. There is certainly no doubt that Descartes conceives himself as an agent throughout the *Meditations,* and we have stressed that conception, for Descartes, is a "making" in the sense of techne. Despite this, action
is different not only from thinking, but from even conceiving oneself as an
agent. Insofar as he acts, Descartes is not res cogitans.* This is no problem,
however, since only the body-machine acts. But is even conceiving oneself as an
agent, or volition in general, a mode of thought, despite its name?

That it is doubtfully so is sufficiently clear from the equivocations on "understanding" that we observed in our discussion of the modes of thought. Thinking
as such is understanding, which we explicated as the cognition or conception
of the instruments of the mind with respect to their value for knowing the
world. Thereafter, understanding is duplicated in the division of the two
principal modes volition and understanding. Volition is not a mode of conception or perception; it "adds" something to perceptions. Although it may be
thought about, it is no less distinct from perception than is action. It is a
thought only in the trivial prephilosophic sense of something of which we are
conscious, something "within us." But this is not the required sense. The threat
to res cogitans is that the unity claimed for it, which alone makes it a true
concept of mind, seems to be wanting. The modes of thought are not uniform
in virtue of a single concept, but appear to be patched together from several

---

* Voluntary motion, as distinguished from perception of volition, is expressly excluded from
res cogitans (HR II, 52/AT VII, 161).

concepts, whose differences are in a fashion acknowledged—as in the division between modes or the recognition of "confused thoughts"—but whose consequences for res cogitans are not acknowledged.

The implications of these observations for the Cartesian mind doctrine are serious. We shall postpone to the Conclusion a discussion of them. At present our intention is to pursue the problem of res cogitans into the *Passions,* since it is the work devoted to mind-body unity, and therefore to an assessment of volition.

Cogito and Volo in the *Passions of the Soul*

For our purposes it is important to establish that the *Passions* were written as an explicit resumption of the problem with which the *Meditations* close. We have previously explained why it fits the description of the last and culminating part of philosophy. It speaks of the "whole nature of man," which was the topic of the Sixth Meditation; a treatise on the passions is appropriate to this topic because the passions were traditionally recognized as "common" to soul and body.[52] In the *Meditations* Descartes announces that man's greatest perfection is his will; the *Passions* culminate in his pronouncement that "nothing truly pertains" to man but the free "disposition of his will." The radical character of this assertion has not generally been appreciated; res cogitans, to which only thoughts pertain, seems to be altogether revised or even discarded. At the very least it seems to promise an attempt to reconcile the tension between cognition and volition.

Some passages of the work suggest a revision of res cogitans along Spinozist lines, which declares the essence of man to be appetitio. There are two reasons for rejecting these suggestions. The negative reason is that the project would require a thorough reworking of Descartes's *Meditations* doctrine on the relation between perception and judgment, whereas the *Passions* entirely avoid theoretical topics of this kind; they are rather single-mindedly oriented upon the body. The positive reason is that what reconciliation there is in the work between ego cogito and ego volo takes the path of an attempt to assimilate cognition to volition; indeed, this is the main thrust of the argument, which attempts to show how volition may be conceived as a "passion," or a modification of the human machine.

THE DOUBLE PERSPECTIVE OF THE *Passions*

Following scholastic usage, Descartes declares that action and passion are, like cause and effect, corelative concepts and that in any process, the action and passion are "always one and the same." * They are distinguishable only with respect to the different subjects to which the agency and passivity of the indivisible occurrence may be referred. But since no subject acts more immediately on the soul than the body to which it is joined, then "what in the soul is a passion is in the body commonly speaking an action." [53] A passion, therefore, is any perceived result of the action of the body on the soul. Not merely emotions, but sensations of all kinds and imaginations are also passions.

Since this definition of action and passion is scholastic, its significance is easily overlooked. The *Passions* are Descartes's one published treatise in which the physical theory of the genesis of sensations is worked out in detail.† The treatise bases its analysis of the passions on automatism, according to which, the soul is not a spiritual substance impressed by the body, as the wax is impressed by the seal; "soul" is nothing but my thinking, and for a passion to be "in" the soul means only that it is perceived. Consequently, to say that the action and passion are "one and the same" is to assert that the passion, or perception, is identical with the animal spirits that cause it.

The identity thesis is the axis of the argument of the treatise. It presupposes, as factually given, two different points of view—that of "body," or animal automatism, and that of "experience." The identity thesis can be asserted from neither of these points of view alone. They are united by a reflection—the argument of the *Passions*—which interprets the experience of consciousness in the light of automatism and vice versa. Above all, this binocular approach enables Descartes to correct the errors of prejudice that arise from experience of the passions, which is ignorant of their causes.[54] Furthermore, it is the "foundation" of the morality based on true physics because it corrects the "very considerable error" of the ancients, which is the belief that the soul moves the body.[55] It evidently follows that the will does not move the body. This thesis is the foundation both of the ethics of the *Passions* and of the endeavor to assimilate volition to cognition. The *Passions* therefore exactly parallel the procedure of the *Meditations* by attempting to combine a theory of the mind's relation to the world—here in its practical mode—with a theory of mind.

These strands of thought are brought together in paragraph 17, which specifies the nature of res cogitans in light of the first automatism analysis (§§ 4–16), whose purpose is to show what ought to be attributed to body:

---

* *Passions*, § 1. "Actio et passio ita conjunguntur realiter in uno motu seu mutatione, ut nec actio a passione, nec passio ab actione separabilis sit." From Suarez, quoted by Gilson, 1913a, 8.

† This procedure is sanctioned by traditional usage, which recognized the perishable part of the soul primarily with respect to the passions. It was also the topic whose treatment most readily posed the problem of the body's effects upon the soul.

Those [thoughts] which I call [the soul's] actions are all our volitions, because we find by experience that they proceed directly from our soul, and appear to depend on it alone; while on the other hand, we may usually term "passions" all those kinds of perceptions or forms of knowledge which are found in us, because it is often not our soul which makes them what they are, and because it always receives them from the things which are represented by them.

Passions are perceptions in general, which for the most part are generated by the body. Volitions are actions because they "appear" to depend on the soul as their cause, or better, they appear to be spontaneous activity. This division revises the customary classification of thoughts into the two principal modes. The emotions, appetites, and sensations are now classified as perceptions because they "depend" on the body. Volition is transformed from a genus into a species of thought that stands isolated as the exclusive activity of the soul. The reclassification shows that automatism is the instrument whereby "confused thoughts" are, at least nominally, resolved into the concept of res cogitans. It also shows that every perception, with the exception of those that are caused by the will, is evidence of the mind's dependency on the body. What then of the soul's "actions"? The reason adduced for classifying volitions as actions is "experience." But as the *Passions* repeatedly show, experience is defective; for example, it "relates" emotions to the soul as their cause, although the physicist relates them to the body.[56] Since automatism must as a matter of course relate the apparent actions of the soul to the body as well, Descartes eventually replaces the distinction between the free and non-free will, understood with respect to causal genesis, by the distinction between "strong" and "weak" will.[57] In the present context, however, he follows a different approach. Although volitions are actions, nevertheless we cannot will without perceiving that we do; and "because this perception and this will are really one and the same thing, the nobler always supplies the denomination, and thus we do not customarily call it a passion, but only an action."[58] This statement is a decisive proof of the persistence of the empirical res cogitans in the *Passions,* as well as an index of the path to reconciliation of res cogitans with experience of the action of the will. Volition, like external sensation, may be regarded both as an appearance for me, i.e., as a perception, and in the specific quality of the sensation or experience, i.e., as an action or as an externally existing object. To regard volition as a perception is the necessary point of departure for its assimilation to res cogitans. However, Descartes overcomes the incongruities that arise from this strategy by admitting the "action" of the will as an appearance. Its character as appearance is constituted by the experience of the efficacy of the will, corrected by the explanation, based on automatism, of the causal connections that are posited by experience but which it does not know. The reconciliation of thinking with willing occurs when experienced "activity" is perceived or understood as a function of passion, in the broad and narrow sense of the word. That conception is ostensibly achieved through the argument of the *Passions* which explains the dependency of the will on the passions, hence, on the body (the moment of determinism) and also the appearance of freedom, or the ethical "absolute dominion" of the will over the passions.

PASSIONS AND VOLITION

Although animal spirits are the immediate cause of all the passions, they are experienced as if provoked by things perceived, with respect to the ways in which they may be advantageous or harmful. According to the Cartesian analysis which attributes all motive power to the body, their function is not to move the body but merely to "incite" or "dispose" the soul to "will" those motions that the animal spirits impart to the body.[59] They fulfill this function because the passions are "knowledge" of a certain kind; they are "representations" of harm and benefit that may befall the soul insofar as it is attached to the body.[60]

At the basis of all the passions are pleasure and pain as the fundamental representations of good and evil. The latter are not passions but sensations, which are "instituted by nature as testimony to [the] good disposition and [of the body], representing that to the soul as a good pertaining to it . . . thus exciting joy in it." [61] Pain represents to the soul the bad disposition of the body and its weakness in not being able to resist the cause. Consequently, we take pleasure in, or enjoy, all those representations that signify the condition of our strength.[62] This analysis of pleasure and pain is a synthesis of Stoic and Epicurean notions. It is Stoic in its assertion that the first impulse of the soul is toward self-preservation. Pleasure and pain are not goods in themselves, but represent something (strength or power) beyond themselves. On the other hand, the joy of the representation of well-being follows so closely upon pleasure that "commonly no distinction between them is made." The soul takes pleasure in its strength.*

The predominance of the Stoic element in Descartes's understanding of good

---

* Descartes believed that his ethics incorporated the central teachings of the Stoics, Epicureans, and Aristotelians (AT IV, 275). The tug of war in Descartes's thought between the pleasant and the good is definitive for his ethics.

and evil is apparent from the role he ascribes to the will. When some pleasure is perceived, the soul "joins itself" to that thing "willingly," not merely because or insofar as it is pleasant, but because it is represented as being *my own*. The sequence Descartes imagines to exist between pleasure and volition is consequently rather complex. Pleasure represents well-being or strength to the soul, the apprehension of which causes the emotion of love, which disposes the soul to possess the pleasant thing as its own. To will the good, then, is in all cases to will the possession of what "belongs" to oneself.* What is at issue in the reconciliation of ego cogito and ego volo is that the I who wills "consents" to a representation as its own—it is the I who is a "possessor." The thinking ego, however, knows thoughts as representations for me. Ego cogito therefore requires a contemplative stance toward the whole range of willing, which extends downward to the first impulses of nature and upward to what the scholastics call "rational will."

The mediating step between this point in the exposition and generosity, as the culminating position, is an analysis of the "enslavement" or "irresolution" to which the will is reduced by the strife that exists in the soul. Descartes rejects the traditional analysis of this strife as a struggle between the higher and lower faculties, e.g., between reason and passion, or as an opposition between the concupiscent and irascible parts of the soul. His ground is the unity of res cogitans: that which senses is also rational, and all appetition is also volition.[63] The basis of the strife is not the soul at all, but contrary movements that the pineal gland is able to excite, e.g., when it disposes the body both to flee from danger and to halt to combat it. The contrary corporeal movements translate into an irresolute condition of will because they excite contrary passions (such as fear and shame) that dispose the will to consent to incompatible representations of what is good, i.e., its own. In Stoic terminology, there arises a conflict between the will to get and the will to avoid. The remedy for this condition, which for Descartes is the basis for all ethical evil, is the achievement of harmony between conduct and conviction. It is achieved by "firm and determinate judgments respecting knowledge of good and evil" which provides the "proper arms" and "firm foundation" of virtue.

In order to distinguish good from bad foundations, or true knowledge of

---

* From the correspondence we know that Descartes had been reading the *Symposium* during the time that he composed the ethics; the description of one's own as his "other half" (*Passions,* §§ 82, 83, 90) is evidently taken from the speech of Aristophanes, who certainly does not believe that the good is virtue, which in turn is knowledge. Descartes's oscillation on this question is part of the unresolved antitheses of his ethics.

good and evil from undependable and unreliable knowledge, Descartes introduces a distinction between the judgments of reason and of the passions. If whatever excites pleasure, love, and joy were never bad for us, the ethical good would be to follow these passions, without regard to knowledge.[64] But since reflective experience teaches the contrary, the wise man will appraise the value of each thing according to the judgment of reason, and he will "consent" only to those goods, whether they be pleasures or the joys of the soul, that pass the muster of reason's judgment. Virtue, we may almost say, is knowledge, and vice ignorance.*

Almost, but not quite. In order to explain how the judgments of reason translate into control of the passions and the corporeal movements that they accompany, Descartes introduces the principle upon which, as he says, his psychophysical analysis rests. Neither will nor reason have any power to move the body directly nor to subdue passions that are strongly aroused.† But, since each thought and each passion is connected with some motion of the gland, which in turn controls the movements of the body; and since the association between thoughts is also a concurrence of gland motions, which control body movement, the passions can be mastered by conditioning that establishes the desired associations among thoughts.[65] Naturally strong souls condition themselves by forming "firm and determinate judgments," whereas weak souls can be conditioned by the right upbringing. In either case, what liberates the will from its dependency on the passions is not the exercise of an efficacious will, but the chaining of associations. Thus, the principle of association shows how the most extreme dependency of the soul on the body is compatible with the "absolute dominion" of the will over the passions.

The psychophysical principle of association holds a crucial place in the reconciliation of volition with cognition. In effect, it generates a concept of will ostensibly compatible with automatism by redefining the meaning of "free will." The will's bondage is not specifically its incapacity to control the passions,

---

* *Passions,* §§ 144, 160, 212, 28; HR I, 217/AT IX-2, 22; AT IV, 86, 284; AT V, 83–84. As Röd has seen very well (1964, 190–92), the texts cited here show that virtue, and the sovereign good, are nothing but the resolution to follow reason in all things, which gives the ethical sense of generosity as portrayed in the *Passions* and by the first rule of the provisional morality. Krüger's analysis runs in the same direction, although he was the first to discern the connection between theory and practice as united in generosity, and the only commentator who has expounded it in a convincing fashion (Krüger, 1933, 250–60).

† The decisive texts for the problem of free will vs. determinism in the *Passions* are §§ 41 and 44. In the former, the "whole action of the soul" is said to consist in the power of the will to move the pineal gland, solely because it wills something. In the latter, this volition is likened to the power of volition to enlarge the pupil of the eye when it wishes to view something at a distance.

but the irresolution that arises from its "consenting" to contrary passions; conversely, the freedom of the will is not specifically its efficacy, but its harmony with itself. The general solution of how that harmony is achieved, that is, precisely what chaining of associated thoughts renders the will firm and resolute in its judgments, is determined by the problem to be surmounted. The bondage of the will is a function of its assent to a multitude of contrary passions as contrary representations of good and evil. What is required, therefore, is a single representation of good and evil that controls the will's consent to the goods and evils represented by all the particular passions. That representation is the passion of generosity.

GENEROSITY AS PASSIVE ACTION

The precedence of generosity over the other passions presupposes that it represents true knowledge of good and evil, because only the truth is fixed and unwavering. But generosity is itself a species of wonder and its precedence must be deduced from the precedence of wonder over the other passions. The passions generally dispose the will to consent to something represented as good or evil, i.e., harmful or beneficial to ourselves; however, wonder is an exception to this rule, for in this state we "consider with attention objects which seem . . . rare and extraordinary," without regard to the harm or benefit they may bestow.[66] It is the one passion that precedes "consent"; hence, it is the "objective" passion. In this respect Descartes follows the traditional appreciation of wonder as the beginning of knowledge.[67] The immediate effects of wonder are the most subjective passions, esteem and disdain, according to whether it is the "greatness" or "smallness" (i.e., the strength and nobility or their opposites) of the object at which we wonder. One of the principal objects of wonder is the soul itself, and in this way we arrive at self-esteem based on true knowledge. Such self-esteem is generosity understood as consciousness that one's worth consists entirely in the good use that one makes of the only thing that truly pertains to oneself—free will.[68] Self-esteem for any other reason—bodily condition, wealth, honors, or whatever—is a misrecognition of the nature of the soul which therefore leads to vice. But why is that the case? To esteem oneself for anything but his will means that the will in such a case consents to a representation of a good other than the will itself. Consequently, the will embraces as its own something other than itself—wealth, health, honors, etc. But none of these things are absolutely within our power, since circumstances may deprive us of them. The will is thus deprived of what it falsely believes is its own, which renders the soul bitter and full of remorse. Similarly, pursuit of these goods necessarily leads to affirming contrary things as good, which causes repentance and irresolution. Bad conscience and the bondage of the will owing to its embracing as its own things other than itself are the evidence that the only thing completely within our power, hence the only thing that is truly our own, and thus the only thing that truly pertains to oneself, is the will. Accordingly, the foundation of virtue is to will the will, to embrace it as the only enduring, entirely reliable, and solid good. The "firm and constant resolution to use [the will] well" is thus the determination of the generous soul to consent to nothing that reason does not approve, and those external goods which reason approves should be willed only in light of the universal necessity by which we should regulate our desires.

The effect of generosity is to turn the will back upon itself both ethically and epistemologically, and it is the coincidence of these two reflections which guarantees virtue as knowledge, thereby achieving that reconciliation between thinking and willing of which the Cartesian principle is capable. The coincidence of virtue with knowledge depends upon the coincidence of a power strong enough to control all other passions with the power that enables us to recognize the true nature of the human good. It is the self-assertion of the will which is also the truth of the will. The strength or resolution of this self-assertion depends, as we saw, upon nature's collaboration in producing a strong soul. Knowledge of nature's collaboration, as given in the theory of automatism, enables us to grasp volition as a passion in the twofold sense of a powerful agitation of the soul and as a perception, specifically, as an appearance for me. Volition is a rare and extraordinary appearance, compared with the homogeneity of nature, that causes us to perceive it with wonder: the "action" of the soul embracing the will as its own coincidence with the perception of volition as truly as its own.

The Heterogeneity of Thinking and Willing

In the *Passions,* perhaps more than in any other writing, the loose ends and incommensurables of Cartesian philosophy affect the sense and direction of the work. In presenting the foregoing interpretation, an effort has been made to bring out the argument which has the greatest internal consistency and which exhibits the most intimate connection with the remainder of the system. But that argument fails both because of internal inconsistencies and errors of fact, and because of contrary tendencies in the *Passions.*

At stake in the *Passions* is the adequacy of the theory of mind as res cogitans and ultimately the success of the plan to unite a scientific epistemology with a theory of mind. The problem of that program, as articulated in the Sixth Meditation, is how prejudice or confused thoughts may be integrated with res cogitans. The *Passions* restrict attention to two modes of prejudice, passions and volitions in the narrow sense of those terms, and attempt to show that they may be assimilated to res cogitans. The failure to assimilate the passions obtrudes just at the point at which Descartes reasserts the res cogitans doctrine against the traditional view that the soul is composed of parts that are related in a hierarchical structure. There is no strife within the soul, he claims, because it is a unity. Yet Descartes reintroduces this strife by his distinction between reason and passion as sources of opposed representations of good and evil. The basis of the distinctions as he draws it is that the representations of the passions are immediate judgments that arise from the body, whereas the judgments of reason are reflective. But this suffices to establish a distinction of "parts" in the soul; indeed, the traditional distinction is based on just such evidence. Finally, Descartes even recognizes that the rational "part" is higher than the passions, since the judgments of reason are preferable to the passions because they correct their errors. Descartes even attempts to show, by appeal to the theory of association, that reason can achieve sovereign dominion over the passions. Having admitted this, it is not convincing to appeal to perception as the unity common to reason and passion. Even if the theory of association successfully proved that all operations of the soul are mechanical, reason and passion would remain distinguishable, even as Descartes distinguishes them when he refuses to assign any positive role to passion in his methodological writings.

The great difficulty with the Cartesian concept of volition is its want of unity. The notion of willing as embracing something "as one's own," as his "other half," is derived from appetition, in particular, love. But volition is distinct from appetition, as is illustrated by Descartes's incongruous and probably ironical remark that the foetus embraces its nutriment by "free will." [69] Similarly, common volitions such as shifting the eyes or imagining and recollecting hardly have anything about them that resembles the idea of possession, although they too are said to be volitions. [70] And despite Descartes's extremely corporeal orientation toward volition, the generous man conceives his will in abstraction from his body; he is, as it were, unaware that body "pertains" to himself. This is no exaggeration. A highly developed Stoic line is evident throughout the treatment of generosity; it leads him to "esteem very little" all those things that can be "taken away" even though the passions and appetites may "will" them with great energy. [71] This tendency to homogenize and confuse differences, to describe the higher in terms of the lower, and vice versa, issues from Descartes's attempt to replace the classical notion of the soul as a hierarchy of parts by a unitary concept in which the principal attribute is common to all the modes. They are difficulties that spring directly from the interpretation of the soul as a thinking thing.

The difficulties are especially acute in the concept of the generous soul. Generosity is the passion that makes us conscious of our worth as consisting exclusively in willing; but it is also the resoluteness of the will. The action and the passion are "one and the same thing." Despite his heroic effort to detach the experience of activity from the prejudiced attribution of causal efficacy to the will, thus conceiving the activity as appearance, it remains true that the appearance persists, even as we continue to sense the pain as in the foot, despite automatism. To call it a passion in the equivocal sense of a perception and an emotion merely thrusts the problem back to the question of the compatibility of emotions with the concept of thoughts. Descartes certainly wants to retain the appearance as such, and to anchor in it the appetitive phenomena of possession. But he is able to give this move a semblance of plausibility only by sublimating appetition into an essentially Stoic conception of volition. It is amazing that Descartes thought he could achieve the reconciliation of thinking and willing by embracing will as an appearance. His philosophy of mind actually is more suited to a rejection of the will because it is an appearance, along the lines of a Buddhist annihilation of the will. The status of the problem of the will is parallel to belief in the external existence of sense objects. However thoroughly that belief may be dissected, we nevertheless see the chair in the corner when we open our eyes. No matter how you judge that perception, there is only one way to perceive it. Similarly, there is only one way in which something can be willed, and that is to will it; perception is no substitute. The aliquid amplius that Descartes "adds" to his ideas remains as ineluctably heterogeneous to thinking as the pain in the foot or the chair in the corner. The idealist premise of res cogitans, hence res cogitans itself, founders on the reef of prejudiced sensibility.

7 Conclusion: Some Incommensurables of Cartesian Philosophy

The fountainhead of Cartesian rationalism is a certain willfulness manifest by the "resolution" to attain absolute and immutable certitude. Since this objective borrows its plausibility from the indubitability of mathematics, Descartes framed a program to extend mathematical evidence to all of philosophy. The result is a perpetual struggle, or "irresolution," within Cartesian philosophy between the demand for certitude and the intractability of the subject matter. We will conclude this study by outlining some of the major perturbations produced by this clash.

Descartes's enduring problem is to reconcile the purported sufficiency of the intuitive evidence of clear ideas with the acknowledged need for discursive reflection. The problem makes its first appearance with the theory of simple natures. If there are intuitions of simples at all, that they are simple must be recognizable from the intuition. If the simples are also known to be exhaustive, the world is apprehended *sub specie aeternitatis;* the menial task of discursive reason is to sort out the simples from the ambiguities of experience. Juxtaposed with the purported intuitive apprehension of simples is a theory or discursive argument to the effect that the existence of simples can be inferred from the indubitability of mathematics, and that the simples must be just mind and body. The tension between these points of view is signaled by the inconsistency between the claim that simples can be known "without taking pains" or "without meditation," and the discursive argument of the methodological and metaphysical foundations, which acknowledges the elusiveness of simples. We do not know extension by a single act of "mental vision"; it must be unpacked by an argument meant to prove that such unlikely things as motion and number are "modes" not "really" distinct from extension. The very need for the discursive argument casts doubt upon his claim that we can have an intuition of thought and extension as simples. That Descartes required a *theory* of simple natures at all proves that his evidence for them was not intuition, as the theory claims, but the theoretical reasoning that posited simples. But if simples are made known by reasoning, then they cannot be simple to intuition.

The tension between the adequacy and insufficiency of intuition dominates the foundational problem. The difficulty posed by the use of hypothesis in science especially merits notice. Descartes always stresses that certitude in physics requires a deduction from irrevisable first causes or principles. His conviction that he knew those causes never wavered. But he recognized the inductive hiatus created by the introduction of hypothetical causes, since deduced effects do not prove the hypothesis. His last word on the subject combines this acknowledgment with an attempt to escape its consequences: while we cannot infer to the truth of isolated hypotheses, still, when one considers that so many effects are deduced with mathematical rigor, we can only deem God a deceiver if they are not true.[1] The suggestion is that we substitute one breathtaking leap for many isolated inductions. Just here, where he should have doubted, his assurance of the coincidence of certainty and truth asserts itself. The problem is not, as he portrays it, a question regarding certainties whose falsity is unknowable, as if an omnipotent God might deceive us, but whether reason is in fact immutable. Descartes could not acknowledge the mutability of reason without admitting that his first principles were revisable and hypothetical. Although the work of Galileo and Kepler, not to mention his own scientific studies, provided Descartes with examples of science that were both hypothetical in principle and mathematical in demonstration, he resisted the suggestion that science in its entirety might be of that character. His position on the Copernican theory, which he appears to have consistently conceived as a clash between reason and faith, indicates that he never attained a clear concept of the profound methodological insight latent in the ecclesiastical position. We say he resisted the insight because to have embraced it would have cost him the dogmatism of simple natures, to which he was firmly committed.

The foundational endeavor is meant to establish that reason is immutable and its principles irrevisable. The contrary view implies that the order of knowledge is estranged from the order of things; according to an authoritative current interpretation, the order of things is approached by successive approximation, whose criterion of progress is the coherence of theory with a growing body of experimental data. Descartes's conception of the relation between these two orders is quite different. The theory of simple natures permanently fixes the order of cognition and the order of nature. The problem of science is to surmount the confused thought of prejudice. For this reason he found it plausible to argue that the science could be placed on an unshakable foundation by demonstrating that there is a point of intersection—corporeal ideas—between the two orders. The argument is of course circular—the true Cartesian circle,—since it purports to show that thought and extension exhaust reality by first assuming these principles. But the circle accurately reflects the basic dilemma of the foundational search for certainty, for the circle provides a certain coherence and completeness to a system whose foundation otherwise rests exclusively upon intuition.

As has been discussed, there are inconsistencies produced in res cogitans by the contrary claims of intuition and discursive reason. Although res cogitans is mediated by the dualist physical theories, Descartes wavers between incorporating the mediation into res cogitans, in which case it is a concept, and taking "I think" as an unmediated intuition. This uncertainty merely continues the ambiguity regarding simple natures. When mediation is acknowledged, res cogitans is a product, a concept; when refused, it deteriorates into a perception. A clear grasp of the mediation would probably have led Descartes to recognize the dependency of intuition upon discursive argument, which would have led in turn to recognition of the revisability of first principles and to the conclusion that thinking mediates being in a stronger sense than he is prepared to acknowledge. Instead, he retreats into the immediate certainty of prephilosophic consciousness, and thereby commits himself to the impossible attempt to restore immediacy at the level of reflection, via the distinction between real and apparent clear ideas. Cartesian consciousness therefore cannot be said to be one thing; it oscillates between philosophical self-consciousness aware of its mediation, and scientific empirical consciousness that tends, in Descartes's expositions, to degenerate to the immediacy of prephilosophic consciousness. The oscillation is the clearest index of Descartes's failure to find a satisfactory interpretation of the role of experience in science.

The attempt to restore the intuitive immediacy of clear and distinct ideas inspires the thesis that to think is to perceive. Mind is ostensibly known by a "non-reflexive act" such that self-consciousness is fully given in any cognition. The homogeneity and concurrence of consciousness of self and of objects reduces the methodological-metaphysical reflection to the "single level of reason" proper to mathematical physics. Such a unitary science is the necessary condition for the absolute certainty of an introspective reflection that would found science. It is also needed to maintain the parallelism between modes of thought and extension presupposed by the intersection, in corporeal ideas, of thought and extension. But the interpretation of thoughts as perceptions exacts a heavy price. Perceptions are passive-adventitious, whereas conception is active-factitious. Although the *Meditations* acknowledge this difference, Descartes is unable to find a concept that embraces whatever is common to both while preserving their difference. The term "idea," which was meant to answer this purpose, is a universal equivocation that has no meaning distinct from the properties of the particular modes of thought to which it is applied. The magnitude of Descartes's problem is indicated by the distinction between understanding and volition, which completely separates conception from activity by assigning all activity to the will. It is therefore not surprising that the *Meditations* do not adequately incorporate the methodological insight that thinking is active-productive techne.

The outstanding example of methodological activity in the *Meditations* is the attempt to overcome the adventitiousness of prejudice by the effort of thought. But the intuitive-perceptive criterion asserts itself even here. Prejudice is quarantined by declaring that it is only apparently clear and distinct; the appearance is said to arise owing to unnoticed willfull additions to ideas. Therefore prejudice, which to all appearances is surely adventitious, according to Descartes's theory is active-constructive, whereas conception, which to all appearances is surely factitious, according to the theory is adventitious. Only by this total reversal of experienced thought can Descartes save the primacy of intuition as a sufficient criterion. The actual deed of the *Meditations,* however, diverges from this theory. Self-consciousness distinguishes itself from consciousness of objects by reflecting upon the value of perceptions for knowledge of the world. The appraisal metamorphoses mere perceptions into differentiated ways of cognizing objects, with the result that all thinking, as distinguished from prephilosophic perceiving, is active-constructive cognition. From this perspective, intuition is only the facility of thought that arises from the institution of the scientific capacity; qua immediate certainty it does not differ at all from the capacity of prejudice. Descartes implicitly acknowledges this important point when he grounds the certitude of the Cogito upon the natural tendency of thought.

The unresolved conflict between thought as perception and conception pulls Cartesian philosophy in opposite metaphysical directions, toward Aristotle and toward German Idealism. Throughout this essay we have emphasized Descartes's agreement with Aristotle that philosophy attempts to know things exactly as they are. But the ambiguities of his position invite a Kantian interpretation along the following lines.[2] Descartes's methodological beginning signifies rejection of the ontological orientation that is intent upon knowing the world as it is; instead, one is content with an epistemological orientation whose criterion is certitude commensurate with the subjective conditions of knowledge. The doctrine of the creation of the eternal truths is the metaphysical correlate of the methodological foundation. God might have created a world whose principle is not extension, a world, therefore, unknowable to reason. The creating God, a correlate of the creating mind, functions as a limiting concept that enables reason to grasp the limits of knowledge with complete clarity; it accordingly enables us to embrace with equanimity the necessities of reason even though they are unfounded in the things themselves. We have rejected this interpretation because Descartes associates the creating God with the anti-science of the biblical God, both of which are incompatible with the veracious God. It is nevertheless true that the ambiguities of the Cartesian foundation are truly such as to lead to the transformation of the veracious God or creating God into an unknowable *Ding an Sich* and the associated distinction between phenomenon and noumenon.

Owing to his attempt to conceive man as a unitary thinking thing, Descartes's practical philosophy reproduces many of the problems of theoretical philosophy. The "perfection" of morality is ambiguous between the good as the pleasant and the self-admiration of generosity. It can hardly be said that Descartes successfully reconciled the Stoic and Epicurean strands of his thought. One line of argument reduces good and evil to pleasure and pain; pleasure is by nature good. The other attributes all goodness to the honorable will that has heroically subdued the passions and elevated itself beyond circumstances outside the power of the will to control. But we have no power not to take pleasure in the pleasant, nor is pleasure-taking a reason for self-esteem. The strife between these two goods reflects the competing claims of passive perception and active construction. Its far-reaching implications become apparent only when the sage master of the passions is combined with the sage master of nature. For him, nature is not good, but is the main impediment to the autonomy of will or reason, which alone is good. Mechanical nature is neutral in the distinction between good and evil. Its moral significance is only that it presents the sage technician the greatest opportunty for the exercise of his autonomous power, from which self-admiration springs. Mere pleasure-taking is noncognitive, therefore non-human —bovine. To believe, as Descartes apparently did, that the pleasure of generosity reconciles these two points of view is analogous to his belief that perception is common to all thoughts: only the name is common. Pleasure is due entirely to nature, while the joy of generosity is due entirely to our own efforts. The same ambiguity is present in the perfection that Descartes projects into the future. It is unclear whether the final purpose of the mastery of nature is a calculus of pleasures based on the technical possibility of fulfilling all desires, or the achievement of autonomy. Descartes's failure to write a political philosophy may be due in part to this problem. Perhaps the solution is a brave new world of animal contentment, instituted and maintained by technical masters whose existence is creative; but it is difficult to imagine why the masters should admire their handiwork.

The conflict between pleasure and the good will is subsumable under the more general inconsistency between freedom and necessity. Descartes intensified this legacy from Stoicism and spread its paradoxes to all parts of philosophy. Everywhere we find the objectivity of science in collision with the subjectivity of thinking. Man is a reflex automaton, yet a proud, ambitious automaton who rebels against necessity—a spiritual automaton. Matter is unaffected by thought, yet man would bend nature to his will. He is yoked to the serfdom of passive perception, but he is also the sovereign knowing subject. He is an insignificant part of nature, yet a point outside it. He yearns for security, but would realize it by audacious and hazardous enterprises. He seeks to master the passions, yet his whole good is to enjoy them. These and other oppositions grow from Cartesian dualism. As is proper for the commentator, I have sought throughout this study to argue the coherence of the Cartesian principle. But I must also acknowledge that the greatness of Descartes's philosophy is due less to the problems it solves or to the certainties it produces than to the depth of its contradictions. Their depth may be appreciated by observing that although nearly every significant thinker of the past century was a critic of dualism, none surmounted it. So long as our concept of nature is mechanical, it is improbable that it can be surmounted. Dualism seems to both necessary and impossible: a skeptical predicament. But there is no bar to conceiving that predicament in the Socratic manner, as an occasion to philosophize.

Appendix A: The Copernican Theory

From the correspondence with Mersenne between November 1633 and April 1634, the following points are clear: Descartes not only believed the Copernican theory, but thought if it were false then the "foundations" of his philosophy would be destroyed; he feared that he would suffer Galileo's fate if he espoused the theory; and he was aware that the ruling of the Inquisition against the theory was not de fide (AT I, 270–71, 281–82, 285, 288). From this period until the publication of the *Principles* (1644) there is no writing in which a change of mind is announced. On the contrary, he wrote to Mersenne in 1640, "nothing prevented me up to now from publishing my philosophy, except the interdiction of the motion of the earth, from which I do not know how to separate it" (AT III, 258–59). The argument that Descartes abandoned the Copernican theory must therefore be drawn entirely from the *Principles* and one letter written after the *Principles*.

Descartes offers his theory of planetary motion as an alternative to those of Copernicus and Tycho. Believing the movement of the earth absurd and contrary to common sense, Tycho, Descartes explains, propounded an explanation according to which the sun and fixed stars rotate about the earth (*Prin*. III, § 18). But if his theory is thought through, one comes to the conclusion that Tycho attributes less movement to the earth "in words," but more "in effect" than did Copernicus, because the reasons he attributes motion to the heavens and rest to the earth are "imaginary," whereas the reason for which he ought, on his own theory, attribute motion to the earth is "evident and certain" (*Prin*. III, §§ 18, 38). Considered as hypotheses, the theories of the two do not differ at all (*Prin*. III, §§ 17, 19). (The reason Tycho gave for his dissatisfaction with the Copernican theory—the absence of an observed parallax for the fixed stars —is not mentioned by Descartes.)

Descartes undertakes to "deny the motion of the earth more carefully than Copernicus, and more truthfully than Tycho" (*Prin*. III, § 19). The essentials of the theory are easily stated. He assumes a heliocentric system in which the planets, including the earth, rotate about the sun. The denial of the earth's motion is premised upon a particular explanation of this motion. The planets are entrained in vortexes that provide them motive force (*Prin*. III, §§ 26, 28). The planets are like vessels in a river, or passengers in the vessel, who are at rest with respect to the water or the vessel, respectively (*Prin*. III, § 29). This relative rest is the whole meaning of Descartes's "careful" denial of the earth's motion; the account itself is identical to that offered in *The World* (AT XI, 56–72).

In appraising this question, bear in mind the condemned opinion that Descartes allegedly shuns in his account: *Terra non est centrum mundi, nec immobilis, sed secundum se totam movetur, etiam motu diurno.* Descartes does not even try to hide the evident fact that his theory dislodges the earth from the center of the universe; on the contrary, he expressly asserts it (*Prin*. III, § 40). Moreover, he forthrightly styles the belief that the earth does not move a "prejudice" of childhood (*Prin*. I, § 71; III, § 29); and in many passages he unobtrusively attributes motion to the earth (*Prin*. III, §§ 33, 37, 40, 41, 150, 151) or asserts that all bodies whatever move: "But if we think that in the whole universe there is not any point that is truly immobile (and it will be recognized in what follows that this admits of *demonstration*) we conclude that there is no location of anything in the world which is *firm* and *fixed*, except that we fix it in our thought" (*Prin*. II, § 13; see also *Prin*. II, §§ 25, 27, 32).

Statements of this kind were apt to suggest to Descartes's readers that he was somewhat disingenuous in denying the earth's motion. A correspondent in fact raised this question, to which Descartes responded:

> I believe that at first one will judge that it is only in words that I deny [the earth's motion], in order to avoid censure, since I retain the system of Copernicus. But when one examines my reasons, I am sure that he will find them serious and solid, and that they show clearly that it is necessary rather to say that the earth moves, in following the system of Tycho, than in following Copernicus, explicated in my way. For if one is not permitted to follow either of these two, it is necessary to return to Ptolemy, to which I do not believe that the Church has ever obliged us, seeing that it is contrary to experience. And all the passages of Scripture which are against the movement of the earth do not regard the system of the world at all, for it is only a way of speaking. I entirely satisfy these passages when I prove, as I have, that to speak properly, it is necessary to say that the earth does not move, in following the system I expound (AT V, 550).

The gist of this remark is that it is necessary only to satisfy the Scriptural passages that appear to deny the motion of the earth, which can be done simply by denying its motion "in words." But Scripture does not regard the system of the world at all; it merely speaks in terms commonly understandable in order to accommodate the capacities of the "simple and the ignorant," as when it attributes passions and members to God, although he is incorporeal (AT III, 23, 502; V, 169). To set aside the Copernican theory on such grounds is to commit the double error of misunderstanding Scripture and missing the scientific truth.

Descartes's earliest biographer, Baillet, wrote that Descartes required the example of Catholic mathematicians and scientists "whom the decree of the Inquisition did not cause so much fear as him" before he resolved to publish his cosmology (*La Vie de Monsieur Des-Cartes,* I, 252). And in the same place he continues:

> But M. Descartes saw later in Liège a manifesto or report, published on Sept. 20, 1633, on the occasion of the condemnation of Galileo, in which was written: "Although [Galileo] simulated that [he presented the Copernican theory] only as an hypothesis"; so he then judged that, despite the permission of 1620, the intention of the gentlemen of the Inquisition was to forbid the use of this hypothesis in astronomy, and he changed his resolution in regard to these ecclesiastics.

Descartes's modern biographer and editor, Charles Adam, was so impressed by Descartes's expressions of fear of the consequences of Galileo's condemnation that he claims that Descartes invented his metaphysics as a "camouflage" for his system, with the result that it is impossible to say what the system really is (AT XII, 177f.).

For discussions of this question, see Milhaud, 1921, 2–21; Laporte, 1945, 391–404; Röd, 1964, 143–54.

Appendix B: Klaus Oehler on Ancient and Modern Philosophical Self-Consciousness

In *Die Lehre vom noetischen und dianoetischen Denken bei Platon und Aristoteles,* Oehler expounds the difference between ancient and modern self-consciousness by means of a thorough study of the concept of thinking in Plato and Aristotle. As the natural complement to the present work, it deserves comment.

It is characteristic of moderns to begin philosophy by a reflection upon thinking that constitutes self-consciousness as sovereign and self-sufficient vis-à-vis the world. Self-consciousness is self-sufficient because it can know itself independently of the world; it is sovereign because its measure of truth is a design that it projects upon the world (pp. 1–2, 105, 260). The classical reflection upon thinking begins with things and is always world-related; thinking is grasped from the perspective of its dependence on ontologically prior objects. Plato in particular took notice of the path that modern philosophy was to make its highway, but rejected it as absurd. The difference between ancients and moderns, it may be said, is the difference between realism and idealism. The so-called Platonic idealism asserts only the priority of noetic entities to sense phenomena; it is not the modern view that the forms of consciousness are prior to the world (pp. 112, 258, 260).

Oehler's contrast is most forceful where Kant and his successors are taken as the paradigm of modern philosophy. But even allowing the paradigm, our study suggests that the contrast underestimates the importance of consciousness and the activity of thought to antiquity, even as it neglects the role that the passivity of thinking plays in modern thought. Given Oehler's premises, it is natural to surmise that ancient skepticism is the closest point of contact between ancients and moderns, for it might seem that skepticism achieves the turn from world to self that becomes the modern principle. Oehler thinks this not the case. Skepticism does not depart from the universal recognition, in antiquity, of the reality of objects (*Ansichsein des Seienden*). "It does not attain the degree of modern skeptical radicality, recognizing only what is objectified by consciousness, but rather doubts only the knowability of objects whose existence it does not dispute" (p. 104). If the Protagorean position, as dissected in the *Theaetetus,* leads to "absolute subjectivism," it is certain that Protagoras did not draw these conclusions himself and that Plato, who did, rejected them as absurd (p. 104, n.). The characteristic modern denial of the independent reality of the world is therefore known to antiquity, but only as an impossible consequence of sophist doctrine.[1] Elsewhere in the study, however, a different evaluation of the sophists appears. Their challenge to the unreflective, self-evident stance of the ancient physicists toward the external world shattered naive confidence in the possibility of objective knowledge, and precipitated awareness of the knowing subject; the "relativist" and "subjectivist" conclusions that Socrates drew from sophist doctrine became for him fundamental to the problematic of knowledge (p. 259). Socrates' close, if negative, approximation to the modern position suggests that an investigation of the post-Socratic Skeptics would be fruitful. Oehler unfortunately does not carry his study that far. Still, we may examine skeptical doctrine in the light of his assertions.

According to Sextus Empiricus, the skeptical criterion of existence (*hyparxis*) is the phenomenon, understood as an impression (*phantasia pathetike*); the dispute with the dogmatists is whether phenomena or impressions suffice for knowledge of their cause (the hypokeimenon).[2] Skepticism therefore begins with the thesis that we have immediate knowledge of impressions or thoughts only, and its negative conclusion is that impressions do not suffice for knowledge of the cause. But if impressions or phenomena are the criteria of existence, the negative conclusion asserts that there is no evidence for the existence of the independent external world (hypokeimenon). This position is difficult to distinguish from denial of the *Ansichsein des Seienden,* which Oehler attributes exclusively to modern thought, nor is it easy to find the difference between Kant's *Ding an Sich* and the skeptical hypokeimenon. Both the Skeptics and Kant take impressions as passively received by the subject, thereby implying an independent external world; but it was the modern Kant, not the ancient Skeptics, who tried to prove its existence. Modern skepticism reaches its term in doubt of the external world, causal connection, and the unity of mind. Ancient skepticism went further down the road to doubt even the apprehensibility of extension and of the mind, the validity of logic and every positive science, including ethics. A skepticism more radical than the ancient version is inconceivable, since it undertakes to doubt every dogmatic assertion; that there is none more radical in execution can be ascertained by comparing the ancients with the modern rivals.

We showed previously that the Skeptics, no less than Socrates, take consciousness rather than the world as the principle of philosophy owing to the problems that arise from ancient physics. We have also argued at length that Cartesian self-consciousness is mediated in even a more positive and emphatic way by physics. What differentiates ancients and moderns is not the relatedness or unrelatedness of the mind to the world, but the specific way in which that relationship is conceived. With this proviso, we agree with Oehler that the stress on the active-constitutive role of thinking characterizes modern philosophy, although thinkers such as Spinoza do not fit this mold.

In the absence of a treatment of the Skeptics, we may establish our argument by examination of Oehler's contrast between Socratic knowledge of ignorance and a self-consciousness independent of objects. The rupture of the mind's natural relatedness (or "intentionality") toward objects is the condition of this independence, and its consequence is that subject and object, knower and thing known, are identical (p. 111). Plato rejects this identity as impossible, for relatedness to objects is the minimum condition of knowledge: "Intentionality or non-intentionality is the sole criterion, for Plato, which decides whether or not there exists something like a knowledge of knowledge without the inclusion of the content of knowledge" (p. 107). Because knowledge without content is impossible, for Plato there is, strictly speaking, no self-consciousness, or consciousness of consciousness. "When Socrates knows himself, that is the intentionally-determined knowledge of his soul, not knowledge that makes itself into its own object, in which subject and object are one" (p. 108). Oehler believes that these conclusions are supported not only by the manifest tendency of the Platonic writings, but by the *Charmides* in particular. It is true that the *Charmides* rejects the possibility of knowledge of knowledge because it would lack an object, and hence, content. Yet the premise of the argument there is that knowledge of knowledge includes knowledge of ignorance. If the former is impossible, so is the latter. What then becomes of Socrates' knowledge of ignorance? The suggestion that knowledge of ignorance is knowledge of the soul is contradicted by *Phaedrus* 230a, when Socrates includes his own soul among the things of which he is ignorant.

The anti-Socratic argument of the *Charmides* may be understood by contrasting it with the *Theaetetus*. In the former, Critias advances roughly the Socratic position, but under questioning proves unable to defend it. The incapacity proves that Critias does not possess knowledge of knowledge or of ignorance, but only opinions about them. Socrates extracts this admission by asking him to explain how there can be knowledge that is not knowledge of some particular kinds of objects, such as mathematics or grammar. In the *Theaetetus,* however, his questioning moves in the opposite direction. When Theaetetus attempts to answer the question, "What is knowledge?" by citing particular kinds of knowledge, Socrates criticizes the form of the answer by pointing out that he had asked for a general definition; he requires, in other words, knowledge of knowledge. The fact that the three definitions of knowledge discussed in the dialogue meet the requirement of correct form appears to prove that knowledge of knowledge was an intelligible notion to Plato; the negative result of the discussion is knowledge of ignorance. The fault of Critias is not so much with his thesis as with his failure to understand that it requires a dianoetic articulation, which would provide, as the *Theaetetus* shows, the necessary reference to particular knowledge whose absence Socrates criticizes in the *Charmides.* In a way, though, Oehler's formulation of the Socratic position fits our understanding of it. Knowledge of knowledge, if it were available, would be knowledge of the ideas, of objects independent of consciousness, rather than knowledge of consciousness; but what we know, thanks to the *Theaetetus* and similar investigations, is the incompleteness of our grasp of what would make knowledge perfect. That is why knowledge of ignorance defines the Socratic principles as a species of philosophical self-consciousness.

These disagreements do not diminish the solid scholarship, dialectical skill and sensitivity to complex problems that characterize Oehler's fine study.

Notes

Chapter 1

1 Alquié, 1950, 10; also 12–13, 103.
2 Ibid., 5–10.
3 AT I, 308/AM I; 267, AT I, 271; *Prin.* IV, § 205.
4 Gueroult, 1953, I, 23.
5 Alquié, 1950, 4; Gueroult, 1953, I, 9; 1962, 172–73.
6 Alquié, 1950, 11–12.
7 AT II, 276; AT III, 523.
8 HR I, 203/AT IX–2, 1–2.
9 Ibid.
10 HR I, 205/AT IX–2, 4.
11 HR I, 211/AT IX–2, 14.
12 HR I, 213–14/AT IX–2, 18.
13 HR I, 213/AT IX–2, 17.
14 HR I, 215/AT IX–2, 20.
15 Hamelin, 1921, 21.
16 HR I, 210/AT IX–2, 13.
17 HR I, 212/AT IX–2, 16.
18 HR I, 212–13/AT IX–2, 16–17.
19 HR I, 126/DM 71.
20 AT XI, 326.
21 HR I, 118/DM 59.
22 *Prin.* II, § 40.
23 *Passions,* § 5. Descartes wrote More that the *Passions* prove that "all the movements of the members which accompany the passions are mechanical" (AM VIII, 210).
24 See especially the distinction between "René Descartes" and "Cartesius" in Balz, 1952, 66–72.
25 Heidegger, 1961, II, 167–68.
26 Beck, 1965, 110, 116; Röd, 1964, 95–96.
27 More, 1925, 184; also 186, 193–94, 197, 198.
28 La Mettrie, 1960, 191.
29 d'Holbach, 1774, II, 150; also 148.
30 Leibniz, 1965, IV, 300; also 283, 299.
31 AT XII, 306. See Gilson 1913b, 3, 441, 442; DM 289–90.
32 Maritain, 1945, 41–42.
33 Krüger, 1933, 246; Laberthonnière, 1935, I, 16–17.
34 *Encyclopédie,* 1778, I, xxvi. For a collection of quotations from Descartes's writings that provoked the opinion that he dissembles, see Blondel, 1896, 552–54. The problem is mentioned in most of the standard histories of Cartesian philosophy, usually to be laid to rest by a "balanced" acceptance of some lack of candor on certain points.
35 For short surveys of 20th-century continental Cartesian studies, see Rodis-Lewis, 1951, and Fetscher, 1955. Sebba's *Bibliographia Cartesiana,* with its notes to the listings, is the unrivalled extensive survey of the recent literature, although it gives scant attention to the quite large literature in the analytic tradition.
36 Laporte, 1945, 299–300; also 465. Consider also Gouhier, 1937, 418–19.
37 HR I, 118/DM 60.
38 Ibid.
39 HR I, 124/DM 69. The subtle humor that Descartes injects into his writings provides some index of his irony. Defending himself in advance against "misunderstanding," he writes: "I am very glad to have the opportunity here of begging my descendants never to believe that what is told to them proceeded from myself, unless I expressly divulged it" (HR I, 124/DM 70). The bachelor Descartes's only progeny was a natural daughter who was at that time about a year old.
40 Laporte, 1945, 398; see 393.
41 Ibid.; AT III, 259.
42 Laporte, 1945, 394.
43 AT IV, 256–57.
44 HR I, 95/DM 23.
45 HR I, 90/DM 15.
46 AT III, 297–98.
47 Above, pp. 11–12.

48 At I, 282. On the role of Scheiner in the Galileo affair, see Santillana, 1955, 185, 188–89, n.; 290–91, n.
49 AT V, 178.
50 AT VII, 575, 576, 577, 578, 581; also AT IX-2, **7.**
51 *Passions,* § 211; also AT VII, 247.
52 Caton, 1971, 362–68.
53 HR I, 206/AT IX-2, 5–6. Descartes's reduction of Aristotelianism to Platonism has an ancient precedent. In Cicero's *Academica* (I, 17–18, 22; II, 15) Lucullus claims that the teaching of the Old Academy and of the Peripatetics was a single system with two names. He also notes that the dogmatism of these schools was contrary to Socrates' critical spirit.
54 *Meno* 80 a–b; *Symposium* 218 a–b; *Gorgias* 467 b, 481 b.
55 HR I, 313–316/AT X, 509–15.
56 *Theaetetus,* 156. Socrates' exposition of Protagoras's thesis traces its parentage to so many sources that in the end it is only nominally Protagoras's child. It seems likely that the historical Protagoras did not expound his thesis in this fashion, and that Plato's amended version is meant to be what Protagoras should have said had he attained greater clarity about his own position.
57 *Theaetetus* 160 c.
58 Ibid., 161 c.
59 Appendix B.

Chapter 2

1 HR I, 82–83/DM 3.
2 HR I, 83, 126/DM 3–4, 71. Cf. HR I, 89/DM 15.
3 HR I, 125/DM 68–69; HR I, 203/AT IX-2, 1; HR I, 309, 323/AT X, 502, 522–23. On the popularity of the *Discourse,* see HR I, 130/DM 78–79.
4 *Encyclopédie,* 1778, VI, 415 (Article "Cartésianisme").
5 DM 1, 4: 8–10, 18: 20, 22: 25, 27: 10, 28: 31.
6 HR I, 130/DM 77.
7 HR I, 82/DM 2–3.
8 HR I, 107/DM 42–43.
9 HR I, 87/DM 10.
10 HR I, 98/DM 28.
11 HR I, 83/DM 4.
12 HR I, 85/DM 7; HR I, 4/AT XI, 364–65.

13 HR I, 86/DM 8.
14 HR I, 3/AT X, 363.
15 HR I, 84/DM 6.
16 HR I, 84/DM 7.
17 *Passions,* § 1.
18 HR I, 108/DM 62.
19 Ibid.
20 HR I, 86/DM 9–10.
21 HR I, 311/AT X, 505.
22 HR I, 86/DM 8–9.
23 HR I, 85/DM 7.
24 HR I, 88/DM 13.
25 HR I, 89/DM 13–14.
26 HR I, 119/DM 62.
27 HR I, 121/DM 64–65.
28 HR I, 89/DM 13.
29 HR I, 91/DM 17.
30 HR I, 91/DM 19.
31 HR I, 93/DM 19–20.
32 Beck, 1952, 200–201; Klein, 1968, 178–80.
33 Klein, 1968, 181. See also Gilson, 1913a, 229.
34 HR I, 26/AT X, 398.
35 HR I, 27/AT X, 399. For other enumerations of simple natures, see HR I, 15, 41, 42/AT X, 382, 422, 423.
36 HR I, 45–6/AT X, 425.
37 *Prin.* I, § 10; also HR I, 324/AT X, 524; AT XI, 35.
38 HR I, 43/AT X, 422; also HR I, 45/AT X, 424 and Rule XI.
39 HR I, 45/AT X, 425.
40 HR I, 46/AT X, 427.
41 *Prin.* II, § 64; AT III, 39; AT XI, 47, 39.
42 AT I, 417. To this remark Monchamp comments: "It is true that Descartes never expressly denied the existence of any energy other than impulsive force; but since he expressly affirms that all the actions of bodies are due exclusively to this force, it is necessary to conclude to the non-existence of any other force." (Monchamp, 1886, 56–57). This reasoning is typical of what Descartes's readers must do in order to unravel his countless rhetorical feints.
43 Aristotle, *N. Ethics* 1139 b20–1140 a15.
44 Quoted by John of St. Thomas, 1955, 12.
45 Risse, 1963, 285–88. Although John of St. Thomas generally opposes Fonseca, he recognizes the validity of his approach to logic by granting it a place under the heading "doctrinal logic" (John of St. Thomas, 1955, 33, 38–39, 47).

46 HR I, 9/AT X, 271–72.
47 HR I, 29/AT X, 401.
48 Ibid.
49 *Summa Theologica* Ia, I, 5.
50 HR I, 116/DM 57.
51 Aristotle, *Pos. An.* 72 b4; 75 b20–25; 88 b30–35; 99 b15–20; 100 b5–12.
52 *Passions,* § 153.
53 Ibid., § 206.
54 Epictetus, *Discourses,* I, i, xx; II, viii.
55 Cicero, *Academica,* I, xi, 40–42; Pohlenz, 1950, 43; Bréhier, 1951, 86–106; Sex. Emp., *Adv. Log.,* I, 227.
56 *Passions,* § 48.
57 Epictetus, *Discourses,* I, xii; IV, i.
58 HR I, 96/DM 25.
59 HR I, 89/DM 13–14.
60 HR I, 95/DM 23. Baillet's biography confirms by many details Descartes's studied conformism in matters of no importance to philosophers.
61 HR I, 96/DM 24.
62 HR I, 90/DM 14–15.
63 Krüger, 1933, 239.
64 *Passions,* §§ 153, 160.
65 Ibid.
66 Ibid., § 190. Generosity is equated with good conscience also in AT IV, 266.
67 HR I, 89/DM 13.
68 HR I, 119/DM 62.
69 For a discussion of Cartesian politics as the politics of enlightenment, see Kennington, 1963, 379–96.
70 HR I, 119/DM 62.
71 HR I, 100/DM 30.
72 Ibid.
73 HR I, 99/DM 29.
74 HR I, 108/DM 43.
75 HR I, 108/DM 43; HR I, 203–04, 208/ AT IX–2, 2, 10; HR I, 310/AT X, 505; AT II, 141.
76 AT I, 144.
77 AT II, 141; also AT I, 144.
78 AT II, 142–32, 197ff.; *Prin.* III, §§ 4, 46, 47; IV, §§ 1, 204.
79 AT I, 562, 563.
80 HR I, 94/DM 21–22.
81 HR I, 100/DM 30.
82 Ibid.
83 AT I, 182.
84 Gilson, 1913b, 441, 334–35, 312.
85 Koyré, 1922, x.
86 AT III, 233.
87 AT III, 306.

88 HR I, 107/DM 41.
89 HR I, 123/DM 67.

Chapter 3

1 AT I, 249.
2 Sabra, 1967, 99–100.
3 Taliaferro, 1964, 12–13.
4 HR I, 107/DM 42.
5 AT XI, 3–4; also, *Prin.* I, §§ 71–74; II, §§ 1–3.
6 *Regulae,* XII, XIV; AM VII, 133.
7 Spinoza, 1951, II, 39.
8 Olscamp, 1965, 89/AT VI, 112.
9 Ibid.
10 Ibid., 90/AT VI, 113.
11 Sabra, 1967, 47, n. 7. For an account of Ibn al-Haytham's work and its influence in Europe, see Polyak, 1941, 114–17, 121–23; Ronchi, 1957, 28–32; Sabra, 1967, 72–83.
12 *De An.* 416 b33–35.
13 *Par. An.* 667 b22–25; *De Juv.* 469 a30–33; *De Som.* 462 a9.
14 *De Sen.* 449 a7–20; *De An.* 413 a1–6; see Hicks's commentary to 425 a25 (Hicks, 1907).
15 *De An.* 418 a18–19, 425 a25–27; *De Sen.* 442 b8–17.
16 *De An.* 431 b31, 432 a15.
17 AT XI, 36.
18 Olscamp, 1965, 70/AT VI, 88.
19 Ibid.
20 Ibid., 93/AT VI, 115. According to Polyak (1941, 138), the first record of this experiment is Scheiner's *Rosa Ursinus,* which Descartes had read.
21 Sabra, 1967, 65.
22 Olscamp, 1965, 105/AT VI, 134.
23 Ibid., 103/AT VI, 133.
24 Ibid., 106/AT VI, 137–38.
25 Ibid., 107/AT VI, 140–41.
26 AT XI, 31; AT I, 179.
27 Daniel, 1694, 36, 43; Gilson, DM 391–92; Koyré, 1939, III, 149; Sabra, 1967, 50.
28 AT XI, 31–33; HR I, 107/DM 41–42.
29 AT XI, 35; HR I, 108/DM 43.
30 AT XI, 35.
31 Ibid., 36–37.
32 Ibid., 42.
33 Liard, 1882, 39.
34 Ibid., 39–42.
35 HR I, 56, 67/AT X, 441, 454–55.
36 AT XI, 120; HR I, 116/DM 57.

37 AM VIII, 134–35.
38 *De Motu* 701 b10–702 a21, 703 a30–39; *Gen. An.* 734 b10.
39 AT XI, 201–02. Italics added.
40 For descriptions of these machines by Descartes's contemporaries, see AT XI, 212–15.
41 AT XI, 170–71.
42 AT XI, 172, 174.
43 Ibid., 170, 172.
44 Ibid., 183.
45 Ibid., 176–77.
46 Olscamp, 1965, 85/AT VI, 107; *Passions,* § 44.
47 *Passions,* § 41.
48 AT XI, 181.
49 *Passions,* § 50.
50 AT XI, 179, 184.
51 HR I, 87/DM 10.
52 HR I, 117/DM 58.
53 AT XI, 200, 202.
54 AT I, 41; AM VIII, 335–37.
55 AT I, 413.
56 AM VIII, 135; *Passions,* § 50.
57 Vartanian, 1960, 58.

Chapter 4

1   HR I, 139/AT VII, 10.
2   HR I, 140/AT VII, 13.
3   HR I, 139/AT VII, 9.
4   AT II, 276.
5   Gueroult, 1953, I, 13; also ibid., I, 18, 22, 63; II, 288–89.
6   Ibid., I, 25–27. The textual basis for Gueroult's argument is HR II, 48–51/AT VII, 155–58.
7   Ibid., I, 16–17, 80–81; also Gueroult, 1962, 179–80.
8   Gueroult, 1953, I, 23–24.
9   Ibid., I, 17.
10 Ibid., I, 31–32.
11 Ibid., I, 58; also 38, 52–53.
12 MM I, 8.
13 AT V, 146.
14 *Prin.* IV, § 206.
15 HR I, 198–99, 143/AT VII, 89, 16.
16 HR I, 37/AT X, 413.
17 MM I, 2.
18 HR II, 33/AT VII, 133. Gouhier (1962, 51–56) has properly stressed the Platonism of the withdrawal of the senses, although

it should more accurately be ascribed to Augustine.
19 Sex. Emp., *Outlines,* I, 5, 32–33, 192, 202–03.
20 *Prin.* I, § 71.
21 MM VI, 6.
22 HR I, 106/DM 40; HR II, 78/AT VII, 196; *Prin.* I, § 30.
23 MM III, 3.
24 HR II, 252/AT VII, 245.
25 MM I, 7.
26 *Prin.* I, § 5; also *Prin.* I, § 13.
27 HR II, 27, 40/AT VII, 124–25, 143–44.
28 HR II, 41/AT VII, 144; also MM III, 4.
29 *Prin.* I, § 30.
30 HR II, 39, 245/AT VII, 141, 428.
31 MM I, 12.
32 MM II, 6.
33 MM II, 9.
34 MM III, 4.
35 HR I, 134/AT VII, 3.
36 AT V, 8/AM VII, 297–98.
37 AT V, 8/AM VII, 299.
38 2 Cor. 5:7. This passage is frequently cited by the Patriarchs.
39 *Summa Theologica* Ia. I, 6.
40 AT I, 271; also Appendix A.
41 HR I, 8/AT X, 370; HR II, 43/AT VII, 147–48.
42 *City of God,* XIX, ix.
43 MM III, 4.
44 *Prin.* I, § 43.
45 HR II, 251/AT VII, 436.
46 MM I, 3.
47 *Passions,* § 166.
48 Krüger, 1933, 246.
49 MM III, 4.
50 MM VI, 1.
51 MM V, 15.
52 HR I, 429/AT VIII–2, 353.
53 MM IV, 9, 16.
54 Beck, 1965, 135.
55 Ibid., 136, 147.
56 AT V, 223–24. Also AT I, 145; AT IV, 118; AT V, 272/AM VIII, 128–29; HR II, 250–51/AT VII, 435–36.
57 HR II, 250–51/AT VII, 435–36; AT I, 145, 149–50.
58 AT V, 223–24, 272.
59 HR II, 42/AT VII, 145–46.
60 HR II, 41/AT VII, 144.
61 Gueroult, 1953, I, 232–33, 244–45; Röd, 1961, 136–38.
62 Röd, 1961, 137, 138.

Chapter 5

1 HR II, 38/AT VII, 140; HR II, 127/AT IX-1, 205.
2 HR I, 324/AT X, 523.
3 HR II, 38, 241, 244-45/AT VII, 140, 442, 427.
4 HR I, 324-25/AT X, 524.
5 HR I, 7-8/AT X, 369.
6 HR I, 42, 43/AT X, 420, 421; Beck, 1952, 75-78; Beck, 1965, 86.
7 HR I, 43/AT X, 421.
8 Leibniz, 1965, V, 391 (*Nouveaux Essais* IV, 7, 7); similarly, Heidegger, 1961, II, 161.
9 HR II, 49/AT VII, 156.
10 *Prin.* I, § 8.
11 *Prin.* I, § 12. Observe that the error is committed by Polyander in the *Search for Truth*, HR I, 318/AT X, 517.
12 AT V, 147; HR II, 38/AT VII, 141; HR II, 127/AT IX-1, 205; *Prin.* I, § 59.
13 HR II, 80/AT VII, 197.
14 AT III, 247-48.
15 This is especially clear in the *Search*, HR I, 323-24/AT X, 522-24.
16 MM II, 3.
17 *Prin.* I, § 11.
18 Beck, 1965, 92.
19 Spinoza, 1963, 16.
20 HR I, 317/AT X, 516.
21 MM II, 5.
22 Ibid.
23 MM II, 6.
24 HR II, 81, 83/AT VII, 199, 201.
25 HR I, 319/AT X, 518.
26 HR I, 208/AT IX-2, 9-10; *Prin.* I, § 7.
27 HR II, 138, 195/AT X, 260, 336.
28 HR II, 210/AT VII, 356.
29 Gueroult, 1953, I, 71.
30 *Prin.* I, § 32.
31 This point is acknowledged in MM II, 9 and MM III, 3.
32 HR II, 207/AT VII, 351.
33 *Prin.* I, § 12.
34 HR II, 252/AT VII, 438.
35 *Prin.* IV, § 197.
36 MM II, 6.
37 Noted also by Röd, 1959-60, 185-86.
38 HR II, 140-41/AT VII, 263.
39 *Prin.* I, §§ 32, 48; MM II, 5.
40 *Prin.* I, §§ 64, 65; MM VI, 3, 10.
41 *Prin.* I, § 59.

42 HR II, 134/AT IX-1, 216, n.
43 HR II, 98-99/AT VII, 222; HR II, 134/AT IX-1, 216; HR II, 213/AT VII, 360.
44 MM III, 19; AM VIII, 122-23.
45 HR II, 63/AT VII, 175.
46 AM VIII, 122.
47 HR II, 252/AT VII, 438; also HR II, 33, 213/AT VII 132-33, 360.
48 AT II, 37-38.

Chapter 6

1 MM V, 3; also MM III, 21.
2 MM VI, 1.
3 HR II, 52/AT VII, 161-62; also HR II, 67-68/AT VII, 181.
4 HR I, 36/AT X, 411-12.
5 Ibid.
6 HR I, 38, 39/AT X, 414, 416.
7 HR I, 39/AT X, 416.
8 HR I, 58-59/AT X, 443-45.
9 HR I, 60/AT X, 446.
10 Ibid.
11 Ibid.
12 HR I, 57-58/AT X, 442-43.
13 Ibid.; also HR I, 62/AT X, 449.
14 HR I, 61/AT X, 447-48.
15 Ibid.; also *Prin.* II, § 8.
16 HR II, 38/AT VII, 141.
17 HR I, 37/AT X, 412.
18 HR I, 121/DM 64-65.
19 MM III, 3.
20 *Prin.* II, § 9.
21 Liard, 1882, 38, 50.
22 Ibid., 49. Descartes's references to Viète in his correspondence is summarized in AM VIII, 468-69.
23 Ibid., 50.
24 Ibid., 44.
25 Ibid.
26 Boutroux, 1900, 34.
27 Ibid.
28 Ibid., 35.
29 Ibid., 33.
30 HR I, 39-40, 67/AT X, 416-17, 455.
31 Ibid.
32 HR I, 40/AT X, 417.
33 HR I, 92/DM 18.
34 HR I, 67/AT X, 455.
35 HR I, 66/AT X, 455.
36 HR I, 68/AT X, 456-57.
37 Viète, 1968, 325.
38 Klein, 1968, 206.

39 HR I, 140–41/AT VII, 13–14; HR II, 48, 62/AT VII, 154, 175; HR II, 133/AT IX-I, 215.
40 HR I, 137/AT VII, 8.
41 HR II, 81–83/AT VII, 198–201; HR II, 196/AT VII, 337.
42 HR I, 141/AT VII, 13.
43 MM VI, 20–21.
44 MM VI, 20.
45 MM VI, 15.
46 MM VI, 21, 23.
47 MM VI, 13.
48 MM VI, 15, 17; *Prin.* I, §§ 46, 67.
49 *Prin.* I, §§ 67, 68.
50 *Prin.* I, § 9; HR II, 52, 244/AT VII, 161, 427.
51 MM VI, 22.
52 Gilson, 1913a, 206.
53 *Passions*, § 1.
54 For example, *Passions*, §§ 23–25.
55 *Passions*, § 4.
56 Ibid., §§ 23–25.
57 Ibid., § 48.
58 Ibid., § 19.
59 Ibid., §§ 40, 52, 111, 137.
60 Ibid., §§ 49, 56, 59, 79, 80, 91, 93, 120.
61 Ibid., § 94.
62 Ibid., § 95.
63 Ibid., § 47.
64 Ibid., §§ 139–42.
65 Ibid., §§ 50, 136, 161, 211.
66 Ibid., §§ 53, 70.
67 Gilson, 1913a, 215.
68 *Passions*, §§ 152–53, 160.
69 Ibid., § 107; also §§ 79, 47.
70 Ibid., §§ 20, 36.
71 Ibid., §§ 203, 147–48.

Chapter 7

1 *Prin.* IV, § 206. For other statements on the use of hypothesis, see AT I, 559ff.; AT II, 141–43, 197ff., 268; AT III, 39; AT X, 33–47; *Prin.* II, §§ 4, 64; III, §§ 4, 15, 46–47; IV, §§ 1, 200–206. For recent discussions of Descartes's position, see Olscamp, 1965, v–xxxiv; Beck, 1952, 251–53; Sabra, 1967, 30–45.
2 Rosen has called attention to these ambiguities in Rosen, 1969, 29–34.

Appendix B

1 Pp. 103–104. Oehler's appraisal of Protagoras's position vis-à-vis the moderns is similar to that of Heidegger (1961, II, 168–73; 1957, 94–103). For some strange reason, neither consider ancient skepticism, specifically Sex. Emp., in appraising the extent and character of subjectivity in antiquity and modernity. Heidegger's differentiation of the positions of Protagoras and Descartes depends upon attributing to the former the interpretation of truth as "unconcealedness." In this way he obfuscates Protagoras's express interpretation of truth in terms of sensibility, which is the key to the subjectivity of Protagoras's position.
2 Sex. Emp. *Outlines*, I, 22.

Bibliography

Alquié, Ferdinand. *La découverte métaphysique de l'homme chez Descartes.* Paris: Presses universitaires françaises, 1950.

———. "Notes sur l'interpretation de Descartes par l'ordre des raisons." *Revue de métaphysique et de morale* 61 (1956): 403–18.

Aquinas, St. Thomas. *Summa Theologica.* London: Eyre and Spottiswoode, 1964–

Aristotle. *De Anima.* See Hicks, R. D.

———. *Works.* Translated into English under the editorship of W. D. Ross. 12 vols. Oxford: Clarendon Press, 1908–52.

Armin, H. F. A. *Stoicorum veterum fragmenta.* Stuttgart: Teubner, 1964.

Augustine, St. Aurelius. *Oeuvres de Saint Augustin.* Texte de l'édition bénédictine, traduction, introduction, et notes. Paris: Desclée De Brouwer, 1948–

Baillet, Adrien. *The Life of Monsieur Des Cartes . . . ,* translated from the French by S. R. London: Printed for R. Simpson, 1693.

Balz, A. G. A. *Cartesian Studies.* New York: Columbia University Press, 1951.

———. *Descartes and the Modern Mind.* New Haven: Yale University Press, 1952.

Beck, L. J. *The Method of Descartes.* Oxford: Clarendon Press, 1952.

———. *The Metaphysics of Descartes.* Oxford: Clarendon Press, 1965.

Blanchet, Léon. *Les antecédents historiques du "je pense, donc je suis."* Paris: Alcan, 1920.

Blondel, Maurice. "Le christianisme de Descartes." *Revue de métaphysique et de morale* 4 (1896): 551–69.

Boeder, Heribert. "Parmenides und der Verfall des kosmologischen Wissens." *Philosophisches Jahrbuch* 74 (1966): 30–77.

———. "Der Ursprung der 'Dialektik' in der Theorie des Seienden." *Studium Generale der Albert-Ludwig Universität* (Freiburg im Br.) 21 (1968): 184–202.

Bohatec, Josef. *Die cartesianische Scholastik in der Philosophie und reformierten Dogmatik des 17. Jahrhunderts.* Leipzig: Deichert, 1912.

Bouillier, Fransisque. *Histoire de la philosophie cartésienne.* 2 vols. 3d ed. Paris: Delagrave, 1868.

Boutroux, Pierre. *L'imagination et les mathématiques selon Descartes.* Paris: Alcan, 1900.

Bréhier, Émile. *Chrysippe et l'ancien stoicisme.* Paris: Presses universitaires françaises, 1951.

Brochard, Victor. *Les sceptiques grecs.* 2d ed. Paris: Vrin, 1932.

Brunschvicg, Léon. *Les étapes de la philosophie mathématique.* Paris: Alcan, 1912.

Canguilhem, Georges. *La formation du concept de réflexe au XVIIᵉ et XVIIIᵉ siècles.* Paris: Presses universitaires françaises, 1955.

Caton, Hiram. "On the Interpretation of the *Meditations.*" *Man and World* 3 (1970): 224–45.

———. "The Problem of Descartes' Sincerity." *Philosophical Forum* 2 (1971): 355–69.

Cicero. *De natura deorum & Academica.* With English translation by H. Rackham. Cambridge, Mass.: Harvard University Press, 1933.

Cronin, Timothy J. *Objective Being in Descartes and in Suarez.* Rome: Gregorian University Press, 1966.

Daniel, Gabriel. *A Voyage to the World of Descartes.* Translated by T. Taylor. 2d ed. London, 1694.

Denissoff, Élie. *Descartes, premier théoricien de la physique mathématique.* Louvain: Bibliothéque philosophique de Louvain, 1970.

Descartes, René. *Correspondance publiée avec une introduction et des notes par Charles Adam et Gérard Milhaud.* 8 vols. Paris: Alcan and Presses universitaires françaises, 1936–63. Cited as "AM."

———. *Correspondence of Descartes and Constantijn Huygens, 1635–1647.* Edited by Leon Roth. Oxford: Clarendon Press, 1926. See Huygens.

———. *Discours de la méthode: texte et commentaire.* Edited by Étienne Gilson. 3d ed. rev. Paris: Vrin, 1962. See Gilson.

———. *Discourse on Method, Optics, Geometry, and Meteorology.* Translated by Paul J. Olscamp. Library of Liberal Arts, no. 211. New York: Bobbs-Merrill, 1965. See Olscamp.

———. *The Geometry of René Descartes.* Translated by D. E. Smith and M. L. Latham. New York: Dover, 1954. See Smith, D. E.

———. *Oeuvres de Descartes.* Edited by Charles Adam and Paul Tannery. 13 vols. Paris: Vrin, 1957–68. Cited as "AT."

———. *The Philosophical Works of Descartes.* Translated by E. S. Haldane and G. R. T. Ross. 2d ed. New York: Dover Publications, Inc., 1967.

Encyclopédie, ou Dictionnaire raisonné des Sciences, des Arts, et des Métiers. 3d ed. Geneva and Neufchâtel, 1778.

Epictetus. *Discourses.* With English translation by W. A. Oldfather. 2 vols. London: Heinemann, 1926.

Fessard, Gaston. *La dialectique des "Exercices Spirituels" de Saint Ignace de Loyola.* Paris: Aubier, 1956.

Fetscher, Iring. "Das französische Descartesbild der Gegenwart." *Philosophische Rundschau* 3 (1955): 166–98.

Frankfurt, Harry. *Demons, Dreamers, and Madmen: The Defense of Reason in Descartes's Meditations.* New York: Bobbs-Merrill, 1970.

Georges-Berthier, Auguste. "Le mécanisme cartésien et la physiologie au XVIIᵉ siècle." *Isis* 2 (1914): 37–89; 3 (1920): 21–58.

Gibson, Boyce. *The Philosophy of Descartes.* London: Methuen, 1932.

Gilson, Étienne. *Index scolastico-cartésien.* Paris: Alcan, 1913. (Date cited as "1913a")

Gilson, Étienne. *La liberté chez Descartes et la théologie.* Paris: Alcan, 1913. (Date cited as "1913b")

———. *Études sur le rôle de la pensée médiévale dans la formation du système cartésien.* 2d ed. Paris: Vrin, 1930.

———. *Discours de la méthode: texte et commentaire.* 3d ed. rev. Paris: Vrin, 1962. Cited as "DM."

Gouhier, Henri. *La pensée religieuse de Descartes.* Paris: Vrin, 1924.

———. "Descartes et la religion. Note méthodologique." Pages 417–24 in *Cartesio nel terzo centenario del Discorso del metodo.* Milan, 1937.

———. *Essais sur Descartes.* 2d ed. Paris: Vrin, 1949.

———. *La pensée métaphysique de Descartes.* Paris: Vrin, 1962.

Gueroult, Martial. *Descartes selon l'ordre des raisons.* 2 vols. Paris: Aubier, 1953.

———. "De la méthode prescrite par Descartes pour comprendre sa philosophie." *Archiv für Geschichte der Philosophie* 44 (1962): 172–84.

Hamelin, Octave. *Le système de Descartes.* Paris: Alcan, 1921.

Heidegger, Martin. *Holzwege.* Frankfurt: Klostermann, 1957.

———. *Nietzsche.* 2 vols. Pfüllingen: Neske, 1961.

———. *Die Frage nach dem Ding.* Tübingen: Niemeyer, 1962.

Heimsoeth, Heinz. *Die Methode der Erkenntnis bei Descartes und Leibniz.* Giessen: Topelmann, 1912–14.

Hertling, Georg. "Descartes' Beziehungen zur Scholastik." In *Historische Beiträge zur Philosophie.* Munich, n.p., n.d.

Hicks, R. D. *Aristotle's De Anima.* Edited, with translation, introduction, and notes. London: Cambridge University Press, 1907.

Hintikka, Jaakko. "*Cogito, Ergo Sum*: Inference or Performance?" *Philosophical Review* 71 (1962): 3–32.

d'Holbach, Baron. *Système de la nature, ou des lois du monde physique et du monde morale.* Paris: Masson, 1774.

Huxley, Thomas H. *Method and Results.* New York: Appleton, 1897.

Huygens, Constantijn. *Correspondence of Descartes and Constantijn Huygens, 1635–1647.* Edited by Leon Roth. Oxford: Clarendon Press, 1926.

John of St. Thomas. *The Material Logic of John of St. Thomas.* Translated by Yves R. Simon, John J. Clanville, and G. Donald Hollenhorst. Chicago: University of Chicago Press, 1955.

Kennington, Richard. "Descartes' 'Olympica.'" *Social Research* 28 (1961): 171–204.

———. "René Descartes." In *A History of Political Philosophy.* Edited by Joseph Cropsey and Leo Strauss. New York: Rand McNally, 1963.

———. "The Finitude of Descartes' Evil Genius." *Journal of the History of Ideas* 32 (1971): 441–46.

Kenny, Anthony. *Descartes: A Study of His Philosophy.* New York: Random House, 1968.

———. "The Cartesian Circle and the Eternal Truths." *Journal of Philosophy* 67 (1970): 685–700.

Klein, Jacob. *Greek Mathematical Thought and the Origin of Algebra.* Translated by Eva Brann. Cambridge, Mass.: M.I.T. Press, 1968.

Koyré, Alexandre. *Essai sur l'idée de Dieu et les preuves de son existence chez Descartes.* Paris: Leroux, 1922.

————. *Études galiléennes.* 3 vols. Paris: Hermann, 1939.

————. *From the Closed World to the Infinite Universe.* Baltimore: The Johns Hopkins University Press, 1957.

Krüger, Gerhard. "Die Herkunft des philosophischen Selbstbewusstseins." *Logos* 22 (1933): 225–72.

Laberthonnière, Lucien. *Études sur Descartes.* 2 vols. Paris: Vrin, 1935.

La Mettrie, Julien Offray de. *L'Homme machine.* Critical edition with an introductory monograph and notes by Aram Vartanian. Princeton: Princeton University Press, 1960. See Vartanian.

Laporte, Jean. *Le rationalisme de Descartes.* Paris: Presses universitaires françaises, 1945.

Leibniz, G. W. *Die philosophischen Schriften.* 7 vols. Edited by C. F. Gerhardt. Hildesheim: Olms, 1965.

Lenoble, Robert. "La psychologie cartésienne." *Revue internationale de philosophie* 4 (1950): 160–89.

Leroy, Maxime. *Descartes, le philosophe au masque.* Paris: Rieder, 1929.

Liard, Louis. *Descartes.* Paris: Baillière, 1882.

Liddell, E. G. T. *The Discovery of the Reflexes.* Oxford: Clarendon Press, 1960.

Linksz, Arthur. *Physiology of the Eye.* 3 vols. New York: Grune & Stratton, 1952.

Mach, Ernst. *Analysis of Sensations.* New York: Dover Publications, 1959.

Malebranche, Nicolas. *De la recherche de la vérité.* Edited by Geneviève Rodis-Lewis. 2 vols. Paris: Vrin, 1962

Marc-Wogau, Konrad. "Der Zweifel Descartes' und das cogito ergo sum." *Theoria* 20 (1954): 128–52.

Maritain, Jacques. *The Dream of Descartes.* Translated by M. L. Andison. New York: Philosophical Library, 1945.

Mesnard, Pierre. *Essai sur la morale de Descartes.* Paris: Bowin, 1936.

Milhaud, Gaston. *Descartes savant.* Paris: Alcan, 1921.

Monchamp, Georges. *Histoire du cartésianisme en Belgique.* Brussels: Hayez, 1886.

More, Henry. *The Philosophical Writings of Henry More.* Edited by F. Mackinnon. New York: Oxford University Press, 1925.

Natorp, Paul. "Le développement de la pensée de Descartes depuis le Regulae jusqu'aux Méditations." *Revue de métaphysique et de morale* 4 (1896): 416–32.

Oehler, Klaus. *Die Lehre vom noetischen und dianoetischen Denken bei Platon und Aristoteles.* Zetemata: Monographien zur klassischen Altertumswissenschaft, vol. 29. Munich: Beck Verlag, 1962.

Olscamp, Paul J. *Discourse on Method, Optics, Geometry, and Meteorology.* New York: Bobbs-Merrill, 1965.

Passmore, John A. "William Harvey and the Philosophy of Science." *Australasian Journal of Philosophy* 36 (1958): 84–94.

Plato. *Theaetetus.* With English translation by H. N. Fowler. Cambridge, Mass.: Harvard University Press, 1966.

Pohlenz, Max. *Stoa und Stoiker.* Zürich: Artemis, 1950.

Polyak, S. L. *The Retina.* Chicago: University of Chicago Press, 1941.

Reymond, Arnold. "Le 'cogito,' vérification d'une hypothèse métaphysique." *Revue de métaphysique et de morale* 30 (1923): 539–62.

Risse, Wilhelm. "Zur Vorgeschichte der Cartesischen Methodenlehre." *Archiv für Geschichte der Philosophie* 45 (1963): 270–91.

Röd, Wolfgang. "Zum Problem des premier principe in Descartes' Metaphysik." *Kantstudien* 51 (1959–60): 176–95.

———. "Zur Problematik der Gotteserkenntnis bei Descartes." *Archiv für Geschichte der Philosophie* 43 (1961): 267–302.

———. *Descartes: Die innere Genesis des cartesianischen Systems.* Munich: Reinhardt, 1964.

Rodis-Lewis, Geneviève. "Bilan de cinquante ans d'études cartésiennes." *Revue philosophique de la France et de l'étranger* 141 (1951): 249–67.

Ronchi, Vasco. *Optics: The Science of Vision.* New York: New York University Press, 1957.

Rosen, Stanley. "Thought and Touch: A Note on Aristotle's *De Anima.*" *Phronesis* 6 (1961): 127–37.

———. "A Central Ambiguity in Descartes." Pages 17–35 in *Cartesian Essays.* Edited by B. Magnus and J. B. Wilbur. The Hague: Nijhoff, 1969.

Sabra, A. I. *Theories of Light.* London: Oldbourne, 1967.

Santillana, G. de. *The Crime of Galileo.* Chicago: University of Chicago Press, 1955.

Scholz, Heinrich. *Mathesis Universalis.* Edited by H. Hermes, F. Kambartel, and J. Ritter. Stuttgart: Schwabe, 1961.

Sebba, Gregor. *Bibliographia Cartesiana: A Critical Guide to the Descartes Literature, 1800–1960.* International Archives of the History of Ideas, 5. The Hague: Nijhoff, 1964.

Sextus, Empiricus. *Outlines of Pyrrhonism.* With English translation by R. G. Bury. 4 vols. Cambridge, Mass.: Harvard University Press, 1933.

Sirven, J. *Les annés d'apprentissage de Descartes (1596–1628).* Paris: Vrin, 1930.

Smith, D. E. and M. L. Latham. *The Geometry of Descartes.* New York: Dover Publications, 1954.

Smith, N. Kemp. *Studies in the Cartesian Philosophy.* London: Macmillan, 1902.

———. *New Studies in the Philosophy of Descartes.* London: Macmillan, 1952.

Spinoza, Benedict de. *Benedicti de Spinoza Opera.* Edited by J. van Vloten and J. P. N. Land. 4 vols. The Hague: Nijhoff, 1911.

———. *The Chief Works of Benedict de Spinoza.* Translated by R. H. M. Elwes. 2 vols. New York: Dover Publications, 1951.

———. *The Earlier Philosophical Writings.* Translated by Frank A. Hayes. New York: Bobbs-Merrill, 1963.

Strauss, Leo. *Persecution and the Art of Writing.* Glencoe, Ill.: The Free Press, 1952.

Taliaferro, T. Catesby. *The Concept of Matter in Descartes and Leibniz*. Notre Dame Mathematical Lectures, no. 9. Notre Dame: Notre Dame Press, 1964.

Trendelenburg, Adolf. *Historische Beiträge zur Philosophie*. 2 vols. Berlin: Bethge, 1855.

Vartanian, Aram. *La Mettrie's l'Homme machine: A Study in the Origins of an Idea*. Princeton: Princeton University Press, 1960.

Viète, François. *Introduction to the Analytical Art*. Translated by J. Winfree Smith. Printed in Klein, 1968 (q.v.). Cited as "Viète, 1968."

Virieux-Reymond, Antoinette. *La logique et l'épistémologie des stoiciens*. Chambéry: n.p., n.d.

Vuillemin, Jules. "Sur la difference et l'identité des méthodes de la metaphysique et des mathematiques chez Descartes et Leibniz." *Archiv für Geschichte der Philosophie* 43 (1961): 267–302.

Walsh, W. H. *Metaphysics*. London: Hutchinson University Library, 1963.

Bibliography of Descartes Literature, 1960–1970

Although Gregor Sebba's *Bibliographia Cartesiana* lists titles published as late as 1962, the omissions from 1960 forward are so numerous that I have begun with 1960. Articles published after December 1970 have not been listed. Systematic search for book and monograph titles also ends with that date, but such titles as came to my attention until September 1972 have been included.

Doney's bibliography (see below) contains important supplements to Sebba for the years prior to 1960, especially in the field of analytic literature. Croissant's bibliography (see below) has not been available to me for examination. Sebba does not list it.

All merely nominal Cartesian writings, e.g. on Cartesian tensors, have been eliminated. Limitations of space dictated the following additional omissions: all items listed by Sebba; book reviews; most rejoinders and replies; popular editions and translations other than those in English. Collections have not been listed separately. Reprints and new editions have been included. An asterisk against a title indicates that it could not be verified from a reliable source.

The scope of the title search is largely confined to the reference works consulted: *Bibliographie de la philosophie; Bulletin signalétique; Essay and General Literature Index; Internationale Bibliographie der Zeitschriftenliteratur; The Philosopher's Index; Répertoire bibliographique de la philosophie.*

Titles were initially compiled by Mr. David Kipp and Dr. E. M. Curley. Mrs. Jocelyn Harding completed the compilation and verified all titles. Mrs. Elizabeth Short did the proofreading. These labors were facilitated by Professor John A. Passmore, Head of the Department of Philosophy, Research School of Social Sciences in the Australian National University. To all these persons I am very grateful. Final responsibility for the bibliography is mine.

I. Texts and Translations

Descartes, René. *Discours de la méthode.* With a biographical and philosophical introduction by André Robinet. Paris: Larousse, 1969. 130 pp.

———. *Discourse on Method and Other Writings.* Translated by F. E. Sutcliffe. Harmondsworth: Penguin Books, 1970.

———. *Discourse on Method, Optics, Geometry, and Meteorology.* Translated with introduction by P. J. Olscamp. Indianapolis: Bobbs-Merrill, 1965. xxxvi, 361 pp.

———. *The Essential Descartes.* Edited with introduction by Margaret D. Wilson. New York: The New American Library of World Literature, 1969. xxxiii, 384 pp.

———. *Il Mondo. Trattato della luce. L'Uomo.* Translated by Maria Garin. Introduction by Eugenio Garin. Piccola biblioteca filosofica Laterza, n.s. 48. Bari: Laterza, 1969. 237 pp.

———. *Oeuvres de Descartes.* Edited by Charles Adam and Paul Tannery. 12 vols. 1896–1910. A reprint of these volumes, with the addition of the Descartes-Huygens correspondence, 1635–47, as edited by Leon Roth, 1926, has been issued and reissued at intervals since 1956 by J. Vrin, Paris.

———. *Oeuvres de Descartes.* Edited by S. Silvestre de Sacy with introduction by G. Rodis-Lewis. Paris: Le Club français du livre, 1966. 1040 pp.

———. *Oeuvres philosophiques.* Edited by Ferdinand Alquié. 2 vols. Paris: Garnier, 1963–67. 856 pp.; 1149 pp.

———. *Opere.* Translated by E. Garin [et al.], with introduction by E. Garin. 2 vols. Classici della filosofia moderna. Bari: Laterza, 1967.

———. *Opere filosofiche.* Edited by Bruno Widmar. Turin: Unione Tipografico Ed. torinese, 1969. 901 pp.

———. *Philosophical Essays: Discourse on Method, Meditations, Rules for the Direction of the Mind.* Translated, with an introduction and notes, by Laurence J. Lafleur. Indianapolis: Bobbs-Merrill, 1964. xxiv, 236 pp.

———. *Philosophical Letters.* Translated and edited by Anthony Kenny. Oxford: Clarendon Press, 1970. 270 pp.

———. *Regulae ad directionem ingenii.* Critical text by G. Crapulli, with the first Dutch translation. The Hague: M. Nijhoff, 1966. 164 pp.

———. [*Réponses aux objections de Gassendi*]. See Gassendi, Pierre. *Disquisitio metaphysica . . .* in section IV.

———. *Textes de Descartes.* Edited by R. Lefèvre. Paris: Bordas, 1967.

———. *Treatise of Man.* French text with translation and commentary by Thomas Steele Hall. Cambridge, Mass.: Harvard University Press, 1972. 232 pp.

———. *Über den Menschen* (1632) and *Beschreibung des menschlichen Körpers* (1648). Translated, with a historical introduction and notes by Karl Eduard Rothschild. Heidelberg: L. Schneider, 1969. 202 pp.

II. Textual Criticism and Computer Studies

Beaude, Joseph. "Une Page inédite de Descartes." [On the permanence accidents in the Eucharist.] *Archives de philosophie* 3 (1971): 47–49.

Dibon, Paul "Note critique sur deux lettres de la correspondance de Descartes." *Journal of the History of Philosophy* 9 (1971): 63–67.

Ehrmann, P. "Descartes: Une édition détruite en 1667 réapparaît en 1961. Conséquences. [Une édition Théodore Girard Paris 1667 de la version française des *Méditations*]." In *Congrès de Sociétés de philosophie de langue française. 12th, Brussels and Louvain, 1964. La Vérité; Actes.* Vol. 1, pp. 282–85. Louvain: Editions Nauwelaerts, 1964.

———. "Descartes: Histoire d'une préface méconnue en France et inédite en Hollande." *Philosophia reformata* 25 (1960): 36–45.

———. "Complément à l'histoire d'une préface méconnue." *La Bouquiniste français* 42 (1962): no. 40, pp. 98–107; no. 41, pp. 133–42.

Fenzl, Richard. "Pseudo-cartesianisches." *Neusprachliche Mitteilungen aus Wissenschaft und Praxis* 20 (1967): 230–32.

Heinekamp, Albert. "Ein ungedruckter Brief Descartes an Roderich Dotzen." *Studia Leibnitiana* 2 (1970): 1–12.

Morris, John. *Descartes' Dictionary.* New York: Philosophical Library, 1971. 247 pp.

———. "A Computer-Assisted Study of a Philosophical Text." *Computers and the Humanities* 3 (1969): 175–78.

Robinet, A. "Descartes à l'ordinateur." *Les Études philosophiques* 2 (1970): 219–23. Discusses J. Morris's computer studies.

Schiff, Janet. *A Word Index to Descartes' "Discours de la méthode."* University Park: Pennsylvania State University, 1970. 52 pp.

Sebba, Gregor. "A 'New' Descartes Edition?" *Journal of the History of Philosophy* 1 (1963): 231–36. Reply: by Henri Gouhier, ibid. 2 (1964): 71.

III. Bibliographies

Croissant, Jeanne. "Bibliographie cartésienne." *Morale et enseignement* 9 (1960): 44–50.

Doney, Willis. "Bibliography." In his *Descartes: A Collection of Critical Essays,* pp. 369–86. New York: Anchor Books, 1967.

Sebba, Gregor. *Bibliographia Cartesiana: A Critical Guide to the Descartes Literature, 1800–1960.* Archives internationales d'histoire des idées, 5. The Hague: Nijhoff, 1964. xvi, 510 pp.

IV. Books and Monographs

Allard, Jean-Louis. *Le Mathématisme de Descartes.* Ottawa: Éditions de l'Université d'Ottawa, 1963. 232 pp.

Arata, Carlo. *Discorso sull' essere e ragione rivelante.* Milan: Marzorati, 1967. 263 pp.

Balz, A. G. A. *Descartes and the Modern Mind.* Reprint of 1952 edition. Hamden, Conn.: Shoe String Press, 1967. 492 pp.

Barjonet-Huraux, Marcelle. *Descartes.* Paris: Éditions sociales, 1963. 176 pp.

Beck, Leslie J. *The Metaphysics of Descartes: A Study of the "Meditations."* London: Oxford University Press, 1965. 307 pp.

Berti, Giuseppe. *Introduzione al pensiero religioso di René Descartes.* Padua: Cedam, 1964. 50 pp.

*Blondel, Maurice. *Dialogues avec les philosophes: Descartes, Spinoza, Malebranche, Pascal, Saint Augustin.* Paris: Aubier-Montaigne, 1967. 296 pp.

Bohatec, Josef. *Die cartesianische Scholastik in der Philosophie und reformierten Dogmatik des 17. Jahrhunderts.* Reprint of 1912 edition. Hildesheim: G. Olms, 1966. 158 pp.

Bonnot, Gérard. *Ils ont tué Descartes: Einstein, Freud, Pavlov.* Paris: Denoël, 1968. 255 pp.

Broadie, Frederick. *An Approach to Descartes' "Meditations."* London: Athlone Press, 1970. x, 230 pp.

Carbonara, Cleto. *Renato Cartesio.* Naples: Libreria scientifica editrice, 1965. 190 pp.

Chauvois, Louis. *Descartes, sa méthode et ses erreurs en physiologie.* Preface by Jean Rostand. Paris: Editions de Cèdre, 1966. 154 pp.

Chavagne, A. *Descartes. Problèmes,* 4. Brussells: Editions Labor, 1965. 127 pp.

Collins, James Daniel. *The Continental Rationalists: Descartes, Spinoza, Leibniz.* Milwaukee: Bruce, 1967. 177 pp.

———. *Descartes' Philosophy of Nature. American Philosophical Quarterly* Monograph series, 5. Oxford: Blackwell, 1971.

Crapulli, Giovanni. *Mathesis universalis: Genesi di un' idea nel XVI secolo.* Lessico intellettuale europeo, 2. Rome: Edizioni dell' Ateneo, 1969. 287 pp.

Crapulli, Giovanni, and E. Giancotti-Boscherini. *Ricerche lessicali su opere di Descartes e Spinoza.* Lessico intellettuale europeo, 3. Rome: Edizioni dell' Ateneo, 1969. 186 pp.

Cronin, Timothy J. *Objective Being in Descartes and in Suarez.* Analecta Gregoriana, 154. Rome: Gregorian University Press, 1966. vii, 276 pp.

Daniel, Gabriel. *Voiage du monde de Descartes.* Photomechanical reprint of the 1690 Paris edition. Amsterdam: Rodopi, 1970. 439 pp.

De Angelis, Enrico. *La Critica del finalismo nella cultura cartesiana: Contributi per una ricerca.* Istituto di Filosofia dell' Università di Pisa. Florence: F. le Monnier, 1967. 152 pp.

De Feo, N. M. *Dio, uomo e mondo da Cartesio a Nietzsche.* Naples: Morano, 1966. 210 pp.

Del Noce, Augusto. *Riforma cattolica e filosofia moderna.* Vol. 1: *Cartesio.* Bologna: Il Mulino, 1965. xii, 708 pp.

Denissoff, Élie. *Descartes, premier théoricien de la physique mathématique: trois essais sur le 'Discours de la méthode.'* Bibliothèque philosophique de Louvain, 22. Louvain: Publications universitaires de Louvain, 1970.

Dennert, Jürgen. *Die ontologisch-aristotelische Politikwissenschaft und der Rationalismus. Eine Untersuchung des politischen Denkens Aristoteles', Descartes', Hobbes', Rousseaus und Kants.* Beiträge zur politischen Wissenschaft, 11. Berlin: Duncker und Humblot, 1970. 382 pp.

*Faggioto, Pietro. *Il Problema della metafisica nel pensiero moderno.* Part 1: *Bacone, Galilei, Cartesio, Hobbes, Spinoza, Locke.* Padua: Cedam, 1969. 244 pp.

Fleckenstein, Joachim Otto. *Naturwissenschaft und Politik, von Galilei bis Einstein.* Munich: Georg D. W. Callwey, 1965. 255 pp.

Frankfurt, Harry G. *Demons, Dreamers, and Madmen: The Defense of Reason in Descartes' "Meditations."* Indianapolis: Bobbs-Merrill, 1970. ix, 193 pp.

Frondizi, Risiere. *Descartes.* Buenos Aires: Centro Editor de América Latina, 1967. 124 pp.

Gabaude, Jean-Marc. *Liberté et raison: la liberté cartésienne et sa réfraction chez Spinoza et chez Leibniz.* Vol. 1: *Philosophie réflexive de la volonté.* Vol. 2: *Philosophie compréhensive de la nécessitation libératrice.* Publications de la Faculté des lettres et sciences humaines de Toulouse, sér. A, 13.14. Toulouse: Association des Publications de l'Université, 1970, 1972. 434 pp, 347 pp.

Gassendi, Pierre. *Disquisitio metaphysica seu dubitationes et instantiae adversus Renati Cartesii metaphysicam et responsam.* Edited, with translation and notes, by B. Rochot. Bibliothèque des textes philosophiques. Paris: J. Vrin, 1962. xiv, 658 pp.

*Gewirth, Alan. *Descartes.* London: Macmillan, 1972.

Gouhier, Henri. *Les grandes Avenues de la pensée philosophique en France depuis Descartes.* Louvain: Nauwelaerts, 1966. 96 pp.

———. *La Pensée métaphysique de Descartes.* Paris: J. Vrin, 1962, 412 pp.

Halbfass, Wilhelm. *Descartes' Frage nach der Existenz der Welt: Untersuchungen über der cartesianischen Denkpraxis und Metaphysik.* Monographien zur philosophischen Forschung, 51. Meisenheim: Anton Hain, 1968. 258 pp.

Heimsoeth, Heinz. *Atom, Seele, Monade: historische Ursprünge und Hintergründe von Kants Antimomie der Teilung.* Abhandlungen der geistes- und sozialwissenschaftlichen Klasse, 1960, 3. Mainz: Verlag der Akademie der Wissenschaften und der Literatur, Wiesbaden, 1960. 142 pp.

Ito, Katsuhiko. *Descartes no Ningen-zo.* [The problem of consciousness in Cartesian philosophy]. Tokyo: Keiso-shobo, 1970. 407 pp.

Kalocsai, Dezsö. *Descartes elikaja.* [Descartes' ethics]. Budapest: Akadémia Kiadö, 1964. 217 pp.

Keeling, S. V. *Descartes.* 2d ed. London: Oxford University Press, 1968. xviii, 325 pp.

Kenny, Anthony. *Descartes: A Study of His Philosophy.* New York: Random House, 1968. vii, 242 pp.

Klemmt, Alfred. *Descartes und die Moral.* Monographien zur philosophischen Forschung, 83. Meisenheim: Anton Hain, 1971. 182 pp.

Kujawski, Gilberto de Mello. *Descartes existencial.* São Paulo: Editôra Herder, 1969. 174 pp.

Lefèvre, Roger. *La Pensée existentielle de Descartes.* Paris: Boras, 1965. 176 pp.

Lindborg, Rolf. *René Descartes.* Stockholm: Natur och kultur, 1968. 181 pp.

Lot, Germaine. *Descartes.* Paris: Seghers, 1966. 192 pp.

Löwith, Karl. *Das Verhältnis von Gott, Mensch und Welt in der Metaphysik von Descartes und Kant.* Heidelberg: Carl Winter, 1964. 26 pp.

Mahnke, Detleff. *Der Aufbau des philosophischen Wissens nach René Descartes.* Epimeleia: Beiträge zur Philosophie, 8. Munich: Anton Pustet, 1967. 165 pp.

Marcial de Alcaide, Maria Teresa. *La Filosofia de Descartes.* Santiago del Estero: Dirección General de Cultura de la Provincia [1967?]. 30 pp.

Marciano, Francesco E. *Il Pensiero scientifico di Descartes.* Turin: Società Editrice Internazionale, 1962.

Mesnard, Pierre. *Descartes.* Paris: Seghers, 1966. 192 pp.

Montias, H. *Descartes.* Paris: Gauthier-Villars, 1969. 65 pp.

Morawiec, Edmund. *Przedmiot a metoda w filozofii Kartezjusza.* [Object and method in the philosophy of Descartes]. Warsaw: Akademia Teologii Katolickiej, 1970. 156 pp.

Negri, Antonio. *Descartes politico o della ragionevole ideologia.* Milan: Feltrinelli, 1970. 209 pp.

Pfaff, Rudolph Franz. *Die Unterschiede zwischen der Naturphilosophie Descartes' und derjenigen Gassendis und der Gegensatz beider Philosophen überhaupt.* New York: B. Franklin, 1966. 65 pp.

Picardi, Filippo. *Il Concetto di metafisica nel razionalismo cartesiano.* Milan: Editore Marzorati, 1971. 110 pp.

Polo, Leonardo. *Evidencia y realidad en Descartes.* Facultad de Filosofía y Letras del Estudio General de Navarra. Colección filosófica, 1. Madrid: Ediciones Rialp, 1963. 332 pp.

Pousa, Narciso. *Moral y libertad en Descartes.* La Plata: Universidad Nacional de la Plata, 1960. 42 pp.

Röd, Wolfgang. *Descartes: die innere Genesis des cartesianischen Systems.* Basle: Ernst Reinhardt, 1964. 254 pp.

———. *Descartes' erste Philosophie.* Bonn: Bouvier, 1971. 147 pp.

Rodis-Lewis, Geneviève. *Descartes: initiation à sa philosophie.* Paris: J. Vrin, 1964. 128 pp.

———. *Descartes et le rationalisme.* Paris: Presses universitaires de France, 1966. 128 pp.

———. *La Morale de Descartes.* 3d ed. rev. Paris: Presses universitaires de France, 1970. 136 pp.

Sassen, Ferd. *Descartes.* The Hague: Kruseman, 1963. 157 pp.

Schiavo, Mario. *Il Problema etico in Cartesio.* Rome: Ciranna [1965?]. 240 pp.

Schmidt, Gerhart. *Aufklärung und Metaphysik: die Neubegründung des Wissens durch Descartes.* Tübingen: Nemeyer, 1965. x, 180 pp.

Specht, Rainer. *Commercium mentis et corporis: über Kausalvorstellungen im Cartesianismus.* Stuttgart: F. Frommann, 1966. 185 pp.

———. *René Descartes in Selbstzeugnissen und Bilddokumenten.* Reinbek b. Hamburg: Rowohlt, 1966. 183 pp.

*Spicker, Stuart F., ed. *The Philosophy of the Body: Rejections of Cartesian Dualism.* Chicago: Quadrangle Books, 1970. x, 367 pp.

Spinoza, Benedictus de. *Earlier Philosophical Writings: The Cartesian Principles and Thoughts on Metaphysics.* Translated by Frank A. Hayes, with an introduction by David Bidney. Indianapolis: Bobbs-Merril, 1963. xxxvi, 161 pp.

Taliaferro, Robert C. *The Concept of Matter in Descartes and Leizniz.* Notre Dame: University of Notre Dame Press, 1964. 33 pp.

Toffanin, Guiseppe, *Italia e Francia: Umanesimo e Giansenismo; L'Arcadia e Cartesio.* Bologna: Zanichelli, 1960. 76 pp.

Van den Hoeven, Pieter. *Metafysica en fysica bij Descartes.* Gorinchem: Noorduyn, 1961. 293 pp.

Versfeld, Mathinus. *An Essay on the Metaphysics of Descartes.* Reprint of 1940 edition. Port Washington: Kennikat Press, 1969. 192 pp.

Villoro, L. *La Idea y el ente en la filosofia de Descartes.* Mexico: Fondo de Cultura Economica, 1965. 168 pp.

Vleeschauwer, Herman Jean de. *Le Plan d'études de René Descartes.* Communications of The University of South Africa, C35. Pretoria: University of South Africa, 1962. 64 pp.

Vrooman, Jack R. *René Descartes.* New York: G. P. Putnam's Sons, 1970. 308 pp.

Wegelingh, Willem. *Cartesiaanse uitzichten.* Lochem: De Tijdstroom, 1966. 46 pp.

V. Articles and Chapters of Books

I. SCIENCE AND METHOD

Aulizio, Francesco. "Cartesio e la psicologia moderna." *Pagine di storia della medicina* 11 (1967): 113-19.

Bernier, R. "Expérimentation et spéculation dans la genèse de la conception de la vie chez Descartes." In International Congress on the History of Sciences. *11th, Warsaw, 1965. Actes.* Vol. 2. Warsaw: Polish Academy of Sciences.

Blackwell, Richard J. "Descartes' Laws of Motion." *Isis* 57 (1966): 220-34.

Blake, Ralph M. "The Role of Experience in Descartes' Theory of Method." In *Theories of Scientific Method: The Renaissance through the Nineteenth Century,* by R. M. Blake, Curt J. Ducasse, and Edward H. Madden, pp. 75–103. Seattle: University of Washington Press, 1960.

Bouligand, Georges. "Descartes, Leibniz, Euler et les débuts de l'heuristique moderne." Académie des Sciences, Paris. *Comptes rendus* 256 (1963): 4138–42.

Brüning, W. "Posibilidades y limites de la duda metódica en Descartes." *Revista de humanidades* 6 (1963): 39–63.

Burke, John S. "Descartes on the Refraction and the Velocity of Light." *American Journal of Physics* 34 (1966): 390–400.

Busacchi, Vincenzo, et al. "Descartes e Newton nel pensiero di Claude Bernard." *Pagine di storia della medicina* 11 (1967): 78–82.

Cohen, I. B. " 'Quantum in se est.' Newton's Concept of Inertia in Relation to Descartes and Lucretius." Royal Society, London. *Notes and Records* 19 (1964): 131–55.

Costabel, Pierre. "Essai critique sur quelques concepts de la mécanique cartésienne." *Archives internationales d'histoire des sciences* 20 (1967): 235–52.

Crombie, A. C. "The Mechanistic Hypothesis and the Scientific Study of Vision." In Bradbury, Savile and Turner, G. L. E., eds. *Historical Aspects of Microscopy,* edited by Savile Bradbury and G. L. E. Turner, pp. 66–112. Cambridge: W. Heffer, 1967.

———. "Some Aspects of Descartes' Attitude to Hypothesis and Experiment." In *Collection des travaux de l'Académie internationale d'histoire des sciences,* pp. 192–201. Florence: Bruschi, 1960.

De Angelis, Enrico. "Il Metodo geometrico da Cartesio a Spinoza." *Giornale critico della filosofia itialiana* 43 (1964): 393–427.

Denissoff, Élie. "La Nature du savoir scientifique selon Descartes, et l'Histoire de mon esprit, autobiographie intellectuelle." *Revue philosophique de Louvain* 66 (1968): 5–35.

Dobzhansky, Theodosius. "On Cartesian and Darwinian Aspects of Biology." *Graduate Journal* 8 (1968): 99–117.

Dubarle, D. "Sur la Notion cartésienne de quantité de mouvement." In *Mélanges Alexandre Koyré, publiés à l'occasion de son soixante-dixième anniversaire.* Vol. 2, pp. 18–128. Paris: Hermann, 1964.

Fleckenstein, J. O. "Von Descartes zu Leibniz." *Mathematisch-physikalische Semesterberichte zur Pflege des Zusammenhanges von Schule und Universität* 11 (1964–65): 129–43.

Gabbey, A. "Les Trois genres de découverte selon Descartes." In International Congress on the History of Sciences. *12, Paris, 1968. Actes.* Vol. 2, pp. 45–49. Paris: Blanchard, 1970.

Garagorri, P. "Criterio y método." *Revista de occidente* 5 (1967): 277–300.

Gargani, A. G. "Funzione dell' immaginazione e modelli della spiegazione scientifica in Harvey e Cartesio." *Rivista critica di storia della filosofia* 25 (1970): 250–74.

Giovanni, Antonio di. "Il Mondo, il corpo e l'anima nel pensiero cartesiano." *Pagine di storia della medicina* 11 (1967): 28–38.

Graves, John C. [A discussion of Descartes' reduction of matter to space.] In his *Conceptual Foundation of Contemporary Relativity Theory.* Cambridge, Mass.: M.I.T. Press, 1971.

Hall, A. R. "Cartesian Dynamics." *Archive for History of Exact Sciences* 1 (1961): 172–78.

Hall, T. S. "Descartes' Physiological Method." *Journal of the History of Biology* 3 (1970): 53–79.

Harre, R. "Powers." *British Journal for the Philosophy of Science* 21 (1970): 81–101.

Hoenen, P. H. J. "Descartes' Mechanism." In *Descartes: A Collection of Critical Essays*, edited by Willis Doney, pp. 353–68. New York: Doubleday, 1967.

Janovskaja, S. A. ["The Role of Rigor in the Development of Mathematics, Especially in Regard to the *Géométrie* of Descartes."] In Russian. In *Issledovanie lagicheskikh sistem*, pp. 13–50. Moscow: Nauka, 1970.

Jaynes, Julian. "The Problem of Animate Motion in the Seventeenth Century." *Journal of the History of Ideas* 31 (1970): 219–34.

Klein, Jacob. "The Concept of 'Number' in Descartes." In his *Greek Mathematical Thought and the Origin of Algebra*, pp. 197–210. Translated by Eva Brann. Cambridge, Mass.: M.I.T. Press, 1968.

Kouznetsov, B. "La Notion cartésienne de l'inertie et la science moderne." In *Mélanges Alexandre Koyré, publiés à l'occasion de son soixante-dixième anniversaire*. Vol. 1, pp. 361–66. Paris: Hermann, 1964.

Koyré, Alexandre. "Newton and Descartes." In his *Newtonian Studies*, pp. 53–114. London: Chapman and Hall, 1965.

McGuire, J. E. "Atoms and the Analogy of Nature: Newton's Third Rule of Philosophizing." *Studies in History and Philosophy of Science* 1 (1970): 3–58.

Manzi, Leonello. "Le Passioni dell 'anima' di Renato Cartesio." *Pagine di storia della medicina* 11 (1967): 56–63.

Mayerhofer, J. "Descartes: A New Interpretation of His Ideas on the Philosophy of Nature." In International Congress on the History of Sciences. *11th, Warsaw, 1965. Actes.* Vol. 2, pp. 248–49. Warsaw: Polish Academy of Sciences.

Mesnard, Pierre. "Le Point de vue génétique dans la physiologie cartésienne." *Revue générale des sciences pures et appliquées* 72 (1965): 379–82.

Metz, André. "Descartes et Leibniz: note sur leurs conceptions de la force et du mouvement, à la lumiére de la science actuelle." *Archives de philosophie* 31 (1968): 473–76.

Mullatti, L. C. "Descartes' Philosophy of Nature." 2 pts. *Journal of the Karnatak University* (Humanities) 3 (1967): 24–34; 4 (1968): 1–8.

Nádor, Georg. "L'Importance de la doctrine heuristique de Descartes dans l'histoire de la science." *Dialectica* 16 (1962): 25–38.

Ohana, J. "Note sur la théorie cartésienne de la direction du mouvement" *Les Études philosophiques* 16 (1961): 313–16.

Olaso, E. de "Leibniz y la duda metódica" *Revista de filosofía* (Argentina) 14 (1964): 37–56.

Ostrowski, A. M. "On Descartes' Rule of Signs of Certain Polynomial Developments." *Journal of Mathematics and Mechanics* 14 (1965): 195–200.

Pastore, Nicholas, et al. "The Orientation of the Cerebral Image in Descartes' Theory of visual Perception." *Journal of the History of the Behavioural Sciences* 5 (1969): 385–89.

Powell, Betty. "Descartes' Machines." *Proceedings of the Aristotelian Society* 71 (1970–71): 209–22.

Prenant, Lucie. "Sur les Références de Leibniz à Kepler contre Descartes." *Archives internationales d'histoire des sciences* 13 (1960): 95–97.

Quinton, A. "Matter and Space." *Mind* 73 (1964): 332–53.

Risse, Wilhelm. "Zur Vorgeschichte der cartesischen Methodenlehre." *Archiv für Geschichte der Philosophie* 45 (1963): 269–91.

———. "Descartes und die Zirbeldrüse." In *Wissenschaft, Wirtschaft und Technik: Studien zur Geschichte. Wilhelm Treue zum 60. Geburtstag*. Edited by K.-H. Manegold, pp. 438–47. Munich: Bruckmann, 1969.

Rothschuh, K. E. "René Descartes und die Theorie der Lebenserscheinungen." *Sudhoffs Archiv für Geschichte der Medizin und der Naturwissenschaften* 50 (1966): 25–42.

Sabra, A. I. [Descartes' theory of light: his explanation of the rainbow, of colors, of reflection and refraction.] In his *Theories of Light from Descartes to Newton*, pp. 17–135. London: Oldbourne Press, 1967.

Schrynemakers, Arthur. "Descartes and the Weight-driven Chair-clock." *Isis* 60 (1969): 233–36.

Serres, Michael. "Descartes et Leibniz dans les deux manières de penser le réel et la science." *Critique* 17 (1961): 50–75.

———. "L'Évidence, la vision et le tact." *Les Études philosophiques* 2 (1968): 191–95.

Shugg, W. "Cartesian Beast-Machine in English Literature (1663–1750)." *Journal of the History of Ideas* 29 (1968): 279–92.

Sobotka, M. ["The Conception of Substance and of Movement in the Philosophy of Descartes and Aristotle."] In Czech. *Filosofický Časopis* 18 (1970): 612–27.

Strong, E. W. "Barrow and Newton." *Journal of the History of Philosophy* 8 (1970): 155–72.

Tonnelat, Marie A. "Quelques-unes des difficultés relatives à la vitesse de la lumière dans la physique cartésienne." In International Congress on the History of Sciences. *9th, Barcelona and Madrid, 1959. Actes*, pp. 606–09. Paris: Hermann, 1960.

2. ETHICS

Botson, C. "Descartes et l'art de vivre." *Synthèses* 17 (1962): 129–39.

Buonajuto, Mario. "Liberta e storia." *Giornale critico della filosofia italiana* 23 (1969): 400–45.

Caramella, Santino. "Lo Stoicismo di Seneca e il neo-stocismo di Cartesio." *Crisis* 12 (1965): 253–59.

Chambers, Connor J. "The Progressive Norm of Cartesian Morality." *New Scholasticism* 42 (1968): 374–400.

Collins, James Daniel. [An 80-page discussion of the Cartesian notion of wisdom.] In his *Lure of Wisdom*. Aquinas Lecture, 1962. Milwaukee: Marquette University Press, 1962.

Crippa, R. "Etica e ontologia nella dottrina cartesiana delle passioni." *Giornale di metafisica* 19 (1964): 532–45.

Davidson, N. M. "Descartes and the Utility of the Passions." *Romanic Review* 51 (1960): 15–26.

Frutos, Eugenio. "La Moral de Séneca en Descartes." In Congreso Internacional de Filosofia en Conmemoracion de Séneca. Cordoba, 1965. *Actas*. Vol. 1, pp. 137–61. Cordoba: Presidencia del Consejo Ejecutivo del Congreso Internacional de Filosofia, 1965.

Gagnon, Maurice. "Le Rôle de la raison dans la morale cartésienne." *Laval théologique et philosophique* 25 (1969): 268–305.

Gullace, G. "Sartre et Descartes: le problème de la liberté." *Revue de l'Université Laval* 21 (1966): 107–25.

Heidsieck, François. "Honor and Nobility of Soul: Descartes to Sartre." Translated by J. M. Somerville. *International Philosophical Quarterly* 1 (1961): 569–92.

Kalocsai, Dezsö. "A Propos de la morale 'définitive' et Descartes." In *Études sur Descartes,* by Ervin Rozsnyai et al., 65–133. Budapest: Akademia Kiado, 1964.

———. "Über Descartes moralische Ansichten." *Deutsche Zeitschrift für Philosophie* 12 (1964): 290–309.

Machado, A. R. "O Valor moral e social do autoconhecimento." [Descartes, Montaigne, Stendhal, Nietzsche.] *Ocidente* 64 (1965): 29–33.

Millet, L. "Man and Risk." *International Philosophical Quarterly* 2 (1962): 417–27.

Ohana, J. "Le Sophisme de l'évidence ex terminus: á propos de l'opposition Descartes–Spinoza au suject de la liberté." *Revue philosophique de la France et de l'étranger* 155 (1965): 151–68.

Polin, R. "Descartes et la philosophie politique." In *Mélanges Alexandre Koyré, publiés à l'occasion de son soixante-dixième anniversaire.* Vol. 2, pp. 381–99. Paris: Hermann, 1964.

Régnault, Francois. "La Pensée du *Prince* (Descartes et Machiavel), suivi de quatre lettres sur Machiavel échangées entre Descartes et la princesse Elisabeth avec un chapitre des *Discorsi* de Machiavel." *Cahiers pour l'analyse textuelle* 6 (1967): 21–66.

Rodis-Lewis, Geneviève. "La Domaine propre de l'homme chez les Cartésiens." *Journal of the History of Philosophy* 2 (1964): 157–88.

Schall, J. V. "Cartesianism and Political Theory." *Review of Politics* 24 (1962): 260–82.

Specht, Rainer. "Über Descartes' politische Ansichten." *Der Staat* 3 (1964): 281–94.

3. METAPHYSICS AND EPISTEMOLOGY

Aldrich, V. C. "The Pineal Gland Updated." *Journal of Philosophy* 67 (1970): 700–10.

Allaire, Edwin B. "The Attack on Substance: Descartes to Hume." *Dialogue* 3 (1964): 284–87.

———. "The Circle of Ideas and the Circularity of the *Meditations*." *Dialogue* 5 (1966): 131–53.

Allen, Harold J. "Doubt, Common Sense, and Affirmation in Descartes and Hume." In *Cartesian Essays: A Collection of Critical Studies,* edited by B. Magnus and J. B. Wilbur, pp. 36–54. The Hague: M. Nijhoff, 1969.

Augustyn, W. ["Les fondements du savoir selon Descartes."] In Polish. *Archiwum historii filozofii i mysli spolecznej* 15 (1969): 177–204.

Baillot, A.-F. "Descartes à la recherche de la vérité." *Bulletin de l'Association Guillaume Budé* (1963): 209–15.

Bartley, W. W. "Approaches to Science and Scepticism." *Philosophical Forum* 1 (1969): 318–29.

Battisti, G. "L'Occasionalismo in Descartes." *Giornale critico della filosofia italiana* 50 (1971): 262–98.

Bauer, Johannes. "Der Zweifel und seine Überwindung: Bemerkungen zur Noetik Descartes." *Salzburger Jahrbuch für Philosophie* 12–13 (1968–69): 49–61.

Bennett, Jonathan. "The Simplicity of the Soul." *Journal of Philosophy* 64 (1967): 648–60.

Berquist, D. H. "Descartes and Dialectics." *Laval théologique et philosophique* 20 (1964): 176–204.

Bertocci, Peter A. "Descartes and Marcel on the Person and His Body: A Critique." *Proceedings of the Aristotelian Society* 68 (1968): 207–26.

————. "The Person and His Body: Critique of Existentialist Responses to Descartes." In *Cartesian Essays: A Collection of Critical Studies,* edited by B. Magnus and J. B. Wilbur, pp. 116–44. The Hague: M. Nijhoff, 1969.

Bourassa, André. "Descartes et la connaissance intuitive." *Dialogue* 6 (1968): 539–54.

Bouwsma, Oets Kolk. "Descartes' Evil Genius." In his *Philosophical Essays,* pp. 85–97. Lincoln: University of Nebraska Press, 1965.

————. "Descartes' Skepticism of the Senses." Ibid., pp. 59–63.

————. "On Many Occasions I Have in Sleep Been Deceived." Ibid., pp. 149–73.

Bréhier, Émile. "The Creation of the Eternal Truths in Descartes's System." In *Descartes: A Collection of Critical Essays,* edited by Willis Doney, pp. 192–208. New York: Doubleday, 1967. Also published, in French, in *Revue philosophique de la France et de l'étranger* 113 (1937): 15–29.

————. "La Création continuée chez Descartes." In his *Études de philosophie moderne,* pp. 52–57. Paris: Presses universitaires de France, 1965.

————. "Descartes d'après le P. Laberthonnière." Ibid., pp. 58–68.

————. "L'Esprit cartésien." Ibid., pp. 49–51.

Buchdahl, Gerd. "Descartes: Method and Metaphysics." In his *Metaphysics and the Philosophy of Science, the Classical Origins: Descartes to Kant,* pp. 79–180. Oxford: Blackwell, 1969.

Buonajuto, Mario. "A Proposito delle cartesiane 'nature semplici.'" *Il Pensiero* 6 (1961): 357–70.

Burkill, T. A. "Une Critique de la tendance subjectiviste de Descartes à Sartre." *Dialogue* 6 (1967): 347–54.

Caton, Hiram. "On the Interpretation of the 'Meditations.'" *Man and World* 3 (1970): 224–45.

————. "The Theological Import of Cartesian Doubt." *International Journal for Philosophy of Religion* 1 (1970): 220–32.

Cazabon, Gilles. "Deux Approches antithétiques du problème du comportement." *Revue philosophique de Louvain* 67 (1969): 546–81.

Chandra, S. "Wittgensteinian Technique and the Cartesian Doubt." *Philosophical Quarterly* (India) 33 (1960): 181–89.

Chung, A. C. "The *Meditations* of Descartes." *Chinese Culture* 7 (1966): 61–76.

Clarke, W. Norris. "A Curious Blindspot in the Anglo-American Tradition of Anti-theistic Argument." *Monist* 54 (1970): 181–200.

Cristofolini, Paolo. "Sul Problema cartesiano della memoria intellecttuale." *Il Pensiero* 7 (1962): 378–402.

Cronin, Timothy J. "Eternal Truths in the Thought of Suarez and of Descartes." 2 pts. *Modern Schoolman* 38 (1961): 269–88; 39 (1961): 23–38.

——. "Objective Reality of Ideas in Human Thought: Descartes and Suarez." In *Wisdom in Depth: Essays in Honor of Henri Renard, S.J.,* pp. 68–79. Milwaukee: Bruce, 1966.

Dieth, Paul. "The Feasibility of Hyperbolical Doubt." *Philosophical Studies* 20 (1969): 70–73.

Dilley, Frank B. "Descartes' Cosmological Argument." *Monist* 54 (1970): 427–40.

Doney, Willis. "Descartes' Conception of Perfect Knowledge." *Journal of the History of Philosophy* 8 (1970): 387–403.

Doz, André. "Sur le Passage du concept à l'être chez Descartes et Hegel." *Revue de métaphysique et de morale* 72 (1967): 216–30.

——. "Sur la Signification de 'instar archtype,' Descartes *Troisième Méditation.*" *Revue philosophique de la France et de l'étranger* 93 (1968): 380–87.

Dreyfus, Ginette. "La Réfutation kantienne de l'idéalisme cartésien." In International Congress of Philosophy. *14th, Vienna, 1968. Akten.* Vol. 5, pp. 505–09.

Edie, James M. "Descartes and the Phenomenological Problem of the Embodiment of Consciousness." In *Cartesian Essays: A Collection of Critical Studies,* edited by B. Magnus and J. B. Wilbur, pp. 91–115. The Hague: M. Nijhoff, 1969.

Evans, J. L. "Error and the Will." *Philosophy* 38 (1963): 136–48.

Faggiotto, Pietro. "Deduzione matematica e argomentazione dialettica nella metafisica di Cartesio." *Rivista di filosofia neo-scolastica* 59 (1967): 178–94.

Fahrenbach, Helmut. "Endlichkeit des Bewusstseins und absolute Gewissheit bei Descartes." In *Subjektivität und Metaphysik: Festschrift für Wolfgang Cramer,* edited by Dieter Henrich and Hans Wagner, pp. 64–91. Frankfurt: Klostermann, 1966.

Farias, D. "Teologia e cosmologia nelle *Meditazioni* cartesiane." *Rivista di filosofia neo-scolastica* 54 (1962): 267–88.

Fleischer, M. "Die Krise der Metaphysik bei Descartes." *Zeitschrift für philosophische Forschung* 16 (1962): 68–84.

Frankfurt, Harry G. "Descartes' Validation of Reason." *American Philosophical Quarterly* 2 (1965): 149–56. Also published in *Descartes: A Collection of Critical Essays,* edited by Willis Doney, pp. 209–26. New York: Doubleday, 1967.

——. "Memory and the Cartesian Circle. " *Philosophical Review* 71 (1962): 504–11.

Frutos, Eugenio. "Realidad y limites de la resonancia de San Agustí en Descartes." *Augustinus* 13 (1968): 219–48.

Fulton, James Street. "The Cartesianism of Phenomenology." In *Essays in Phenomenology,* edited by Maurice Natanson, pp. 58–78. The Hague: M. Nijhoff, 1966.

Furlán, A. "Descartes: Cuestiones gnoseológicas." *Sapientia* 25 (1970): 209–22.

Furth, M. "Monadology." *Philosophical Review* 76 (1967): 169–200.

Gabaude, Jean-Marc. "Descartes et la notion de nature humaine." *Les Études philosophiques* 16 (1961): 277–80.

Garcia Bacca, Juan David. "Modelo de reinterpretatión sujetivista del universo: Renato Descartes (1596-1650)." *Diánoia* 13 (1967): 1–54.

Gawlick, Gunter. "Die Funktion des Skeptizismus in der frühen Neuzeit." *Archiv für Geschichte der Philosophie* 49 (1967): 86–97.

Giorgiantonio, Michele. "Le 'nature semplici' cartesiane e la dottrina di Epicuro." *Sophia* 29 (1961): 492–94.

Goldschmidt, Victor. "Le Paradigme platonicien et les 'Regulae' de Descartes." In his *Questions platoniciennes,* pp. 231–42. Paris: J. Vrin, 1970.

Goodhue, William Walter. "Pascal's Theory of Knowledge: A Reaction to the Analytical Method of Descartes." *Modern Schoolman* 67 (1969): 15–35.

Grimaldi, N. "La Dialectique du fini et de l'infini dans la philosophie de Descartes." *Revue de métaphysique et de morale* 74 (1969): 21–54.

Gueroult, Martial. "Animaux-machines et cybernétique." In his *Études sur Descartes, Spinoza, Malebranche et Leibniz,* pp. 33–40. Studien und Materialien zur Geschichte der Philosophie, 5. Hildesheim: G. Olms, 1970. Reprinted from *Cahiers de Royaumont* 5 (1965): 7–15.

———. "La Définition de la vérité (Descartes et Spinoza)." In Congrès des Sociétés de philosophie de langue française. *12th, Brussels and Louvain, 1964. La Vérité: Actes.* Vol. 2: Séances plénières, pp. 43–51. Louvain: Nauwelaerts, 1965. Also published in his *Études sur Descartes,* pp. 55–63.

———. "De la Méthode prescrite par Descartes pour comprendre sa philosophie." *Archiv für Geschichte der Philosophie* 44 (1962): 172–84. Also published in his *Études sur Descartes,* pp. 9–21.

———. "Psychologie cartésienne et psychologie malebranchiste." In his *Études sur Descartes,* pp. 144–64.

Gumppenberg, Rudolf von. "Über die Seinslehre bei Descartes: Eine Untersuchung des Seinsbegriffes in den *Meditationes de prima philosophia.*" *Salzburger Jahrbuch für Philosophie* 12–13 (1968): 131–39.

Harries, Karsten. "Irrationalism and Cartesian Method." *Journal of Existentialism* 6 (1965): 295–304.

Hart, Alan. "Descartes' Notions." *Philosophy and Phenomenological Research* 31 (1970–71): 114–22.

Hawkins, Denis John Bernard. "Descartes and the Project of a Critical Theory of Knowledge." In his *Crucial Problems of Modern Philosophy,* pp. 19–29. Notre Dame: University of Notre Dame Press, 1962.

Johnston, Julia M. "Cartesian Lucidity." *Filosofia* 19 (1968): 663–70.

Kenny, Anthony. "Descartes on Ideas." In *Descartes: A Collection of Critical Essays,* edited by Willis Doney, pp. 227–49. New York: Doubleday, 1967.

Lamacchia, Ada. "Il Problema dell' anima nelle *Meditazioni metafisiche* di Cartesio." *Annali della Facoltà di Lettere e Filosofia* (Bari) 7 (1961): 5–39.

Long, Douglas C. "Descartes' Argument for Mind-Body Dualism." *Philosophy Forum* 1 (1969): 259–73.

Manteau-Bonamy, H.-M. "Réflexions critiques sur les 'Méditations' de Descartes." *Revue thomiste* 63 (1963): 37–72.

Maritain, Jacques. "Il n'y a pas de savoir sans intuitivité." *Revue thomiste* 70 (1970): 30–71.

Morris, John. "Cartesian Certainty." *Australasian Journal of Philosophy* 47 (1969): 161–68.

———. "Descartes and Probable Knowledge." *Journal of the History of Philosophy* 8 (1970): 303–12.

———. "Raison, Connaissance, and Conception in Descartes' *Meditations.*" *Sophia* 36 (1968): 265–72.

Najm, Sami M. "The Place and Function of Doubt in the Philosophies of Descartes and al-Ghazālī." *Philosophy East and West* 16 (1966): 133–41.

Neville, R. C. "Some Historical Problems about the Transcendence of God." *Journal of Religion* 47 (1967): 1–9.

Norton, David Fate. "Descartes on Unknown Faculties: An Essential Inconsistency." *Journal of the History of Philosophy* 6 (1968): 245–56.

Noussan-Lettry, L. "Experiencia y trascendencia ontológica en las *Meditaciones* cartesianas." *Philosophia* 26 (1962): 24–49.

Olaso, E. de. "La Distinción entre el alma y el cuerpo." *Revista de filosofía* (Argentina) 15 (1964): 43–49.

Oliver, W. Donald. "A Sober Look at Solipsism." *American Philosophical Quarterly* 4 (1970): 30–39.

O'Neill, William. "Augustine's Influence upon Descartes and the Mind-Body Problem." *Revue des études augustiniennes* 12 (1966): 255–60.

Peukert, K. W. "Der Wille und die Selbstbewegung des Geistes in Descartes *Meditationen.*" *Zeitschrift für philosophische Forschung* 19 (1965): 87–110, 224–47.

Rabada Romeo, S. "Dios y el problema del criterio en Descartes." *Miscelánea Comillas* 47–48 (1967): 369–88.

Reinhardt, L. R. "Dualism and Categories." *Proceedings of the Aristotelian Society* 66 (1965): 71–92.

Renaud, Michel. "La 'Philosophie du corps' selon M. Cl. Bruarie." *Revue philosophique de Louvain* 67 (1969): 104–42.

Ritchie, A. M. "Can Animals See? A Cartesian Query." *Proceedings of the Aristotelian Society* 64 (1963–64): 221–42.

Robert, J. D. "Descartes, créateur d'un nouveau style métaphysique: Réflexions sur l'introduction du primat de la subjectivité en philosophie première." *Revue philosophique de Louvain* 60 (1962): 369–93.

Roberts, G. "Some Questions in Epistemology." *Proceedings of the Aristotelian Society* 70 (1969–70): 37–60.

Rochot, Bernard. "Infini mathématique et infini métaphysique chez Descartes." *Revue de synthèse* 82 (1961): 67–71.

———. "La Pensée métaphysique de Descartes." *Revue de synthèse* 84 (1963): 491–501.

Röd, Wolfgang. "Objektivismus und Subjektivismus als Pole der Descartes-Interpretation." *Philosophische Rundschau* 16 (1969): 28–39.

Rosen, Stanley. "A Central Ambiguity in Descartes." In *Cartesian Essays: A Collection of Critical Studies,* edited by M. Magnus and J. B. Wilbur, pp. 17–35. The Hague: M. Nijhoff, 1969.

Salmon, E. G. "Mathematical Roots of Cartesian Metaphysics." *New Scholasticism* 39 (1965): 158–69.

Sambarino, Mario. "La Hipótesis cartesiana del genio maligno y el problema del valor de la evidencia." *Cuadernos Uruguayos de Filosofía* 2 (1963): 63–92.

Schouls, Peter A. "Cartesian Certainty and the 'Natural Light.'" *Australasian Journal of Philosophy* 48 (1970): 116–19.

Semerari, G. "Sulla metafisica de Vico." *Annali della Facolta di Lettere e Filosofia* (Bari) 13 (1968): 247–74.

Sibajiban. "Descartes' Doubt." *Philosophy and Phenomenological Research* 24 (1963–64): 106–16.

Slote, Michael Anthony. "Empirical Certainty and the Theory of Important Criteria." *Inquiry* 10 (1967): 21–37.

Strasser, J. "Lumen naturale, sens commun, common sense: zur Prinzipienlehre Descartes', Buffiers und Reids." *Zeitschrift für philosophische Forschung* 23 (1969): 177–98.

Tillman, Alexandre, and Pierre Mesnard. "Descartes ou le combat pour la vérité." *Les Études philosophiques* 21 (1966): 391–94.

Toretti, R. "Finitud del hombre y límites del conocimiento en Descartes y Leibniz." *Anales de la Universidad de Chile* 121 (1963): 33–58.

Unger, Peter. "Our Knowledge of the Material World." *American Philosophical Quarterly* 4 (1970): 40–61.

Wagner, Hans. "Realitas objectiva (Descartes-Kant): Rudolf Zocher zum 80. Geburtstag." *Zeitschrift für philosophische Forschung* 21 (1967): 325–40.

Weier, Winfried. "Die introspektive Bewusstseinswahrnehmung beim hl. Augustinus und bei Descartes." *Franziskanische Studien* 50 (1968): 239–50.

Wells, Norman J. "Descartes and the Modal Distinction." *Modern Schoolman* 43 (1965): 1–22.

———. "Descartes and the Scholastics Briefly Revisited." *New Scholasticism* 35 (1961): 172–90.

———. "Descartes on Distinction." In *The Quest For the Absolute,* edited by F. J. Adelmann, pp. 104–34. Boston College Studies in Philosophy. Chestnut Hill, Mass.: Boston College, 1966.

———. "Objective Being: Descartes and His Sources." *Modern Schoolman* 45 (1967): 49–61.

Zaner, R. M. "La Realidad radical del cuerpo humano." *Revista de occidente* 90 (1970): 290–310.

4. COGITO AND PROOFS FOR THE EXISTENCE OF GOD

Alston, William P. "The Ontological Argument Revisited." In *Descartes: A Collection of Critical Essays,* edited by Willis Doney, pp. 278–302. New York: Doubleday, 1967.

Ayer, A. J. "I Think, Therefore I Am." In *Descartes: A Collection of Critical Essays,* edited by Willis Doney, pp. 80–87. New York: Doubleday, 1967.

Beck, Robert N. "Some Remarks on Logic and the Cogito." In *Cartesian Essays: A Collection of Critical Studies,* edited by B. Magnus and J. B. Wilbur, pp. 57–76. The Hague: M. Nijhoff, 1969.

Bouwsma, Oets Kolk. "I Think, I Am." In *The Nature of Philosophical Inquiry,* edited by J. Bobik, pp. 237–51. Notre Dame: University of Notre Dame Press, 1970.

Carnes, Robert D. "Descartes and the Ontological Argument." *Philosophy and Phenomenological Research* 24 (1964): 502–11.

Conche, Marcel. "Le 'Cogito' axiologique." In International Congress of Philosophy. *12th, Venice and Padua, 1958. Atti.* Vol. 12, pp. 101–08. Florence: Sansoni, 1961.

Connelly, R. J. "The Ontological Argument: Descartes' Advice to Hartshorne." *New Scholasticism* 43 (1969): 530–54.

Dalsgàrd-Hansen, Pool. "Descartes' Cogito-Argument and his Doctrine of Simple Natures." *Danish Yearbook of Philosophy* 2 (1965): 7–40.

Dematteis, Philip B. "The Ontological Argument as Wishful Thinking." *Kinesis* 1 (1968): 1–14.

Derrida, J. "Cogito et histoire de la folie." 2 pts. *Revue de métaphysique et de morale* 68 (1963): 460–94; 69 (1964): 116–19.

Fabro, Cornelio. "Ontological Apriorism and Atheism of the Cartesian *Cogito*." In his *God in Exile: Modern Atheism. A Study of the Internal Dynamic of Modern Atheism, from Its Roots in the Cartesian Cogito to the Present Day,* translated and edited by Arthur Gibson, pp. 91–119. Westminster, Md.: Newman, 1968.

Frankfurt, Harry G. "Descartes' Discussion of his Existence in the Second Meditation." *Philosophical Review* 75 (1966): 329–56.

Gewirth, Alan. "The Cartesian Circle Reconsidered." *Journal of Philosophy* 67 (1970): 668–85.

Grimm, R. "Cogito, ergo sum." *Theoria* (Sweden) 31 (1965): 159–73.

Gueroult, Martial. "Note sur la première preuve 'a posteriori' chez Descartes." *Revue philosophique de la France et de l'étranger* 91 (1966): 487–88.

Hintikka, Jaakko. "Cogito, ergo sum: Inference or Performance?" *Philosophical Review* 71 (1962): 3–32. Also published in *Descartes: A Collection of Critical Essays,* edited by Willis Doney, pp. 108–39. New York: Doubleday, 1967. Replies: Weinberg, J. R. *Philosophical Review* 71 (1962): 483–91; Carney, J. D. Ibid., pp. 492–96. Rejoinder: Hintikka, J. Ibid. 72 (1963): 487–96.

Imlay, Robert A. "Descartes' Ontological Argument." *New Scholasticism* 43 (1969): 440–48. Reply: Humber, J. M. "Descartes' Ontological Argument as Non-Causal." Ibid 44 (1970): 449–59. Rejoinder: Imlay, R. A. "Descartes' Ontological Argument: A Causal Argument." Ibid. 45 (1971): 348–51.

Kelly, Matthew J. "The Cartesian Circle: Descartes' Response to Scepticism." *Journal of Thought* 5 (1970): 67–71.

Kenny, Anthony. "The Cartesian Circle and the Eternal Truths." *Journal of Philosophy* 67 (1970): 685–700.

———. "Descartes' Ontological Argument." In *Fact and Existence,* edited by J. Margolis. Oxford: Blackwell, 1969.

Leyden, W. von. "Cogito ergo sum." *Proceedings of the Aristotelian Society* 63 (1962–63): 67–82.

Magnus, Bernd. "The Modalities of Descartes' Proofs for the Existence of God." In *Cartesian Essays: A Collection of Critical Studies,* edited by B. Magnus and J. B. Wilbur, pp. 77–87. The Hague: M. Nijhoff, 1969.

Malcolm, Norman. "Descartes's Proof That His Essence Is Thinking." *Philosophical Review* 74 (1965): 315–38.

Manzana Martinez de Marañón, José. *"Cogito ergo Deus est": La aportacion de Descartes al problema de la existencia de Dios.* Vitoria: Seminario Diocesano, 1960.

Mathrani, G. N. "Descartes' Idea of God as the Cause of his God-Idea: A Critical Analysis." *Philosophical Quarterly* (India) 33 (1961): 249–54.

Mounier, Emmanuel. "Le Conflit de l'anthropocentrisme et du théocentrisme dans la philosophie de Descartes." *Les Études philosophiques* 21 (1966): 319–24.

Muralt, André de. "Epoché—malin Génie—théologie de la toute-puissance divine." *Studia philosophica* 26 (1966): 159–91.

Nakhnikian, George. "The Cartesian Circle Revisited." *American Philosophical Quarterly* 4 (1967): 251–55.

Nelson, John O. "In Defence of Descartes: Squaring a Reputed Circle." *Dialogue* 3 (1964): 262–72. Reply: Frankfurt, Harry G. Ibid. 4 (1965–66): 92–95.

Obersteiner, Jacob. "Der Weg zur Gotteserkenntnis bei Augustinus und Descartes." *Augustinus* 13 (1968): 283–305.

Peltz, R. W. "The Logic of the 'Cogito.'" *Philosophy and Phenomenological Research* 23 (1962): 256–62.

Plantinga, Alvin. "Alston on the Ontological Argument." In *Descartes: A Collection of Critical Essays,* edited by Willis Doney, pp. 303–11. New York: Doubleday, 1967.

Poulet, Georges. "*La Nausée* de Sartre et le 'Cogito' cartésien." *Studi francesi* 5 (1961): 454–62.

Röd, Wolfgang. "Gewissheit und Wahrheit bei Descartes." *Zeitschrift für philosophische Forschung* (1962): 342–63.

Rose, Lynn E. "The Cartesian Circle." *Philosophy and Phenomenological Research* 26 (1965): 80–89. Reply: Kretzmann, Norman. Ibid., pp. 90–92. Rejoinder: Rose, L. E. Ibid., p. 93.

Santos, B. Edgard. "El 'cogito' y su estructura empirica: Relaciones entre el sujeto cartesiano del conocimiento y el de Santo Tomás." *Franciscanum* 7 (1965): 5–62.

Sarti, Sergio. "Considerazioni sul 'cogito' e sull' idea cartesiana di perfezione." *Giornale di metafisica* 18 (1963): 71–88.

Serres, M. "Un Modèle mathématique du cogito." *Revue philosophique de la France et de l'étranger* 155 (1965): 197–205.

Siegler, F. A. "Descartes' Doubts." *Mind* 72 (1963): 245–54.

Stallknecht, N. P. "The Cogito and Its World." *Personalist* 46 (1965): 52–64.

Williams, Bernard. "The Certitude of the 'Cogito.'" In *Descartes: A Collection of Critical Essays,* edited by Willis Doney, pp. 88–107. New York: Doubleday, 1967.

5. MISCELLANEOUS

Albert, Karl. "Descartes und die französische Philosophie der Gegenwart." *Begegnung* 23 (1968): 61–66.

Astrada, Carlos. "Vico y Descartes." In his *Ensayos filosóficos,* pp. 125–34. Bahia Blanca: Universidad Nacional del Sur, 1963.

Augst, Bertrand. "Descartes's Compendium on Music." *Journal of the History of Ideas* 26 (1965): 119–32.

Beijer, Agne. "*La Naissance de la paix:* ballet de cour de René Descartes." In *Le Lieu théâtral à la Renaissance (Royaumont, 1963): Études,* edited by J. Jacquot et al., pp. 409–22. Colloques internationaux du Centre national de la recherche scientifique: Sciences humaines. Paris: 1964.

Belaval, Yvon. "Leibniz face à Descartes." In *Leibniz 1646–1716: Aspects de l'homme et de l'oeuvre,* edited by M. Gueroult, pp. 189–200. Centre international de synthèse, Journées Leibniz, 1966. Paris: Aubier-Montaigne, 1968.

———. "Premières 'Animadversions' de Leibniz sur les 'Principes' de Descartes." In *Mélanges Alexandre Koyré, publiés à l'occasion de son soixante-dixième anniversaire,* vol. 2, pp. 29–56. Paris: Hermann, 1964.

———. "Vico and Anti-Cartesianism." In *Giambattista Vico: An International Symposium,* edited by Giorgio Tagliacozzo and H. V. White, pp. 77–91. Baltimore, Johns Hopkins Press, 1969.

Bloch, O.-R. "Gassendi critique de Descartes." *Revue philosophique de la France et de l'étranger* 91 (1966): 217–36.

Böhm, Walter. "John Mayow und Descartes." *Sudhoffs Archiv zur Geschichte der Medizin und der Naturwissenschaften* 46 (1962): 45–68.

Bouligand, G. "Sur une affinité dans les textes de Descartes." *Revue philosophique de la France et de l'étranger* 153 (1963): 363–64.

Bracken, Harry M. "Chomsky's Variations on a Theme by Descartes." *Journal of the History of Philosophy* 8 (1970): 181–92.

Busacchi, Vincenzo. "La Chiamata di Cartesio alla cattecha eminente di teorica della mediana nello studio di Bologna nel 1633." *Pagine di storia della medicina* 11 (1967): 9–13.

Cathala, Jean. "Des Bribes arrachées aux actuels introducteurs auprès de M. Descartes et son temps," pt. 1. *Presse médicale* 70 (1962): 847–48.

Chaix Ruy, J. "Vico et Descartes." *Archives de philosophie* 31 (1968): 628–39.

Chaves de Almeida, Lourenco Heitor. "Em Torno de uma exigencia humanistica no ponto de partida da filosofia cartesiana." *Reuista portuguesa de filosofia* 25 (1969): 277–81.

Closset, F. "Kende René Descartes de Nederlandse taal?" *Revue des langues vivantes* 26 (1960): 466–69.

Costabel, Pierre. "Contribution à l'étude de l'offensive de Leibniz contre la philosophie cartésienne en 1691–1692." *Revue internationale de philosophie* 20 (1966): 264–87.

Cropsey, Joseph. "On Descartes' Discourse on Method." *Interpretation* 2 (1970): 130–43.

de Santillana, Giorgio. "Vico and Descartes." In his *Reflections on Men and Ideas,* pp. 206–18. Cambridge, Mass.: M.I.T. Press, 1968.

D'Orsi, Domenico. "Il Tramonto della filosofia moderna, ossia verso la 'quarta età.' Prima puntata: Renato Cartesio." *Sophia* 28 (1960): 167–85.

Feuer, L. G. "The Dreams of Descartes." *American Imago* 20 (1963): 1–26.

Fontan, P. "Une certaine Idée de Dieu: Lectures de Descartes." *Revue thomiste* 71 (1971): 349–66.

Gambier, P. "Un autre Ami de Descartes: le pasteur André Rivet (1571–1648)." *Revue du Bas-Poitou et des provinces de l'Ouest* 75 (1964): 189–94.

Giorgiantonio, Michele. "Il Problema cartesiano." *Sophia* 37 (1969): 109–14.

Golliet, Pierre. "Descartes et les problèmes du style: La lettre latine de 1628 sur Guez de Balzac." In Vlaams Filologencongres. *25th, Antwerp, 1963. Handelingen, pp.* 199–207. Zellik: Secretariaat van de Vlaamse Filologencongressen, n.d.

Gouhier, Henri. "L'Oeuvre de Descartes et sa signification historique." *Gymnasium Helveticum* 16 (1961–62): 166–73.

Grassi, Ernesto. "G. B. Vico und das Problem des Beginns des modernen Denkens." *Zeitschrift für philosophische Forschung* 22 (1968): 491–509.

Gueroult, Martial. "The History of Philosophy as a Philosophical Problem." *Monist* 53 (1969): 563–87.

Gunderson, Keith. "Descartes, La Mettrie, Language, and Machines." *Philosophy* 39 (1964): 193–222.

Haller, R. "Das cartesische Dilemma." *Zeitschrift für philosophische Forschung* 18 (1967): 369–86.

Hoffmann, Paul. "Féminisme cartésien." *Travaux de linguistique et de littérature* 7 (1969): 83–106.

Jager, Bernd. "The Three Dreams of Descartes: A Phenomenological Exploration." *Review of Existential Psychology and Psychiatry* 8 (1968): 195–213.

Jaspers, Karl. "Descartes and Philosophy." In his *Three Essays: Leonardo, Descartes, Max Weber,* translated by Ralph Manheim, pp. 59–185. New York: Harcourt, Brace and World, 1964.

Judrin, Roger. "Sur Descartes." *Nouvelle revue française* 15 (1967): 128–31.

Kennington, Richard. "René Descartes." In *A History of Political Philosophy,* edited by J. Cropsey and L. Strauss. New York: Rand McNally, 1963.

Krutch, Joseph Wood. "One of the Greatest of Men Who Made One of the Greatest of Mistakes." In his *And Even If You Do: Essays on Man, Manners, and Machines,* pp. 289–95. New York: William Morrow, 1967.

Kuntz, Paul G. "The Dialectic of Historicism and Anti-historicism." *Monist* 53 (1969): 656–69.

Kuspit, D. B. "Epoch and Fable in Descartes." *Philosophy and Phenomenological Research* 25 (1964): 30–52.

Lafleur, Laurence J. "Descartes' Place in History." In *Cartesian Essays: A Collection of Critical Studies,* edited by B. Magnus and J. B. Wilbur, pp. 3–13. The Hague: M. Nijhoff, 1969.

Lafrance, Y. "O 'Discurso do método' de René Descartes." *Revista da Universidade católica de São Paulo* 24 (1962): 391–432.

Laporte, J.-M. "Husserl's Critique of Descartes." *Philosophy and Phenomenological Research* 23 (1963): 335–52.

Larsen, Erik. "Descartes and the Rise of Naturalistic Landscape Painting in 17th-Century Holland." *College Art Journal* 24 (1964): 12–17.

Laudan, Laurens. "The Clock Metaphor and Probabilism: The Impact of Descartes on English Methodological Thought, 1650–65." *Annals of Science* 22 (1966): 73–104.

Lauth, Reinhard. "La Constitution du texte des *Regulae* de Descartes." *Archives de philosophie* 31 (1968): 648–56.

———. "Der Entwurf der neuzeitlichen Philosophie durch Descartes." In his *Zur Idee der Transzendentalphilosophie,* pp. 11–41. Munich: Anton Pustet, 1965.

Lefèvre, Roger. "Quand Descartes dîne à Douai." *Revue des sciences humaines* 27 (1962): 313–26.

Lopes de Mattos, Carlos. "Diologando com Descartes." *Revista brasiliera de filosofia* 10 (1960): 471–82.

Mazzeo, Joseph Anthony. "Bacon: The New Philosophy." In his *Renaissance of European Thought,* pp. 161–234. New York: Pantheon, 1966.

Melchiorre, V. "L'Interpretazione di Cartesio nel pensiero di E. Mounier." *Rivista di filosofia neo-scolastica* 53 (1961): 298–313.

Michele, Gianni. "Il 'Traité de l'homme' e una supposita crisi della filosofia cartesiana." *Rivista critica di storia della filosofia* 16 (1961): 315–20.

Moraes, M. "O Cartesianismo de António Cordeiro." *Revista portuguesa de filosofia* 22 (1966): 3–27.

Moreau, Joseph. "Présentacion de Descartes." *Miscelañea de estudos a Joaquim de Carvalho* 8 (1962): 186–28.

———. "Sanchez, précartésien." *Revue philosophique de la France et de l'étranger* 92 (1967): 264–70.

Nádor, Georg. "Eine heraklitische Denkform in Descartes' Werk." *Antike und Abendland* 13 (1967): 96–100.

———. "Métaphores de chemins et de labyrinthes chez Descartes." *Revue philosophique de la France et de l'étranger* 87 (1962): 37–51.

Noussan Lettry, Luis: "La critica de las humanidades en Descartes (Discurso I, parrafos 7° y 8°)." In *Actas de las segundas jornadas universitarias de humanidades,* pp. 207–17. Mendoza: Instituto de Filosofia, 1964.

Oeing-Hanhoff, Ludger. "Der Mensch in der Philosophie Descartes." In *Die Frage nach dem Menschen: Aufriss einer philosophischen Anthropologie. Festschrift für Max Müller zum 60. Geburtstag, edited by Heinrich Rombach,* pp. 375–409. Freiburg: Alber, 1966.

Padovani, Umberto A. "Descartes (il fondatore del pensiero moderno)." *Uidyá* (Marsala) 5 (1967): 1–25.

Paisse, Jean-Marie. "Socrates et Descartes." 2 pts. *Bulletin de l'Association Guillaume Budé* 27 (1968): 241–57; 28 (1969): 89–100.

Peltz, Richard W. "Indexical Sentences and Cartesian Rationalism." *Philosophy and Phenomenological Research* 27 (1966): 80–84.

Perelman, Ch. "Analogie et metaphore en science, poesie et philosophie." *Revue internationale de philosophie* 23 (1969): 3–15.

Prichard, H. A. "Descartes's *Meditations.*" In *Descartes: A Collection of Critical Essays,* edited by Willis Doney, pp. 140–68. New York: Doubleday, 1967. Reprinted from Prichard's *Knowledge and Perception,* pp. 80–104. Oxford: Clarendon Press, 1950.

*Rat, Maurice. "Descartes contre Descartes." *Revue. Littérature, histoire, arts et sciences des deux mondes* 19 (1967): 387–90.

Riley, Gresham. "Self-Knowledge: A Tale of the Tortoise Which Supports an Elephant." *Philosophy Forum* 1 (1969): 274–92.

Rittmeister, J. "Die mystische Krise des jungen Descartes. Mit einem Nachtrag zur heutigen Beurteilung Descartes von A. Storch." *Zeitschrift für psychosomatische Medizin und Psychoanalyse* 15 (1969): 206–24.

Roche, M. "Un homme: Monsieur Descartes." *Humanisme contemporain* 2 (1966): 71–98.

Rombach, Heinrich. "Die Bedeutung von Descartes und Leibniz für die Metaphysik der Gegenwart." *Philosophisches Jahrbuch* 70 (1962): 67–97.

Rozsnyai, Ervin. "Descartes et la philosophie moderne." In his *Études sur Descartes,* pp. 5–63. Budapest: Akademia Kiado, 1964.

Ruiz, Felix. "Reflexiones en torno a Pascal: San Augustin, Pascal, Descartes." *Augustinus* 7 (1963): 411–20.

Salmon, J. H. M. "Descartes and Pascal." *History Today* 21 (1971): 482–90.

Saveson, J. E. "Differing Reactions to Descartes among the Cambridge Platonists." *Journal of the History of Ideas* 21 (1960): 560–67. Reply: Sailor, D. B. "Cudworth and Descartes." Ibid. 23 (1962): 133–40.

Scharfstein, Ben-Ami. "Descartes' Dreams." *Philosophy Forum* 1 (1969): 293–317.

Semerari, Giuseppe. "Intorno all 'anticartesianesimo di Vico." In *Omaggio a Vico*, pp. 193–232. Collana di filosofia, 10. Naples: A. Morano, 1968.

Sommers, Fred. "Predicability." In *Philosophy in America,* edited by Max Black, pp. 262–81. London: Allen & Unwin, 1965.

Specht, Rainer. "Descartes und das Lehramt." *Hochland* 52 (1959–60): 131–38.

Splett, Jörg. "Vérité, certitude et historicité." *Archives de philosophie* 30 (1967): 163–86.

Stempel, Daniel. "*The Garden:* Marvell's Cartesian Ecstasy." *Journal of the History of Ideas* 28 (1967): 99–114.

Tedeschi, F. A. "Ragione e fede in Socrate, Cartesio ed Hegel." *Educare* 12 (1961): 50–61.

Thiébaut, Marcel. "Descartes Masqué?" *Revue de Paris* 67 (1960): 136–52.

Tordai, Zador. "Esquisse de l'histoire du cartésianisme en Hongrie." In *Études sur Descartes,* by Ervin Rozsnyai, et al., pp. 135–68. Budapest: Akademia Kiado, 1964.

Turbayne, Colin Murray. "Analysis and Synthesis: Descartes." In his *Myth of Metaphor,* pp. 28–40. New Haven: Yale University Press, 1962.

Vincenot, Claude. "Jeu, rêve et déduction dans le *Discours de la méthode*." *Revue des sciences humaines* 33 (1968): 355–62.

Vleeschouwer, Herman Jean de. "Le Sens de la méthode dans le discours de Descartes et la critique de Kant." In *Studien zu Kants philosophischen Entwicklung*, pp. 167–83. Hildesheim: G. Olms, 1967.

Vuillemin, Jules. "Sur les propriétés formelles et matérielles de l'ordre cartésien des raisons." In *Hommage à Martial Gueroult: L'histoire de la philosophie, ses problèmes, ses méthodes,* pp. 43–58. Paris: Fischbacher, 1964.

Weber, Jean-Paul. "Commentaire des Règles VII et VIII des 'Regulae' de Descartes: Histoire de texte." *Revue de métaphysique et de morale* 68 (1963): 180–212.

———. "Sur la composition de la Regula IV de Descartes." *Revue philosophique de la France et de l'étranger* 89 (1964): 1–20.

Webster, C. "Henry More and Descartes: Some New Sources." *British Journal for the History of Science* 4 (1969): 359–77.

Weier, Winfried. "Zur Bedeutung des aristotelischen Daseinsbegriffs für die Weiterführung des durch Descartes begründeten Immanentismus." *Archiv für Geschichte der Philosophie* 48 (1966): 277–305.

Weinberg, Kurt. "Zum Wandel des Sinnbezirks von 'Herz' und 'Instinkt' unter dem Einfluss Descartes." *Archiv für das Studium der neueren Sprachen* 203 (1966): 1–31.

Index

NE

ECHEANCE   DATE DUE

Université de Sudbury
University of Sudbury